The Meaning of Friendship

The Meaning of Friendship

Mark Vernon

First published in 2005 as *The Philosophy of Friendship* by PALGRAVE MACMILLAN

This revised edition published 2010 by PALGRAVE MACMILLAN

Palgrave Macmillan in the UK is an imprint of Macmillan Publishers Limited, registered in England, company number 785998, of Houndmills, Basingstoke, Hampshire RG21 6XS.

Palgrave Macmillan in the US is a division of St Martin's Press LLC, 175 Fifth Avenue, New York, NY 10010.

Palgrave Macmillan is the global academic imprint of the above companies and has companies and representatives throughout the world.

Palgrave® and Macmillan® are registered trademarks in the United States, the United Kingdom, Europe and other countries

ISBN-13: 978–0–230–24288–3   paperback

This book is printed on paper suitable for recycling and made from fully managed and sustained forest sources. Logging, pulping and manufacturing processes are expected to conform to the environmental regulations of the country of origin.

A catalogue record for this book is available from the British Library.

Library of Congress Cataloging-in-Publication Data
   Vernon, Mark, 1966–
     The meaning of friendship / Mark Vernon.
        p. cm.
     Summary: "In this book, Mark Vernon offers penetrating insights on the idea of friendship, using philosophy and modern culture to ask about friendship and sex, work, politics and spirituality. He also explores how notions of friendship may or may not be changing because of the internet, and looks at the psychology of friendship" – Provided by publisher.
     Includes bibliographical references and index.
     ISBN 978-0-230-24288-3 (pbk.)
     1. Friendship. I. Title.
     BF575.F66.V47 2010
     177'.62–dc22   2009047551

10   9   8   7   6   5   4   3   2   1
19 18 17 16 15 14 13 12 11 10

Printed and bound in Great Britain by
CPI Antony Rowe, Chippenham and Eastbourne

In memory of Susan Frances Vernon

Contents

Acknowledgements

This book is in part a product of friendships, amongst whom I think of Denise Inge, Craig Mackenzie, Jeremy Carrette, Guy Reid, Chris Biddle, Paul Fletcher, John Inge, Angie Hobbs and Richard Jenkins. I must thank other individuals who have read various chapters and drafts, notably Michael Savage, James Davidson and particularly Lisa Mackenzie. Great thanks also goes to those who signed me up and then steered the book through at Palgrave Macmillan, especially Luciana O'Flaherty, Dan Bunyard and Lisa Dunn, and also to my copy-editor, Peter Andrews.

For the new edition, thanks too for the support of Priyanka Gibbons and Sam Burridge. I would also like to thank those at The School of Life for providing the opportunity to develop my ideas about the subject, by test driving them on folk who have friends. Underpinning all, for me, is the love and friendship of Nick.

List of Illustrations

Introduction

'Their relationship consisted
In discussing if it existed.'

Thom Gunn

For a long time I was single. I relied heavily on friends for company, support and affection. And most of the time I was happy about that. Implicitly, I agreed with Aristotle: who would choose to live without friends even if they had every other good thing, he said. Moreover, I regarded myself as exceptionally lucky with my friends and still do.

But for all that, I was often alone and sometimes lonely. The friendships I enjoyed only went so far.

The limits were most obvious when compared to the relationships I witnessed between lovers or within families. It seemed to me that notwithstanding the occasional exception, friendship simply cannot bear the demands and intimacies, great and small, that are the very stuff of these other relationships of love and blood.

This set me thinking because my experience seemed very different from the way friendship is portrayed at a cultural level. Here it is frequently heralded as nothing less than the defining relationship of our age. In TV soaps, the characters always have their friends to return to when their sexual adventures fail; lovers come and go, but friends remain. Or, according to agony aunts, friendship is the ingredient that makes partnerships work (a suggestion that would have surprised many of those same agony aunts' aunts who might have suggested the ingredient of partnership to make relationships work). For sociologists, a common assumption is that friendship is now most people's relationship of choice, and people often see their friends in opposition to traditional relationships of obligation: as marriage and family flounders, to say nothing of lifestyles becoming more mobile, the belief (or hope) is that friendship will carry them through the serial monogamies and speedy pace of life. And for politicians, the idea of civic friendship is also gaining ground. Here the thought is that democracy can be revivified by a notion of citizenship that includes a concern for others' wellbeing. Such civic friendship would counterbalance disparities between rich and poor, and an individualism that seems so pervasive, as well as provide a way of humanising a civic space which is often otherwise about the exercise of freedoms, an obedience to rules, and a claiming of rights.

All in all, friendship is conceived of positively, as the new social glue to paste over-networked lives: because it is ideally structured to cope with the stresses and strains, great and small, that modern life throws up, it will stop them falling apart.

But will it? My experience told me that whilst friendship can be great, its affections and commitments are often ambiguous. When a lover calls they automatically get first priority and family commitments are, well, family commitments. So perhaps the soaps are romanticising friendship, the agony aunts are falling back on it too fast, and the sociologists and politicians are being overly optimistic?

There is statistical evidence to support the concern too. Professor Ray Pahl, the sociologist of friendship, spoke with about 1,000 individuals. He found that nearly two-thirds say friends are one of the biggest causes of stress in their life; over a quarter that friends are the main cause of arguments with partners and families; around 11 per cent admit to taking a sick day in the previous year due to friendship problems; 25 per cent say they can't cope with making new friends; and well over three-quarters admit to wanting to lose at least 5 'flabby friends' as part of a New Year friendship detox – flabby friends being like those extra pounds that a healthy workout would shed.

In fact, questionable friendships are regularly debated in TV programmes, newspaper columns and learned journals. However, upon further reflection it seemed to me that another, perhaps even more fundamental, question is rarely being asked – and it is one with which philosophy should be able to help. What exactly is friendship? What is its nature, its rules, its promise? How can one differentiate between its many forms? How does it compare to, and mix with, the connections shared between lovers and within families? If at least a kind of friendship is elastic enough to survive the relational stresses and strains of our flexible ways of life, is that friendship also strong enough to bear the burden of the human need to belong, to be connected, to be loved?

These questions are trickier to answer than it might first seem because friendship is hugely diverse. Although it is relatively easy to come up with definitions that account for part of it, it is much harder to find one that does not exclude any of its facets. Aristotle, whose writing on friendship still sets the philosophical agenda to

Figure 1: 'The desire for friendship comes quickly. Friendship does not.' (Aristotle)

this day, found as much 2,500 years ago. Friendship, he proposed, is at the very least a relationship of goodwill between individuals who reciprocate that goodwill. A reasonable starter for ten. However, as soon as he tried to expand it, the definition seemed to unravel.

He looked around him and saw three broad groupings of relationships people called friendship. The first group are friends primarily because they are useful to each other – like the friendship between an employee and a boss, or a doctor and a patient, or a politician and an ally; they share goodwill because they get something out of the relationship. The second group are friends primarily because some pleasure is enjoyed by being together; it may be the football, the shopping, the gossip or sexual intimacy, but the friendship thrives insofar, and possibly only insofar, as the thing that gives the pleasure continues to exist between them. Aristotle noted that these first two groups are therefore like each other because if you take the utility or the pleasure away, then the chances are the friendship will fade.

This, though, is not true of the third group. These are people who love each other because of who they are in themselves. It may be their depth of character, their innate goodness, their intensity of passion or their simple *joie de vivre*, but once established on such a basis these friendships are ones that tend to last. Undoubtedly much will be given and much taken too but the friendship itself is independent of external factors and immensely more valuable than the friendships that fall into the first two groups.

That there are better or higher friendships – different people may call them soul friends, close or old friends, or best friends – as opposed to instrumental and casual friendships, or mere friendliness, is surely right. But to say that great friendship is defined solely by its goodwill seems to miss its essence. Goodwill exists in these best kinds of friendship, but, unlike the lesser types, best friendship – arguably the quintessential sort – is based on something far more profound.

4

Aristotle recognised as much, and whilst his discussion of friendship contains many important and illuminating insights – that we will make much of here – he knew, I think, that ultimately a definitional approach to friendship has its limits.

This ambiguity as to what friendship is reflects, then, the ambiguity that appears to be part and parcel of friendship in life. Try listing some of the friends you have – your partner, oldest friend, mates or girlfriends, one or two family members, work colleagues, neighbours, friends from online chat rooms, family friends, a boss perhaps, therapist, teacher, personal trainer – whoever you might at some time think of as a friend. A look at such a list puts your friends in front of you, as it were, and highlights the vast differences. For example, the friendship with your partner will in certain key respects be unlike that of your oldest friend, though you may be very close to both. Conversely, although friendship is for the most part a far less strong tie than say the connection to family, you may feel less close to members of your family in terms of friendship than others with whom you have no genetic or legal bond. Then again, lovers might make you blush and families can make you scream, but friendship – even soul friendship – is usually cool in comparison.

As you continue further down the list to the friends who are in many ways little more than acquaintances, associates or individuals for whom you have merely a sense of friendliness, it is obvious that friendship stretches from a love you could scarcely do without to an affection that you'd barely miss if it ended. Some people would say there is some minimal quality which means that it makes sense to call all of them friends (perhaps Aristotle's goodwill). Others would disagree: they are the sort who say they have a handful of friends and that others are people they only know. In other words, the ambiguity of friendship extends to the very possibility of prolific and profound friendship-making.

The diverse range of 'friends' that people say they have is entertainingly portrayed in Tim Lott's novel, *White City Blue*. A couple are planning their wedding, trying to sort out the list. He asks her about her friends. She replies:

> For a start there are friends you don't like. I've got plenty of those. Then there are friends you do like, but never bother to see. Then there are the ones you really like a lot, but can't stand their partners. There are those you just have out of habit and can't shake off. Then there's the ones you're friends with not because you like them, but because they're very good-looking or popular and it's kind of cool to be their friend. Trophy friends ... Then there are sports friends. There are friends of convenience – they're usually work friends. There are pity friends who you stay with because you feel sorry for them. There are acquaintances who are on probation as friends.

Personally, I think that Aristotle is on to something in his belief that the closest kind of friendship is only possible with a handful of individuals, such is the investment of time and self that it takes. 'Host not many but host not none', was his formula. He would argue that less is more and it is easy to substitute mere networking for the friendships it is supposed to yield. He actually went so far as to express a fear of having too many friends, 'polyphilia' as it might be called. There is an expression attributed to Aristotle that captures the concern: 'Oh my friends, there is no friend.' Michel de Montaigne, Friedrich Nietzsche and most recently the philosopher Jacques Derrida have picked up on the phrase, though as Aristotle used it, he was not worrying about the loneliness of the modern individual, as Derrida muses on, but rather the dangers of knowing so many people, you really know no one. One of the things I think the philosophy of friendship tells us is that life produces personal relationships of many types, but out of these connections good friendship may or may not grow. Certain associations or institutions like work or marriage can foster friendship but those same associations or institutions need not necessarily be characterised by deep friendship themselves; friendship emerges, as it were, from below up. It is a fluid concept.

Another dimension to the ambiguity of friendship is its apparent open-endedness. Unlike institutions of belonging such as marriage which is supported and shaped by social norms, or work where individuals have contractually defined roles, friendship has no predetermined instructions for assembly or project for growth. People have to create their friendships mostly out of who they are, their interests and needs, without any universally applicable framework. On the one hand, this is a potential weakness, because a friendship may 'go nowhere' or 'run out of steam'. On the other, it is a potential strength because there is also a freedom in this that is crucial to friendship's appeal: it is part of the reason for the diversity within the family of relationships called friendship.

In summary, then, it seems that it is not possible to say unequivocally what friendship is. Sometimes it is intense, sometimes it is thin. Sometimes it appears to embrace many, sometimes only a few.

This might seem to be a bit of a blow if the question is what is friendship. However, far from ambiguity automatically leading to philosophical impasse, an exploration of the very ambiguities of friendship is actually a very good way forward. After all, is not mistaking relationships for what they are not – that is being blind to their ambiguity – arguably the greatest cause of disappointment and failure? A married couple may assume they are friends in some deep sense when really they only have goodwill for each other because of the kids; unless they realise that, when the kids leave home, the marriage may falter too. An employee and a boss may think they are good friends after all the late nights, trips abroad and hours spent together: but when the day arrives for the appraisal or pay rise, and both turn out to be modest, the friendship stumbles and falls.

Alternatively, consider this thought experiment suggested by Nietzsche:

Just think to yourself some time how different are the feelings, how divided the opinions, even among the closest acquaintances; how even the same opinions have quite a different place or intensity in the heads of your friends than in your own; how many hundreds of times there is occasion for misunderstanding or hostile flight. After all that, you will say to yourself: 'How unsure is the ground on which all our bonds and friendships rest; how near we are to cold downpours or ill weather; how lonely is every man!'

Honesty about any relationship is likely to improve it, even if the honest thing to do is not put too much hope in it!

The mistakes that people can make in friendship are also exemplified in some of the things people commonly say about it. For example, many would say that the test of good friendship is being able to pick up immediately where you left off even if you haven't seen the friend for some time. Aristotle, though, thought that good friendship depends on shared living and spending substantial, regular, quality time together. 'Cut off the talk, and many a time you cut off the friendship,' he said. The question is how much time, how much talk is needed?

Or again, are not the Life columns of newspapers and magazines increasingly scattered with tales of friendship's labour lost? A piece on 'Google grief' caught my eye, the twenty-first century phenomenon of learning of the death of an old friend on the web. The writer, Michele Kirsch, complained that having had such a shock, she was not allowed to grieve for her dead friend because those with whom she lived now were implicitly asking, 'If he was so brilliant, why haven't you been in touch for 18 years?' Fair question, she is forced to admit; the friendship she had was nostalgic and only in her head.

And yet, if it is really quite easy to make mistakes by thinking the relationship is something other that what it is, the best kinds of friendship (however that is judged) are essential for a happy life: human beings need people they can call friends and not just people who are relatives, partners, acquaintances, colleagues or associates. In other words, the corollary of friendship's ambiguity is that it is packed with promise and strewn with perils.

This, then, sets the agenda for this book. It is these perils and that promise which I hope to track down, the ambiguities and points of contention that I address. My aim is not to try to produce a comprehensive definition or theory of friendship. Rather, the value of asking about friendship lies in the asking, not necessarily in coming to any incontestable conclusions.

I am taking a lead here from Plato. According to him, at the end of a lengthy conversation on friendship with the Greek youths Lysis and Menexenus, no less a person than Socrates concluded that he had not been able to discover what friendship was. He feared looking ridiculous because paradoxically it also seemed that he, Lysis and Menexenus were friends. But he had good reason for not tying friendship down.

Although everyone has friends of some sort and friendships appear to share similarities, and thus be definable, they are in life as varied as the people who form them. This is the irreducibility of friendship; people have an infinite variety of experiences of it. So another way of putting it is that this is a book of the sort which invites you to test its ideas against your experience. In fact, with a subject like friendship it is almost impossible to do otherwise. It is a search through philosophy for the things that may thwart friendship and for the conditions within which it may best thrive.

Philosophy is frequently overlooked as a resource for thinking through friendship in this way. This has much to do with the fact that only a relatively small number of philosophers have written on the subject at any length. What is more, those who have, although generally agreeing that friendship is essential for a happy life, also say that it provides no automatic satisfaction of human desires for deeper relationships or society's need for connection. Friendship is 'a problem worthy of a solution', as Nietzsche gnomically put it. Or as Aristotle wrote: 'The desire for friendship comes quickly. Friendship does not.' The implication is that the best kinds of friendships are only possible between people who properly value it and who understand how many things from the personal to the political can compromise, undermine and destroy it. There is an art to friendship. Nonetheless, the hope is that philosophy can teach us something about it.

The tradition that we will major on here is that of the west. That said, this is not necessarily to exclude conceptions of friendship from Indian and other Asian traditions. For one thing, it's becoming increasingly clear that Plato and Aristotle derived a lot of their ideas by looking East. Then there is Taxila, in modern day Pakistan, which was a veritable crossroads of the world, a place to which ancient Greek philosophers ventured. Aristotelian and Platonic insights informed the development of Islam too. There's also the fact that whilst Confucian ideas can't have influenced the development of thought in the ancient Mediterranean, Confucian conceptions of friendship aren't always so different: if Confucius envisaged society as a concentric series of circles, with the closest relationships in the centre, rippling out to generate a sense of civic affection and place in the body politic as a whole, then Aristotle has a not dissimilar model in mind too, as we'll see.

Each chapter looks at key ambiguities that may exist in any friendship, testing for the perils, searching for the promise. The first begins with the world of work because work friends frequently exhibit some of friendship's chief ambiguities. On the one hand, the workplace is a good place to find and make friends. But, on the other, it is also one where supposed friends can show remarkable indifference – as in the speed with which the friendship is forgotten when someone leaves the office. The workplace also has an insidious capacity to undermine friendship. The fly in the ointment is the culture of utility that pervades it. People are there to do things, they are paid for doing them, and they are often encouraged to compete against each other in so doing. Of course, all friends use each other from time to time. But friends at work are at risk of coming to feel that they are merely being used. Therein lies the ambiguity of friendship at work. Moreover, the workplace is not an isolated environment in the western world. It informs a culture that tends to colour society as a whole; productivity often counts for more than perspicacity, the professional touch more than the personal touch, being praised more than being praiseworthy, wherever you are. All this is detrimental to friendship and so this chapter also provides us with a first look at friendship in a social context, and how we might thrive in it.

The second chapter considers another source of ambiguity in friendship, namely, sex. The downside is that sex can clearly imperil friendships by its possessiveness or its inappropriateness. The upside is that a friendship which includes a sexual element is the best sort of relationship that many people hope to have. I will argue that the key is to recognise that whilst a sexual relationship will start with physical passion, a passion of a non-sexual sort needs to kick in too if a good friendship is to develop. This is actually a natural if at times delicate step to take because the two kinds of passion are connected: a mature couple will realise that their deeper desires cannot be satisfied only in each other and that their relationship should nurture a search for fulfilment elsewhere too, in wider aspirations and achievements shared together.

This chapter is also a good place to consider a related sort of friendship, passionate friendships that have never had a sexual element, and where to have gone down the sexual route would have destroyed it. The erotic element is here sublimated in the passion that these friends share; we say these friends have a passion for life.

Work and sex are two sources of ambiguity and the third chapter turns to another, exhibited in the way in which friends dissimulate. I am talking here about 'loving deceptions' such as when an individual says they like their friend's new boy- or girlfriend when they do not, or when someone else says that their friend's cooking or clothing or opinion is good or right when they really think it is wrong or bad. Once you start thinking about it, it becomes apparent that these false colourings, evasions and occasionally out-and-out lies pervade friendship. Even close friends will routinely dissimulate because they judge that the time is not right to speak out, that current sensitivities are too great for the honest truth, or more humbly that, even though they are close, equivocation is best because one should not presume to judge another's heart. The particularly odd thing about friendship is that this dissimulation, this feigning friendship, is often necessary for the friendship's sake. The question is what does this say about it? It turns out that the answer again has a plus, for it reveals another aspect of what is possible in the best kinds of friendship. This, in turn, is nothing less than a reflection on what it is to be human itself.

Talking of dissimulation needs naturally to the next chapter, the new phenomenon of friending online. Just what is friendship on sites like Facebook, or in virtual spaces like Second Life, really all about? Is the web a boon for friendship, or a place where it falls apart? Should we be worried about what it is doing to our social lives, or embrace the new without fear, recognising the way it brings people together?

A different kind of ambiguity is explored in the fifth chapter, namely, the ambivalence with which the wider world tends to view friendship. Why do we dislike nepotism, when it's just folk being kind to their friends? Why do we sense tensions between the commitments people have with their families and the ones they'd like to make to their friends? Is democracy itself welcoming of friendship, or actually wary of it, since it encourages favourites and special interests not a vision of the common good? Is friendship the greatest of human loves or actually a corruption of love, because it is irredeemably selfish and particular?

This ambiguity also sets up an observation that might worry us if we believe friendship is necessary for a happy life: why it is that few thinkers today have chosen to tackle the subject at any length, when at certain times in the past – notably in the world of antiquity and the Middle Ages – friendship was a major concern. The suggestion is that in these periods of history, friendship enjoyed a social standing that it does not today. Ancient Greek political life seems to have incorporated quasi-institutions of friendship. The medieval world did so too, to the extent that some people entered 'marriages of friendship'. This stands in marked contrast to our own situation, in which friendship is thought of as an almost wholly private relationship. Are we missing out on this key component of life as a result?

There are what might be called prophets of friendship to be found in the modern world – the area we explore next – in particular in feminism and the women's movement, and more recently in gay and so-called queer thought. Here, friendship is viewed as subversive of social norms and liberating of individual lives. Think of the anxiety provoked by the idea of gay marriage: I suspect that this has little to do with sexual acts and much more to do with forms of friendship that challenge tight notions of family.

This chapter also raises the question of possible differences between the friendships of men and those of women. The evidence on this is mixed and hard to read. On the one hand, there are sociologists who have argued that intimacy has been transformed in the modern world: in the same way that distinct gender roles are eroding at a social level, so differences between male and female friendship are softening too. On the other hand, there are others who argue that the evidence shows that gendered patterns of friendship still form in childhood and continue into adult life: from this view follow conclusions such as that women's friendships are more to do with self-disclosure and empathy, whereas men's friendships are more about the sociability of enjoying or doing things together. It's a fascinating question.

The final chapters return to the question of what friendship ultimately aims at on a personal level, and asks how best to strive for it. I call this the spirituality of friendship, not least because the most profound kind of friendship that people hope for is often referred to as soulmateship. Having said that, this is, I think, a much misused and sentimentalised concept. The philosophical tradition portrays it as an exceptional and difficult love. It necessitates nothing less than being able to overcome the ambiguities of amity – though, if that is never wholly possible, it also suggests how one might live with regards to the very best that can be hoped for in friendship.

So it turns out that philosophy is indeed illuminative of friendship. In fact, I think it offers a better resource for friends than much of what is found in books of self-help. We seek its wisdom, but first we must get to work.

Friends at Work

'In the desert no man meets a friend.'

Eastern proverb

Some people say that they cannot watch *The Office*, the tragi-comic TV docudrama of life at work written by Ricky Gervais, because for all its laughs and for all its humanity, it makes them squirm. It is too close to life. It holds up a mirror to the endless hours people spend in strip-lit rooms and finds the experience wanting.

The friendship between the characters is never far from the surface of the plot. Or rather the edgy, forced relationships that often have to pass for friendship at work. As Tim, the sales rep, comments in one episode: you spend so much time with these people, more time than with your family, and yet you don't know them; all you might have in common with them is that you tread on the same carpet for eight hours a day.

Experience has made Tim sceptical. He has long nursed a love for Dawn, the receptionist. Everyone in the office knows about it and the agony it has caused him. And yet no one is really able to care for him. Gareth, the team leader, wants to make light of it but, like everything else he does, he botches it and ends up just poking fun at Tim. The new woman, who sits opposite Tim, empathises but trivialises his love: wherever she works she is always fancied by blokes, she tells him with a smirk. Then there's Keith, in accounts. He simply rides roughshod over Tim's feelings by offering his, frankly, disgusting advice on how to win women. All in all, the people in the office cannot share Tim's burden, as true friends might, though they know all about it, in embarrassing detail.

We might call this 'pseudo-intimacy', the state in which work colleagues can know so much about each other but can care so little.

However, pseudo-intimacy is not the fundamental problem with which relationships at work must contend. It is, I think, the product of a deeper ambiguity, one which *The Office* also portrays well. Here's another incident.

It features David Brent, the regional manager and fool portrayed by Ricky Gervais. 'You will never have another boss like me,' he boasts. 'Someone who's basically a chilled out entertainer.' By this episode, though, he's been sacked and has taken to coming back to the office with his dog, to catch up with his former employees whom he calls friends. They 'listen in' as he holds court. In this episode Neil, the managing director, arrives and bans David from the office for persistently wasting people's time. David protests, and appeals to his supposed office friends: to show Neil up for the inhumanity of banning him, when he only wanted to visit his friends, David asks cheekily: 'Who fancies a drink after work?'

His request is met with silence. David pleads: he is free tomorrow. Silence. He is free Thursday. Silence. Finally, Tim, out of grudging goodness, volunteers to go for the drink. David grimaces at Neil – the awkward smile of the Pyrrhic victor. The truth is that he not only has no real friends in the office. He barely has any allies.

It is a painful moment but the interesting question for us is why everyone stopped acting as friends the minute David asked them out for a drink? Were they not friendly before? And if not, why were they so two-faced? The answer, I think, lies in the fact that prior to the invitation David gave them something they wanted: a distraction from the working day. There is the disruptive force of his personality too, of course. But they were prepared to show him faux friendship because he broke the tedium of life at the office.

However, to go for a drink with him after work would be another story entirely. That would be a hassle with minimal pleasure; it would risk becoming trapped as David's captive audience, perhaps for hours. And crucially, there would be no benefit in terms of mitigating the dreariness of work. Hence no one wanted to go out for the post-work drink. There is silence.

So, alongside the pseudo-intimacy of work life, there's another factor that shapes such relationships: people's usefulness to one another. Take that usefulness away – in this case, David's purpose as a diversion – and the friendliness tends to unravel too. Put quite generally we have the fundamental source of the ambiguity of many friendships at work. They are determined by their utility.

People's utility at work extends way beyond just being a welcome distraction or even performing a role or a function. It goes to the heart of the working environment, underpinning why people are there at all. They work to do something, for a client, for a team, for a boss. And work is not work without one key utility for the employee, namely, the paycheck. Ideally the work is rewarding, doubly so when there's a sense of achieving something with friends. And if you receive what you believe you are due that generates friendly feeling too.

So, this is not to say that people do not or cannot feel genuine friendship towards one another in the office, or workshop, or on the road. In surveys, friendship routinely comes up as one of the most important factors for people in their working lives. That only makes sense: a friendly face to greet you in the morning humanises the day. Some research from Gallup showed just how good that is. A friendly working environment increases an employee's satisfaction with their employer by nearly 50 per cent. People with good friends at work are twice as likely to think they are well paid. And people with at least three close friends at work are 46 per cent more likely to be extremely satisfied with their job.

The research revealed more. Those 30 per cent of people who report having a best friend at work gain in unexpected ways. They will have fewer accidents, engage more customers and work more productively. They also feel that what they are doing is well aligned with the company's aims, in other words their work feels more purposeful. They are better at being innovative, and are more prepared to share ideas. Further, friends at work provide a sense of belonging: they make you feel that you are informed about what's going on, that your opinions are being heard across the organisation.

Nonetheless, work is not work without sweat and toil. It is the impact of that on friendship we're pursuing here.

On being useful

Think more on this distinctive feature of working life, its utility. Mark Twain captured its characteristic with wit and insight in *The Adventures of Tom Sawyer*. Tom persuades his friends to whitewash Aunt Polly's fence, and he does so by convincing them that they can't afford not to, it's such a rare experience. This deludes them into thinking the work is not work, and they don't really have to do it – though they do, and willingly. Twain reflects on what this means:

> [Tom should comprehend] that Work consists of whatever a body is obliged to do, and that Play consists of whatever a body is not obliged to do. And this would help him to understand why constructing artificial flowers or performing on a treadmill is work, while rolling ten-pins or climbing Mont Blanc is only amusement. There are wealthy gentlemen in England who drive four-horse passenger-coaches twenty or thirty miles on a daily line, in the summer, because the privilege costs them considerable money; but if they were offered wages for the service, that would turn it into work and then they would resign.

That it is the fundamental operating principle in work relationships is revealed in a variety of ways. When people are friendly with the boss, in addition to being civil or polite, is it not at least in part because they depend on the boss for pay, for perks and for a peaceful life – that is, the utility the boss performs for them? Alternatively, why is it so easy to dislike a colleague who doesn't pull their weight, or someone else who makes work for others, even when outside of work they may well be perfectly likeable people? Is it not because at work their likeability is determined by their ability to fulfil their role or function; fail there and friendliness will not follow. Or again: why do people like the postman, the tea-lady or the receptionist? Is it not because they provide the service of being good for gossip and easing the day away? That's the added value they offer, their additional utility. (Incidentally, research shows that gossip at work is good for your health too, so office gossips really are doing something useful.) And what of perhaps the deepest conundrum of all. Why is it that you can have known a colleague for years, enjoyed their company day after day, worked with them, even helped them when personal matters spilt into the workplace, and yet, when they left, it was, overnight, almost as if you had never known them? You might miss them for a day, perhaps a week, and hope their new job is going well. But, in truth, most of the people with whom we were once friendly at work disappear from our lives with little more than a toast in the canteen, or best wishes on a card. It is very odd, when you consider all the time you spend with these people, and the genuine exchange of good feeling. And yet, it is entirely understandable when you realise that the relationship was, at heart, one of utility, based mostly on what was done together. Take that shared activity away, which is what happens when people leave work, and the friendship withers like a cut flower. It is not that they were not liked or had nothing in common with you. It is that the thing held in common – the work – is gone; without doing that together the relationship ceases to have reason or purpose.

The ambiguity of most work friends is also illustrated by what happens to colleagues if they happen to meet outside work. Many will have an inkling of just how unnerving, and amusing, this can be. Clearly few will be pleased to be spotted scanning the job section in the newsagents or to be caught buying luxury moist toilet tissue in the supermarket. But what of this? You're in *beds* at Ikea and through a stack of filing cabinets in *home office* see the person who sits across from you at work; they're in *kitchens*. You spend eight hours a day in the same room as them, and have only friendly feelings towards them. So why do you now put your head down, fake a thorough assessment of the mattresses, and give them ample time to move on, just so you don't have to talk? It feels too awkward, not right for a Saturday morning. Alternatively, at the cinema, heading for the screen, your eyes meet those of someone you've worked with time and time again. You approach, all smiles, and then note: they are of the opposite sex. You have a flush of anxiety. Should you just say 'hi'? Should you merely shake hands? Or should you exchange a kiss? What is appropriate in the non-work context?

The reason for the discomfort is that stripping work relationships of their utility, and the environment in which the relationship makes sense, simultaneously removes their *raison d'être*. So outside work, people find it hard to know how to relate to one another. Typically, they revert to work: talking about what you do together, though you're not actually doing it, feels right, feels friendly. People become awkward because the framework within which they conduct the relationship is gone. (It might also be the case, of course, that someone doesn't want to see their colleagues in the garden centre or at paintball because no matter how nice they might be, they only remind them of work.) Even if your relationships at work involve a drink at the end of the day, or can cope with a casual encounter over the checkout, there will be limits to what they can sustain. This is why team-building away days are so dreaded. They so easily overstep the mark by forcing people together as if they were friends. They are often only saved by the identification of a common enemy, the facilitator or boss, who as the recipient of mutual animosity creates the illusion of friendship in the group.

Work is not the only place where these utility-type friendships predominate. Any friendship that is based primarily upon the fact of doing something together will share similarities with it. Political friends, mostly formed around the business of politics – the art of doing the possible, we might say – are an obvious case in point. In a study of amity and enmity in the highest echelons of

American politics, *Friend and Foe in the U.S. Senate*, Ross K. Baker found that the most common type of interpersonal alliances are based on what he called 'institutional kinship'. These relationships are not really intimate in a personal sense, but instead flourish and flounder insofar as they oil the wheels of political machination. Conversely, close friendships, carrying the everyday sense of personal intimacy, are the rarest. In fact, Baker concludes that they are probably unwise in politics: friendliness provides some 'wiggle room' when the going gets tough, but politically they are a liability. Moreover, if you want to be a leader, the evidence suggests you're better off being a loner. This is not to say that some politicians do not become very good friends, as people may at work. It is just to point out that for most, the friendship lasts only so long as the alliance or advantage does too.

Friendships from those that form between charity workers to those that stem from having been on a TV show provide further examples: take away the charitable work or the show and, for most, the friendship will fall away – if with a warm remembrance of the fun shared or aims achieved. Friendships formed online in virtual communities of interest are like this too. The thing that drives the friendliness of the chat room is the mutual usefulness or common enthusiasm that the internet is so good at propagating. We'll have more to say about this particularly modern manifestation of friendship later, but the suspicion would be that few virtual friendships transcribe into the real world where what is shared online does not dominate.

On not being used

Aristotle identified the principal characteristic of these friendships as he stalked the marketplaces of ancient Greece and Macedonia. He is hard to beat in his examination of the nature of them, characteristic of 'business types', as he put it.

> Those who are friendly with each other because they are useful to each other do not like each other for the person each one is

21

in themselves. They like each other only insofar as it does them some good. They are friendly because it is beneficial to be so.

He identifies the heart of the matter. It's his first type of friendship, the people who share goodwill, at least in the first instance, because they get something out of it. (The first type of friendship may convert into Aristotle's third type, when people know each other for who they are in themselves, and become close friends; but leave that relatively special case to one side for the minute.) Hence people can be friendly with colleagues without necessarily knowing anything much of the person as they are in themselves. And this immediately points to the limitation of this kind of friendship. It's weakness as friendship, and the reason Aristotle believes it is a lesser, if humanising, type of amity, is that it depends on the thing that is done together, on the mutual exchange of utility. The affection finds it hard to reach beyond the benefits gained by being friendly, and if such a friend ceases to perform the function or utility for you – be that because they change jobs or you move on – then the friendliness peters out: you have no other connection to draw on that can sustain this kind of friendship.

Think of the word 'friend' itself, and its conjugates – friends, friendly, friendliness, friendship. I do a lot of freelance work and, consequently, work with a number of different people. I am more or less friendly with them all and imagine that my friendliness is one of the reasons they ask me to work for them again. When working together, we will enjoy friendly conversations, gossip or otherwise; many of them might say of me, 'He is a friend of our organisation.' Others might ask me, from time to time, to do them a favour, which I do, partly to generate goodwill that I hope might have some return in the future, and partly out of friendship. If I'm honest, there's always some of the former motivation in the mix. A relatively small subsection of the individuals I work with might call me 'friend' on occasion, perhaps at a Christmas party. But for most of my work friends, if I heard them describing me as a good friend, perhaps with a capital 'F', say to someone who was a close friend of theirs, I would think that was overstepping the mark. I do not really know them, I would think: I am friends but not really a close friend. The friendliness might share some of the attributes of a deeper friendship, such as trusting and liking one another, and suspecting we might like each other more, if we had the time to put into the friendship outside of work. But it is nothing compared with the friendship founded on the intimacy of knowing and loving someone well, and knowing and loving them regardless of any mutual benefit or common project we share.

There is a risk, when analysing utility friendship in this way, of making it seem that work relationships and the like have more in common with the sycophancy of pleasing superiors, or gratuitous acts of self-interest, than friendship. It raises the question of whether the wise person should be sceptical of any and all friendship at work, and quietly write it off altogether. To do so, though, would be to come down too quickly on work relationships. They will all contain an element of utility, though that does not necessarily imply that they are all merely exploitative. And a work friend might become a close friend, of course.

We need a more subtle language to describe the conditions of friendship in these highly structured environments. It's good to be able to draw distinctions between the ways in which we might profit from the friendliness of other people, on a scale from out-and-out exploitation, through mutual benefit, to an encounter we might come to count as providential. Unmoderated exploitation is never going to provide fertile grounds for friendship. But soft mutual benefit is not only bearable in work relationships but also actually common to all friendships. Indeed, even best friends are, in part, a good thing to have because of what they can do for you, for the function they can perform – from small kindnesses like feeding the cat, to being there to pick up the pieces when life falls apart. Some would say that the defining mark of a good friend is that they are always there for you and thus have a kind of unconditional utility. 'I'll be there, yes I will. You've got a friend', are James Taylor's words. That sounds like a blessing. The

23

difference between that and most relationships at work is that in the office people are friendly generally because of the mutual gain. You are liked first, not for who you are, but for what you give.

And yet, this means that the possibility of genuine friendship at work is not automatically excluded. A common project is an excellent way of bringing people together which must, on occasion, result in good friendship. Some individuals do come to like each other having met at work. Moreover, they can not only survive an encounter at Ikea without embarrassment, but they might even choose to go to Ikea together at the weekend. Work may be one of the best sources of friends, as well as one of the most desirable places to have one. The point is that these relationships are always, at least initially, influenced by the utility factor. The trick is to ensure any nascent friendship is not determined by it.

Figure 2: 'A true friend stabs you in the front.' (Oscar Wilde)

24

This, though, is harder to do than might first meet the eye because the work environment throws up all sorts of hurdles to relationships based primarily on liking someone for who they are, as opposed to what they contribute to a common task. To see the extent of the problem we need to break the matter down into two constitutive elements. One operates at a personal level: how to negotiate the debilitating tendency of the functional nature of friendliness at work. A second operates at a broader, social level: why does the modern workplace cultivate such a powerful culture of instrumentality and how can friends at work cope with it, even overcome it?

On winning friends, not merely influencing people

They're big challenges, and many of Aristotle's thoughts on friendship are focused on them. In chapters VIII and IX of his *Nicomachean Ethics*, his most sustained piece of writing on the subject, he makes a number of suggestions as to tackling the pressures friends at work, and elsewhere, must negotiate. His advice stems partly from his analysis of such friendships and also from the tone he adopts when discussing them. This is important, I think: he has an attitude of unsentimental honesty. The point seems to be that it is vital to recognise work relationships for what they are. Right discernment will show the extent to which any friendliness that they exhibit depends on what the individuals do together and the extent to which a friendship can be deepened into knowing, liking and maybe even loving the individual for who they are themselves.

There are a number of insidious factors that can impede such progress; that they may seem slight contributes to the real challenge. First, Aristotle notes that friendships based on doing something together are easy to form. And second, he notes that they can easily be confused with deeper friendship. They are easy to form for the reason that such friends don't have to reveal much of themselves and can focus instead on what they are up to. That means they don't have to share much of themselves, which

25

anyway takes time, and can instead immediately start to draw on the pool of common experience. We call it the camaraderie of doing things together or, conversely – and perhaps especially at work – the solidarity found in both not wanting to be there. This feature of work friendship might explain why so-called progressive employers increasingly provide things for employees to do alongside the work for which they are employed. Find work with a large enough company and you will not only have a desk but gyms, coffee shops and cafés to hang out in with colleagues. They are locations for the forging of friendships. Is it going too far to suspect that the captains of industry have their eye on statistics such as those thrown up by Gallup? They showed that employee satisfaction increases markedly if staff consider the workplace to be friendly, that they are more likely to be happy with their pay, to engage better with customers and be more productive too.

Such feelings undoubtedly humanise the workplace: the gossip over the photocopier or the emailed joke about the boss are vital too. But such activities are in themselves poor indicators of the possibility for deeper friendship that may evolve from jovial company. For example, a mutually shared indiscretion may be taken as a sign of friendship. 'Did you hear about Jim and Pamela in the store cupboard?' Immediately, you feel the pleasure of being in on the conspiracy against Jim and Pamela. But there need be nothing very intimate about that when it is founded on shallow grounds. The indiscretion may create an illusion of intimacy, when you're just being used as a sounding board, not real confidant. It is readily mistaken as a sign of deeper friendship.

Second, Aristotle sees that friendships characterised by their instrumentality are transient too: the things that bring the individuals together often change – be it the project, the gossip, or the job itself – and in quite arbitrary ways. Once that happens any friendship dissolves as well, for it existed only in relation to that which brought it about. Such transience, may mean that the relationship is over before there was even a chance for anything of any depth to take root.

Third, work friendships can be shaky because the individuals concerned do not always get the same thing out of the relationship. The office joker will demand an audience and think them friends, when the individuals on the receiving end can just feel used. What is more, so-called friendships formed on this basis are not even necessarily with or between pleasant people. The relationships depicted in the movie *Trainspotting* are an extreme version of this. It features a bunch of friends caught up in the underworld of the Edinburgh drug scene. There is the loser, the liar, the psycho and the junkie, and throughout the film they use and abuse each other. The workplace equivalents of the loser, the liar and the psycho are the careerist, the sycophant and the person who will step on anyone in their way: they will be your friends, for as long as it suits them.

This leads us to another set of issues, around what happens when friendships at work go wrong. The problem here is that because they are conditional on mutual benefit, they are also prone to accusation when that benefit is not, or is perceived to have not been, delivered. In the workplace, this can be dangerous. Not only has a possible friend been lost but a possible enemy may have been made. Once the damage is done and bad feeling has set in, one party may then have it in their power, say, to spoil the other person's career prospects. Backstabbing and insidious rumour can cause tremendous trouble. It is for this reason that sociologists of the workplace report that colleagues often pretend to remain friends with others even when they secretly despise them; they'd rather be phony than risk animosity. Similarly, self-help books often advise avoiding friendships at work and letting no one become more than an amicable acquaintance. One title I saw recently, on how to get along with difficult colleagues, expressed such deception perfectly. It was called *The Frog-Snogger's Guide*. Incidentally, it was sat on the shelf bang next door to *The Science of Influence: How To Get Anyone To Say Yes In 8 Minutes Or Less*. The latter tomes' first big tip was to make sure you come across as a friend. If you want to have it your way, you have to secure that illusion within the first four seconds.

Even if people are not so manipulative, the omnipresence of utility can be confusing. It makes for another illusion of friendship that, again, is ambiguous. A friendly character or admirable temperament might look like an attitude of friendship but is still strictly in the service of getting on at work. Or someone may show goodwill towards you that is nothing of the sort. This last possibility is sometimes known as the 'Hawthorne Effect', after an experiment done in Western Electric's Hawthorne factory in 1927. Investigators turned the lights up in the factory and worker productivity went up. They then turned the lights down in the factory and strangely productivity went up a little more. The conclusion they reached was that just an impression of care and goodwill makes workers more productive. In the same way, a letter of thanks from your boss will please you even if you know he doesn't particularly care for you.

Finally, discerning friendliness built on utility from close friendship is difficult because many people want to maintain a degree of privacy at work and are guarded about what they reveal of themselves. For the same reason it is generally deemed inappropriate to enquire into a colleague or employee's personal life – unless, of course, it affects their employability, as in the case of ill health. The result is that, on one level, colleagues assume that they know a great deal about each other, as a by-product of spending all that time together, whilst on another level they actually understand little – the issue of pseudo-intimacy. Similarly, professionalism compromises the extent to which people can get to know each other too. Consider the way people dress: it is usually indicative of their sense of their worth to the company, not who they are in themselves. And experiments with 'dress-down Fridays' prove the point: many would rather wear their usual work clothes even when they have a choice, because it causes them too much anxiety to think how they want to present themselves to their peers otherwise. Jeans or slacks? Shift or top? The fear is of revealing too much, and that mitigates against friendship.

Looking at these problems as a whole, we can see that although an attitude of unsentimental honesty might seem too steely for the fostering of friendship, it has the great advantage of enabling one to discern the amicable wheat from the utilitarian chaff and thereby the relationships from which friendship can grow. If friendship is about knowing someone truly and being known by them, it is also about knowing which relationships are likely to foster good friendships; the relationships that contain the seeds of deeper friendship, as opposed to shallow, instrumental friendliness. It all depends on the attitude people have to their tasks and what they expect of others. And perhaps when genuine good feeling rises above the quest for jolly camaraderie, or devious influence, an admiration for character over professional achievement – a virtuous spiral of regard – can blossom into friendship.

Befriending bosses

Consider now a subset of the personal dimension of work relationships that one must contend with, namely, that of friendliness with the boss. This is inevitably tricky. It might be thought of as the ultimate test. It may be that you like your boss, they like you, they like the work you do for them, and you the rewards you receive in return. But even such happy circumstance is rarely stable. At the heart of the relationship lies an imbalance – in terms of power, money and status. 'Work is of two kinds,' wrote Bertrand Russell. 'First, altering the position of matter at or near the earth's surface...; second, telling other people to do so. The first kind is unpleasant and ill paid; the second is pleasant and highly paid.' Problems for friendship readily arise from such disparity. So is it possible to be friends with the boss?

Some factors touched on already have a bearing on the question. But specifically in relation to this issue, the concerns can be broken down into three parts. First, how are the overtures of friendship that a boss may make to a subordinate to be understood, and the reverse – the friendliness of a subordinate towards the boss? Second, what of the complications that arise if and when work is, at least in part, rewarding for its own sake? And last but not least, what of the business of working for friends?

It is worth doing a little reverse engineering and thinking, first, about the structure of the relationship between employees and bosses. Aristotle is illuminating once more. He divides the relationship into two parts. One is a contractual part, namely, the terms on which someone is employed that has to do with tasks, time and money. 'Not a penny off the pay, not a second on the day,' it is sometimes said. The second is a goodwill part, that is, the human bit of the working relationship, or the extent to which you're prepared to gift your talents free of charge to the boss. The first part being contractual is, by definition, impersonal. The second, goodwill, is where the potential for friendship lies. Unhappiness stems from the confusion of the two.

Perhaps the most common complications stem from the confusion that arises as to the nature of the demands that a boss may make. Are they made on the basis of the contractual part of the relationship or the goodwill part? It is often not easy to tell the difference. For example, if a paycheck is late or it is necessary to work after hours, does the boss call on goodwill or contractual leeway to cope with the immediate crisis? The answer is probably an uneasy amalgam of both.

The confusion is compounded because people are inconsistent when it comes to what they will put up with. Typically, we say that we are happy to give freely, in theory, when in practice we choose what is most beneficial for ourselves. So, it might be an excellent and virtuous thing to do the extra labour without expectation of reward or gain. But when it comes to it, such high-minded character dissolves in the acid of instrumentality: one is primarily there not to indulge goodwill but to earn a living. Hence a boss might think that an extra hour or two in overtime is a small thing, whereas an employee could well regard it as a big deal.

For all that, Aristotle identifies a general rule. When asking employees to go the extra mile, the boss should operate on the side of caution if they want to keep them sweet: financial compensation and clear thanks for what has been given forms the basis of best practice. Moreover, the payment and thanks must be offered up front: that keeps the relationship free of the complications of delayed or unrequited returns. And it must be offered generously, for people vary in their assessment of what they think their efforts are worth: the boss who over-remunerates at the time will reap goodwill in time.

So much for the responsibility of bosses. What of the other situation, when employees ask for something, perhaps time off, and thereby call on the boss's goodwill? Different forces come into play. The fundamental issue is that because the boss is generally in a position to help, the situation is actually loaded against them morally speaking – a friend in need and all that. What is more, the boss may fear losing what friendship they enjoy with their staff if they do not respond positively, and staff may well ask what worth there is in having a friend who is powerful if it does not deliver benefits, at least from time to time. What keeps the issue within the bounds of friendliness are the principles of voluntarism and generosity again. A second rule comes to look very much like the first: when someone calls on the boss's goodwill and asks for a favour, the boss should act reasonably and give freely, and the employee should be reasonable and willingly show gratitude too. True friendship, as Aristotle puts it, does not place the scales centre stage.

What now of work that people enjoy and find rewarding? The complication here is that a job might be thought to be its own reward. This leads to the assumption that friendship can flow more freely between managers and subordinates because financial gain is not such a big issue. Not so, says Aristotle. He tells the story of a lyre player at a party who was promised payment and more, the better he played. When dawn came, he asked for what he thought were his dues. However, his employer regarded himself as something of a connoisseur. After hearing such beautiful music he could not comprehend the demand for more cash: 'Surely, the beauty of the playing is payment enough', he reasoned. 'Your playing is its own reward.' Unsurprisingly the lyre player did not see it that way, and departed bitter and disappointed. The moral of the story is not that the lyre player did not enjoy making music: he may have taken more pleasure from it than anyone. Rather, it is that whilst the party-giver sought music, the lyre player sought a living, and though the former received what he wanted in good measure, the lyre player did not. Work may include its own rewards but for the employee working for someone else it is still a means to an end.

The final scenario is that in which people work for a friend. Once more, the ambiguity of the roles played by individuals in this situation makes it tricky at the best of times. In particular, the money that will necessarily change hands has an inexorable ability to draw all value to itself, sapping the goodwill of even the strongest friendships. The situation is hardly different if the friend in question is not the wage payer, but rather, say, a line manager; being subordinate is quite enough to cause trouble.

Typically, the rot sets in unawares. I once worked for a friend, an arrangement that started off very well. I was deeply grateful to them for the break it gave me; they were glad to offer me a generous share in the rewards of the business, and a good work/life balance. When asked about how it was going by other friends, I told them that we were the exception to the rule: money and friendship can mix!

But that was when the going was good. When the business was hit by a particularly deep cash-flow crisis, I fell into the unhappy confusion between contract and goodwill that Aristotle identifies. It was clear what friendship demanded of me: work for a while without pay. But cash-strapped, I was not able to do so. As it happened, this spared me the harder question of whether I was willing to work unsalaried, but, that aside, I could not deliver for goodwill's sake and I quit. My action inevitably called the friendship into question and things were never the same again. The moral of that story is work for your friend at your own peril.

In general, then, the advice at the personal level is that friendship flourishes best when it can rise above the utility of the workplace, though that is easier said than done. If friendliness is a feature of the office, as you might hope, you're best either not to expect too much or quickly to establish ways of deepening the friendship that have nothing to do with work whatsoever – perhaps by trying a drink together after work, or making an arrangement at the weekend. This will show the relationship up for what it is, so start small: if it is merely a work relationship then the attempt to form a deeper friendship will flounder; if it is truly a friendship, it will flourish. The philosophical principle is that friendships which depend upon doing something together also depend upon the mutual benefit that comes from that. If the benefit is cut for some reason then the relationship will be curtailed too. Such is the fragility of utility-based friendship.

Commercial culture

If the workplace presents barriers to friendship that are difficult to negotiate at a personal level, then the broader culture of work and the economic milieu in general present a challenge to friendship-making too. This is the second dimension of the impact that instrumentality can have on friendship, namely, that the underlying ideals of a commercially-minded society – in which utility, competition, profit and exchange are highly valued – shape a socio-economic climate that people's friendships must contend with too. To develop this aspect, we can turn to another thinker, one of the founding fathers of the modern workplace, Adam Smith.

Smith was actually an optimist about the impact that commerce would have on the opportunities for friendship. He believed commercial life to be democratic and egalitarian, especially when compared to the feudal society of deference and inequality that it pushed aside. Because the industrial economy is a great leveler, people therefore find themselves on a level too which means, he reasoned, that they have better opportunities for friendship.

Among well-disposed people, the necessity or conveniency of mutual accommodation, very frequently produces a friendship not unlike that which takes place among those who are born to live in the same family. Colleagues in office, partners in trade, call one another brothers; and frequently feel towards one another as if they really were so. Their good agreement is an advantage to all; and, if they are tolerably reasonable people, they are naturally disposed to agree. We expect that they should do so; and their disagreement is a sort of small scandal.

Although to the contemporary ear this sounds a bit like the conviviality of a Pall Mall club, Smith is, in fact, that rare thing amongst modern philosophers as a thinker who takes friendship seriously. He resorts to it particularly in his book *The Theory of Moral Sentiments*.

Here, he centres on the concept of sympathy, a notion of compassion, empathy and consideration that underlines the importance of love and friendship in his thought. Having said that, he approaches it ambivalently. Sometimes he appears to take sympathy as meaning the full affectionate feeling that is naturally associated with friendship. At other times sympathy implies merely fellow feeling, as if it were little more than an opinion held in common. This ambivalence is significant, I think. It is as if love and friendship struggle against other less accommodating factors within commercial society, for all that Smith wishes it were otherwise. We are back again amidst the ambiguities of the culture of cost-benefit analysis.

Smith was aware of this predicament and he tried to come up with a theory which showed how people could be friendly not just because they found themselves on the level and involved in a common enterprise, but more powerfully because commercialism itself positively nurtures a culture of friendship. He took an idea from Aristotle. The ancient Greek thought that wellbeing was the goal of life. It could be achieved by moral individuals – people who were increasingly courageous, open-handed, witty and characterful. What is more, he thought that by virtue of having these characteristics, friendship will come their way too.

Smith took this link between the goal of life, individual characteristics and friendship, and adapted it to the world he saw around him. First, he interpreted the goal of wellbeing to mean a culture of flourishing cooperation. If that seems a mediocre thing to aspire to then that is not to say that the virtues of sociality are themselves mundane: if anything quite the opposite, since social cooperation requires individuals to act justly, beneficently and prudently. Moreover, when individuals act in this way, Smith argued, they should attract friends.

The trouble, though, is that although the virtues of social cooperation may be admirable, it is not entirely clear that individuals will readily aspire to them (unlike, say, happiness, which makes its own case as a goal in life). So Smith developed another idea that is not Aristotelian but which would, he hoped, motivate people nonetheless. He called it the 'impartial spectator'.

An impartial spectator is a fictional presence that sees everything an individual does, not to pass judgement, but in order that the individual, believing that they are being watched, will act in the best way they can. If the idea of such an observer seems somewhat fanciful, its very shadowiness is part of Smith's plan too. The point is that the impartial spectator will not satisfy the individual by merely praising them when they behave well; it is not an internalised father-figure. Rather, it operates more like a mirror to encourage the individual to see themselves as they truly are. That, surely, is a frightening thing to behold, quite enough to nudge anyone's bad behaviour in the direction of the good.

The hope is that this will cultivate the individual's desire not for praise, a questionable if understandable goal, but for the perception that they are praiseworthy, a higher aim that nurtures the development of the individual's character and actions. As Smith puts it: 'Man naturally desires, not only to be loved, but to be lovely.' This, then, is what he believes will inspire individuals to act according to the values of social cooperation: they will seek to be praiseworthy, not merely praised. And in turn, because that praiseworthiness makes them lovely, they will find genuine friends, who are lovely too.

What is more, these people of good character should expect many good friends:

> Such friendships need not be confined to a single person, but may safely embrace all the wise and virtuous, with whom we have been long and intimately acquainted, and upon whose wisdom and virtue we can, upon that account, entirely depend.

As an added bonus, Smith also argued these people will be happy because they are content with themselves: 'A great part, perhaps the greatest part, of human happiness and misery arises from the view of our past conduct, and from the degree of approbation or disapprobation which we feel from the consideration of it.'

Figure 3: 'Man naturally desires, not only to be loved, but to be lovely.' (Adam Smith)

Realpolitik

This is the high point in Smith's doctrine of friendship. However, it begs a question. What kinds of behaviour or virtues are thought praiseworthy, and who decides?

On the matter of who decides, Smith is clear that the answer is neither moral philosophers nor priests: however important they may feel their deliberations and dictates to be, they have little impact upon the behaviour of individuals. The best arbiter is the individual themselves, and the dialogue they have with their impartial spectator. Further, because they seek to be praiseworthy, the individual cannot simply justify their actions by saying that what they did seemed right to them; they must consider what society around them might consider to be right too.

But this still leaves the issue as to what is praiseworthy. That is more difficult to decide. The problem is that commercial societies are pluralistic, so there is bound to be some debate as to the standards according to which individuals should behave. One person's praiseworthy efficiency is another's blameworthy zealousness. What seems like pure friendliness to the boss to one looks like toadying up to them to another. Not that Smith is alone in being vulnerable to such moral dilemmas. Deciding cases like these is a problem that any ethical theory has to negotiate, in the absence of moral absolutes. However, a more particular problem stems from the need Smith has for praiseworthiness to itself be thought praiseworthy. If commercial culture is confused about that too – compromising it in favour of utility, profit, exchange and so on – then his theory collapses. The shadowy observer dissipates, as it were, in the harsh winds of what people might call the real world – the realpolitik of commercial activity. People then inevitably return to seeking praise for its own sake.

It seems to me that this is just what happens at work. The determining instrumentality of the workplace means that praiseworthiness is typically secondary to delivery. At work people are praised for the things they do, and chastised for the things that they fail to do: remuneration comes to those who impact the bottom line; people act out of utility – their 'role'. Even intangible qualities that might be thought praiseworthy, like entrepreneurialism or simple human pleasantness, must indirectly prove their worth in terms of profitability to be valued. Employment is not like school where people are rewarded for trying hard regardless of what they achieve, though fat cat directors may be an exception.

To put it another way, if few would challenge the idea that praiseworthiness is praiseworthy in theory, its value stands or falls on whether it is manifest in practice. If a commercial society, of which the workplace is a microcosm, is one in which praiseworthiness is in fact a marginal concern, it seems that friendship will in turn struggle: people will on the whole be merely friendly with each other, rarely truly friends in the sense of loving someone with no thought of gain.

Hence, I think, the equivocation in Smith's notion of sympathy. It is as if he wants the affection that he sees in commercial society to be an expression of the full love of friends. Only when that is set against the conditions of the real world he can only make it stand up as a kind of decent fellow feeling.

Worse yet, there are reasons to think not only that praiseworthiness flounders but also that friendship actually undermines social cooperation itself. Friends regard each other as special. They see each other as praiseworthy, or lovely, typically by way of a contrast with what they regard as unpraiseworthy, or unlovely, around them. Take a value like loyalty. Someone will value the loyalty of a friend because it appears to be absolute compared to the loyalty one might have, say, to a boss, which clearly has its limits. From that it is only a short step to saying something else: if you are my loyal friend, then those others are not. Friendship may promote suspicion not cooperation.

And Smith was wary of this. He argued that people should be 'capable of friendship' but avoid 'ardent attachments'. Or they should restrict their attendance at 'convivial societies' because they will interfere with the 'steadiness of industry'. Far from promoting friendship, commercial society seems to require us to be friendly, but not so close as to foment rebellion or forge alliances. At best, we should be amicable strangers, or 'honorary friends' as the contemporary economist Paul Seabright has put it.

There is also the argument that organisations are inherently suspicious of friendship since they set up networks of loyalties that can act against the organisation's best interests: the activities of friends can easily be viewed as time-wasting, if not nepotistic and subversive – symptoms of cronyism.

Utility spreads

The suspicion that social cooperation values profit and politeness over praiseworthiness and knowing someone well was voiced by another eighteenth-century Scot. According to Adam Ferguson, commercial society is not merely indifferent to deeper friendships but positively cultivates enmity. This is because although it may promote interdependence, it does so at the price of substituting the virtues that would take care of others with those that take care of oneself. He painted a bleak picture of the market society he saw forming around him, 'dominated by a spirit of individualism, competition and legalism where relationships are defined and constrained by contracts and the profit motive'. He accused optimists like Smith of confusing virtue and utility: they would call a cow virtuous, he said, if it produced the right sort of milk. For Ferguson, the workplace is alienating, soul-destroying and isolating, playing to the worst detached and solitary instincts in human beings. In the market economy, man [sic] has therefore, 'found an object which sets him in competition with his fellow-creatures, and he deals with them as he does with his cattle and his soil, for the sake of the profits they bring'.

Karl Marx, the later philosopher who understood the workings of capitalism like no one else, put it even more bleakly. We may work together with the 'utmost amiability,' he noted. But we're in effect constantly passing each other notes that read: 'Dear friend, I give you what you need, but you know the *conditio sine qua non*: you know the ink in which you have to sign yourself over to me; in providing for your pleasure, I fleece you.' Another philosopher, Georg Simmel added a further twist to the impact that work has on relationships. In *The Philosophy of Money*, he notes that modern working lives are characterised by their dependence on technology: he wrote before the invention of the computer, but the way that the silicon chip has revolutionised work in recent decades, in a million intranets and websites, massively underlines his point. And yet, something paradoxical happens when people interact via technology. It simultaneously draws individuals closer together *and* depersonalises their interactions. Hence, in the computer age, individuals become entries on a database, accounts on the other side of the world, information providers, and disembodied email generators to one another. 'What kind of people they are in other respects plays no role here,' Simmel concludes. And if the kind of people they are in other respects does not matter, then the opportunities for friendship are going to be substantially narrowed too.

It should be said that the workplace and the culture of work that now exists in late capitalism has changed massively in the years since Marx, and even Simmel. Today, HR executives in many companies are seriously committed to moving away from command-and-control type management structures and to increasing the choices employees have in the workplace. They want to make time for people in and around work, not only for chores that otherwise eat into their weekends, or even to cultivate churn-quenching work friendships; but also for activities that build praiseworthy aspects of character, from learning a language to taking a sabbatical. I've heard the CEO of one multinational say that he refused to call his employees 'human assets', as the jargon dictates, since he did not own his staff but rather asked them for their time, if in return for certain rewards.

Alternatively, the male-dominated, heavy industry that characterised the industrial revolution of Smith and Marx's time has largely collapsed in the west at least, and with it the grinding days it demanded – though so too have the industrial communities that were arguably excellent environments for nurturing a sense of connection. Or one can point to the place and influence of women in the workplace that might promote a more humanly considerate environment.

However, these gains are themselves under threat, from utility again. Any positive effects are arguably being beaten back by the spread of flexible labour markets and the huge emphasis on productivity in the modern economy. This is nothing if not self-interest with a vengeance. Indeed, many fear that such a culture is deeper now than it was in Smith's day. Is not so-called vocational education little more than preparing students for greater productivity in the workplace, for an ever tighter fit into the cogs of the economy?

The current predicament is well portrayed in Douglas Coupland's novel, *Microserfs*, the story of a group of friends working for Microsoft, the software giant. Dan, the narrator, describes how in the 1970s companies installed showers and sculptures in the workplace, 'to soothe the working soul'. This led in the 1980s to the blurring of the boundary between work and life. And now, inexorably completing the circle, people are asked to become their own corporations: 'Give us your entire life or we won't allow you to work on cool projects,' he says of Microsoft's attitude to its employees. Certainly, the number of hours people spend at work competes with time for friends elsewhere, to say nothing of what is owed to the family. This is doubly detrimental to friendship because apart from the adverse effects of time constraints, good friendships depend too on individuals nurturing a range of interests – a hinterland that modern work practices are quite possibly depleting.

In other words, the spectre of utility still haunts the workplace today. Whilst the poles may have shifted, there is little reason to think that the challenge posed by it is any less strong. Perhaps it is stronger because it is more subtle: if social cooperation in commercial society has mutated into social productivity under capitalism, our work culture is at least as indifferent towards friendship as ever it was. It's a big theme, and will take more unpicking as a problem that has a tangible impact on us all, living as we do in a culture that assesses much more than just our productivity via cost-benefit analysis. Deeper friendships may form yet, but perhaps in spite of, not because of, commercialism.

Friends and Lovers

'If you wanna be my lover, you gotta get with my friends.'
The Spice Girls

The year is 1559 during the brief reign of Mary Queen of France, also known as Queen of Scots. The scene is a festival in the renaissance town of Bar-le-Duc. Two pairs of eyes meet across the crowd, a meeting which one of them later described thus:

> We were seeking each other before we set eyes on each other, and at our first meeting, we discovered ourselves to be so seized by each other, so known to each other and so bound together that from then on none was so close as each was to the other.

A question: was this the start of an affair or a friendship?

Move forward, just over a hundred years, across the channel to springtime in Deptford, South East London. A man and a woman are in the grips of love, attested to by their prolific letters now in the British Library. Their relationship began the year turbulently, though Margaret is beginning to feel less anxious again for all John's intensity. She writes:

> What mean you to make me weep and break my heart by your love to me? Take me and all I have, give me but your love, my dear friend. Tuesday is longed for by me and nights and days move a tedious pace till I am near you.

A question: is it lovers or friends that will be reunited?

Now to the present day, and a crematorium in North London, at the end of a relationship. At the funeral, the man who survives recalls:

> I was barely coherent, shaking violently through the music, trembling, wobbly-voiced, as I read the Maupassant, taking

deep breaths to fight off tears: 'We must feel. That is every-thing. We must feel as a brute beast filled with nerves feels, and knows that it has felt and knows that each feeling shakes it like an earthquake. But we must not say that we have been so shaken. At the most we can let it be known to few people who will respect the confidence.'

The question again: does the man remember his lover or his friend?

The passion described in each case might suggest that these couples were lovers. They were, in fact, all friends. The first is Michel de Montaigne, the essayist and author of one of the best philosophical pieces of writing on friendship, prompted by his relationship with Etienne La Boëtie. This excerpt, from that essay, usually published with the title 'On friendship', describes their first meeting. The second comes from a letter of Margaret Godolphin, a maid of honour at the court of Charles II, who had a 'seraphic' friendship with John Evelyn, a friend of Samuel Pepys. The third comes from a book by the actor Simon Callow, enti-tled *Love Is Where It Falls: An Account of a Passionate Friendship*, a memoir of his relationship with the theatrical literary agent Peggy Ramsay.

And of what passion, for the fervent obsession within which each of these friendships flourished is arresting precisely because none of them were sexual. Montaigne and La Boëtie were both men and though same-sex relationships were a marginal concern of his, Montaigne thought them 'rightly abhorrent to our man-ners'. Of the second couple, one might easily come to the con-clusion that they used Restoration religiosity as a cover for what would have been an affair, had Evelyn not been married. But that would be to misunderstand them: sex was never on the cards. It turns out that they enjoyed an intense friendship of a sort that had a long tradition up to the seventeenth century and is now largely forgotten. For Simon Callow and Peggy Ramsay the ques-tion of whether they would have a sexual relationship or not was relatively easily answered by numerous contingencies from Callow being gay to Ramsay being 40 years his senior. They excluded the possibility, though this is not to say that their relationship was not charged with erotic elements and troubled at times because of that. So, the friendships are intriguing. As what are often referred to as 'Platonic relationships', their passionate quality focuses us on a second set of ambiguities that can cause problems for friendship – now not revolving around the matter of utility but rather the question of sex.

Sex and friendship

This ambiguity is perhaps as familiar. At their best, sexual attraction and the feelings that exist between friends are both types of love. Sometimes, notably in the case of committed partners, this love shows itself as a happy synthesis of erotic and friendly affection. However, at other times, friendship and erotic love, whether or not actually expressed, form an unstable amalgam.

It may be that two friends come to sense a sexual undercurrent between them that far from sweeping them off their feet makes them feel decidedly unsteady. That discomfort leads to the question of whether or not to engage in an affair for fear of the threat it poses to the friendship. The clichéd case in point is the routine confession made on daytime TV: 'I had sex with my partner's best friend!' It generates such good material because friendship and erotic love can be so explosive.

Conversely, it may be that two lovers, brought together by a powerful sexual attraction, start to realise that there are no grounds for any real friendship between them, and as a result the relationship begins to fall apart. It was this scenario that was portrayed in Bernardo Bertolucci's film, *Last Tango in Paris*. Paul, played by Marlon Brando, meets Jeanne, played by Maria Schneider. An affair between them begins, though Paul insists they share nothing of their personal lives. Then, one day, Paul disappears. The affair is apparently over, until they bump into each other on the street, and in an attempt to renew the relationship, go to a tango bar, where he begins to tell her about himself. The bubble of erotic fantasy bursts for Jeanne. Knowing about each other is too much like friendship. The movie does not end happily. Bertolucci reportedly explained that the film grew out of his own fantasy of 'seeing a beautiful nameless woman on the street and having sex with her without ever knowing who she was'. That's a fantasy of sex without any of the complications of friendship, though as a fantasy the suggestion is it's not real.

A third predicament is when sex hangs a question mark over a friendship even when a physical relationship is barely thought of. Imagine a man and woman becoming friends at work – good friends – and deciding to go out for dinner together as an apparently natural extension of the friendship. Then, as they're sat across the table from each other – starched linen, candles and a rose between them – they start to feel awkward. Unwittingly, they have been drawn into uncharted waters as dinner for two is the sort of the thing that lovers do, not friends. The evening is one of embarrassment, and the friendship flounders. What's happened is that cultural assumptions about the activities associated with a sexual relationship have imperilled a friendship quite as effectively as any actual erotic attraction itself. That Montaigne and La Boëtie, Evelyn and Godolphin, and Callow and Ramsay were able to overcome any such issues in their otherwise highly passionate friendships is what makes them so intriguing.

There is, then, a play between sex and friendship that can be great, or conversely can complicate things terribly.

It's an issue that is arguably particularly critical today. The tectonic plates of marriage are shifting ground, giving rise to a new geography of the institution that, at least in part, is based on an ideal of sexual friendship: individuals desire the ecstasies of marriage to be shared with a person who is simultaneously their soulmate. Hence, perhaps, one of the reasons that people are marrying later. They're prepared to wait.

You can see how much ideas of marriage have changed by comparing these descriptions of a good marriage. The first was penned only 150 years ago by Robert Louis Stevenson, author of *Treasure*

Island. 'The two persons more and more adapt their notions one to suit the other, and in process of time, without sound of trumpet, they conduct each other into new worlds of thought.' It sounds like a prison sentence to the modern ear, which is why Stephanie Coontz, author of *Marriage: A History*, describes the ideal now in this way: 'Individuals want marriage to meet most of their needs for intimacy and affection and all their needs for sex... Married couples should be best friends, sharing their most intimate feelings and secrets.'

It's a dream that is reflected in many ways. There are sitcoms such as *Friends*, *Sex and the City* and *Will and Grace*. They thrive on the ambivalences of what the author Ethan Watters calls the 'tribe years' – the period when people are in their twenties and thirties, during which they remain unmarried and order their lives around long-standing friends. The TV shows endlessly toy with their characters' sexual liaisons, and the prospect of a perfect relationship, whilst keeping the friendships firmly centre stage. If and when the individuals do get married, or settle down, it is a sexual friendship that they want. Similarly, the tremendous success of *Bridget Jones' Diary* stems in large part from the seriousness with which the book explores modern friendship and its relationship to sexual promise. She's desperate to be married, and yet finds all her married friends – the 'smug marrieds' as she calls them – almost unbearable, not least when they offer her their patronising advice on how to make her single life as perfect as their married one.

Now, on one reading it may seem easy to untangle the ambiguities of sex and friendship. It just seems ridiculous to suggest in some pop-Freudian kind of way that all friends of the opposite sex would go to bed with each other everything else being equal. The point was well made by the philosopher John Stuart Mill who had an intense and, before they married, controversial friendship with Harriet Taylor: 'We disdained, as every person not a slave of his animal appetites must do, the abject notion that the strongest and tenderest friendship cannot exist between man and woman without sensual relation.'

Figure 4: 'We disdained, as every person not a slave of his animal appetites must do, the abject notion that the strongest and tenderest friendship cannot exist between man and woman without sensual relation.' (John Stuart Mill)

Alternatively, Freud had a point. The problem is not that the sex part always explicitly gets in the way, but rather that it hangs a question mark over the friendship unconsciously or from time to time: there could be a 'faint undercurrent of excitement' even between a St Francis and a St Clare. This erotic possibility, rather than a sexual inevitability, is no less powerful a manifestation of the possibly damaging play between sex and friendship.

Another rather different way in which the question of sex can spoil friendship is in the realm of same-sex attractions. Here, the faint undercurrent does not need a boy and a girl to stir it up and given that the fear of homosexuality is as much of a threat as any actual homosexuality, even in our liberated times, just a suggestion of same-sex attraction is potentially enough to muddy the waters of friendship. This is not to impute anyone and everyone with an innate gayness, like the suggestion that C. S. Lewis objects to so strongly in his essay on friendship, that 'the absence of smoke proves that the fire is very carefully hidden'. Rather, homosexuality complicates same-sex friendship primarily because of homophobia, that is the fear of gayness that may be taken as implied by a close friendship between two men (and I think it is fair to generalise that it is largely a male anxiety.) This means that the individuals concerned feel the need to demonstrate their lack of sexual attraction and make that explicit. They must prove to themselves, and to the rest of the world, that they are not homosexual. Physical intimacy is therefore monitored; emotional affection controlled – all to the detriment of the friendship.

Philosophically speaking, the sources of the confusion stem from the fact that erotic love and friendship are similar in certain respects, and different in others. The similarities mean that people can easily, and happily, come to share the affections that are associated with both. The differences mean that less appropriate affections can then arise, generating the tension.

Similarities and difference

So consider, first, the ways in which erotic relationships and friendship are the same. For starters, both are excellent things to hope for, part of life in all its fullness: love and friendship both call us into and are constitutive of human happiness. We are 'political animals', thought Aristotle, by which he didn't mean that we are invariably scheming but rather that we do not do well on our own. Alone, the human creature feels incomplete and unfulfilled. 'It is not wrong to want to be happy, but it is wrong to want to be happy all alone,' thought Albert Camus.

What is more, whilst both love and friendship stem from the need to be with others, both help us rise above pure self-interest: a lover who demands sex and sex alone is usually thought exploitative; someone who only wants friends for what they can get out of them uses his friends, in a pejorative sense, and any friendships he or she manages to form are doomed. For similar reasons, both loves are defined according to their ideals, for all that those ideals may be hard or impossible to achieve. If we offer the opinion that 'Katie is in a manipulative relationship' or 'Joe has an exploitative friend,' there is an implicit contrast

49

drawn with what the relationship could be like at its best. Someone will say, 'He only loved me for my money', thinking that love is so much more. Someone else will realise, 'She is only interested in me for what she can get out of me', implying that they hoped for so much more too.

Lovers and friends seem alike for what we might call technical reasons too. Both relationships are entered into voluntarily, unlike the relationship one has with country, class or family. Lovers and friends must both share a degree of trust, understanding and forbearance. Both loves can be jealous, one out of avarice, the other out of enmity. And both can operate apart from the law: sexual desire is antinomian, though marriage and tax laws try to channel and control it; and friendship would, in E. M. Forster's famous phrase, betray country before it betrayed itself.

There're some similarities. The other half of the story is the ways in which friendship and erotic love are different. It might be said that friendship is calm, reasonable, harmonious and sober, whereas erotic love is spontaneous, irrational, wild and orgiastic. Or that friendship tends towards the mind, conversation and the spiritual, whereas erotic love is nothing without the body, touch and lust. Alternatively, friendship seems to develop over time: it loves to dwell on what has past and to ponder what is to come. Erotic love, though, delights in immediacy; it exclaims, 'Now!'

Other differences apparently widen the gap. If friendship is not reciprocated it quickly loses its intensity and rapidly makes little sense: it is nonsense to say that someone is my friend but I am not their friend. Erotic love, in contrast, can quicken regardless of whether the passion is returned. Indeed, unrequited love produces eros' most exquisite passion – infatuation: a lover can be besotted with their beloved even in secret. Another difference concerns the relative ease with which friendships and erotic relationships can be formed. Friendship seems easier, in the sense that every new day holds the promise of meeting a new friend, if only in a casual sense. Love, though, seems harder: falling in love may come readily to some, but being in a successful relationship requires work. And everyone knows the frustration of unattainable love. How many, though, have sleepless nights over unattainable friendship?

Or again, once a friendship has formed, it seems reasonable to expect that it will mostly bring out the best in people: friendly affection and moral behaviour appear to conspire together in a virtuous circle of love, since friends want the best for each other. Should something slip, so that enmity comes to dominate the relationship, we'd say the friendship was over, or that at best, the friend became a frenemy. (Merriam-Webster Dictionary: 'One who pretends to be a friend but is actually an enemy.' You know you have a frenemy if your stomach knots as they walk into the room. You know you are a frenemy if a red mist falls across your vision when you see your 'friend' approaching.)

The same does not follow in erotic relationships at all and it is easy to imagine all sorts of situations in which the purely erotic passion of lovers can descend into abuse, violence and hatred – and yet still the individuals concerned could believe they are in love. A quarter of all murders are committed by a lover, far more than are committed by someone who was a friend.

In summary, friendship tends to be reasonable, whereas erotic love is irrational; friendship warms to the mind, whereas sexual attraction wants the body; friendship must be reciprocated to make sense, love need not; and friendship is mostly virtuous, whereas eros can be murderous.

Inasmuch as that is right, it offers one way of understanding how sex can hang a question mark over friendship, or vice versa. It happens when the similarities between the two loves are forced into too close proximity with the differences. A friendship is disturbed by undercurrents of sexuality – be that because of personal chemistry or an awareness of contravening social norms: what is to be done about it? The early days of a passionate affair become the months and years shared by a man and his mistress: so can eros' lion lie down with friendship's lamb? Even a happily committed couple will from time to time be aware of the conflict between the loves their relationship otherwise manages to synthesise. Eros' possessiveness may be threatened by friendship's desire to welcome others in – as when one partner becomes good friends with someone else of the opposite sex. Or friendship's reasonableness may still occasionally find eros' spontaneity irksome – at bedtime, for example, after a hard day's work. Eros is perhaps then like the sand in the oyster's shell. It is the grit around which a smooth, lustrous coating of friendship may form. But pearls have flaws and if they crack, the grit will be re-exposed.

Just what's going on here might be thought of in this way. The love that is called friendship could be defined as the love that longs to know someone else, and be known by them. That love, then, wants the other person to remain another person, in order that there be someone else to get to know. Hence, say, friends love to talk: there is a separateness implicitly in the together-ness of conversation.

The love that is labelled erotic, though, is different. It can be defined as the love that longs to have someone else, and be had by them. That love wants the other person, period. Any gap that is sensed between will seem like a threat. Hence, lovers long to be with each other, body and soul. And to be apart is pure agony, unlike friends who are quite happy not to see each other every day, or week, or month.

These distinctions are provisional. For we've the ideal of sexual friendship in mind, and possibly still ahead of us. And it is philosophy, I think, that has resources to shed a different and refreshing light on the matter, and to suggest a path towards a synthesis. First, we will look at what Plato says on the matter, because he almost uniquely amongst philosophers has a theory of love that offers a path of reconciliation between sexual desire and friendship. Second, we will use Aristotle's thoughts again to consider how to negotiate the dynamics that arise out of the ambiguity of sexual and friendly feeling: in this respect, his ideas can be thought of as practical outworkings of Plato's theory. And third, we will turn to the case of passionate friend-ships – for it turns out, I think, that when passion, as opposed to sexual feeling, characterises a relationship, friendship is most able to flourish.

Immortal longings

Modern philosophy has typically fought shy of exploring the ins and outs of sexual love, though the increasing prominence of women's voices is changing that. Men may fear looking like the trendy vicar who gives sex talks based upon the biblical Song of Songs. They may also worry about inadvertently divulging too much information, for, no matter how abstracted, thoughts on sexual matters are autobiographical to a higher degree than most: this kind of philosophy is done 'in the bedroom', as the Marquis de Sade delighted in repeating. However, it was not always like this. Ancient philosophers were intrepid, none more so than Plato.

For one thing, the chaste phrase now associated with his name – Platonic love – is a misnomer. His writing does try to guide us towards more spiritual longings but that is not to say Plato thought human beings were or should be free of physical desires. It is in his portrayal of Socrates that he works out what he thinks is the best attitude to have towards the starts, stirrings and satisfaction of sexuality. Indeed, Socrates, who was famous for claiming to know nothing for sure, made one exception to his wise ignorance: he was fully conversant with the wiles of erotic love. I think Plato suggests that there is a relationship between sex and friendship, and thus there is a link between friends and lovers. He argues that eros should lead to, though not necessarily be superseded by, friendship. How this might be possible is therefore of great interest in trying to unravel the harmony and discord that can be created by the interaction of the two loves.

The sexual constellation that fascinated Plato the most was the desire that existed between a young man and a youth. It's a tricky area on a number of counts. Given that the homosexual element is not in itself thought illicit, it is, first, male sexuality that Plato appears to explore – though actually that's not quite fair. He gives his best lines on eros to Diotima, a woman, and also discusses how eros longs to give birth and to nurture. So. I think there's more in Plato on feminine desire than might first appear. Second, though, there is the matter of the age difference between the male Greek lovers and the concern to modern minds that their inherent inequality breeds abusive relationships. Third, there is the related anxiety over the criterion that the Greeks used to determine the ability to give consent – the appearance of a beard on the youth. We prefer the less ambiguous, and in practice more conservative, measure of age. So what can be made of these issues?

What is often overlooked is that ancient homosexuality worried Plato too, and for reasons that are close to our own. One of the places in which he raises the matter is in the *Symposium*. This dialogue portrays a dinner party at which various characters make speeches on love. One of the participants, Pausanius, argues that the reason why it is appropriate to love youths only after their beard has appeared is that it is only then that they can be thought to have developed a mind of their own, which means that the older partner will not be able to take advantage of the younger. In fact, Pausanius claims, with an optimism that would outdo most liberals, that the older partner will then want to share everything he has with his beloved and even spend the rest of his life with him. He goes on to express the opinion that individuals whose urges lead them to seduce any boy, regardless of maturity, are debauched; every legal obstacle should be placed in their path. Not that this is any reason to ban homosexuality outright, for all the clarity that comes with prohibition: that would be both tyrannical and would foster a dull and stupid attitude towards sexual matters. Rather, he believes that the ambiguity of the customs and conventions that govern sexual behaviour is, in fact, their strength and virtue. They can steer the complexity of human desire without being oppressive. In other words, Plato saw perfectly clearly that sexuality is tricky. But the power of such feelings is no reason to don an emotional chastity belt. Rather, the trick is to steady yourself and take advantage of them. The question is how.

Plato's answer stems from a key insight. He draws a distinction between sexuality, on the one hand and on the other, erotic desires considered more broadly. Sexuality, for him, is a fundamental component of human experience, but it is just one manifestation of a deeper force. This is eros, and Plato believes it drives us to penetrate more profoundly into things, to reach beyond ourselves, and to attempt to integrate and unify. It is a power of the mind and spirit as well as the body. It is the source of human creativity and innovation. It lies behind the scientific quest of discovery and the religious impulse for meaning. So sex is part of eros, perhaps the part of which we are most conscious; but it is only a part.

He also thought that erotic love can lead to philosophy, as much as the bedroom, because both erotic love and philosophy – the love of wisdom – ultimately aim at the same thing, that is, immortality. To borrow a phrase of Oscar Wilde, lovers are in the gutter but they may also look to the stars. For Plato, love roots us in our bodies and transcends the purely material. It's both/and not either/or. Strictly speaking of course, what is immortal is beyond the reach of human beings as mortal creatures. But glimpses of immortality are possible, do in fact come in many shapes and guises, and it is these experiences that link eros to philosophy.

Consider one example, that of having children. According to the woman's voice in the *Symposium*, Diotima, parents have children not merely as a by-product of their sexual congress but because of this broader desire for immortality. Sex provides a first taste of immortality because its 'petit mort' is ecstatic, which means literally to take you out of yourself. And children secure a deeper satisfaction of immortal longings because, in their offspring, parents live on. Bertrand Russell raised a similar possibility when he argued that the joy of having children comes in large part from the sense of contributing to the never-ending 'stream of life'.

Having said that, children are poor guarantors of such satisfaction since they rebel, change, and often died, until relatively
recently. So, Diotima thought, individuals seek alternative inti-
mations of immortality too. Achievement in sport and the accumulation of money are two: immortality here is sought in fame
and fortune – which perhaps explains why celebrity and money
are thought of as sexy, or at least have pulling power. However,
they are fallible too, depending on various contingencies, not least
pure luck.

Thus, Diotima suggests, the best way to gain as great a share in
immortality as is humanly possible is philosophy, the pursuit of
wisdom. Wisdom imparts the best sense of immortality since it is
timeless, beautiful and true. A wise insight, she says, is like a child
of the soul and it can never be lost. The seeker after wisdom is,
therefore, very close to the passionate lover. Or, as many teachers
of adolescents know, knowledge is not just power, it is sexy – and
if you play your cards right makes you seem something like a
god.

There other ways in which eros inspires the search for wisdom.
Anyone who has fallen in love understands the lure of the beautiful. They also know how love can transform and transcend the
humdrum. It is these same things – the beautiful and the good,
transformation and transcendence – that matter to the ancient
philosophers, the lovers of wisdom. Moreover, since eros is operating in all of us, Plato believed that love can make philosophers of
us all.

In ancient Greece, the way that young men conducted their
youthful affairs encouraged such links to be made. Lovers, of the
sort that Pausanias discussed, were ideally supposed not only to
enjoy sexual passion but from that to develop a passion for things
of the mind and spirit. Such an association between eros and
learning was manifested in one of the best-known institutions of
the ancient world, the gymnasium. Derived from the Greek for
naked, *gumnos*, gymnasia were places for exercising and socialising. They were both sexually charged – somewhere to watch and
be watched – and were a key location for conversing, debate and

instruction. To the ancient Greek mind, the two things went hand in hand.

When it comes to the details of how these two elements might shape a relationship between a young man and a youth, there is currently some debate amongst scholars. However, the ideal would seem to be that the young man offered a mode of education to the younger, through talking with him, socialising with him, and introducing him to the virtues and vices of public life. The youth would reciprocate that attention with genuine pleasure and feeling, perhaps with, perhaps without, genital expression.

Today, models of courtship are different (in case you hadn't noticed.) I suppose that places of exercise may play a part, in the shape of the schoolyard and college court. What hasn't much changed, though, is that falling in love is a complex, chaotic affair. It can lift the eyes to higher concerns, though it may equally prefer to dwell on things lower down. The beautiful body can come to dominate an individual's desire so completely that they have no energy left for much else. Plato understood this. It lay at the heart of his worry about sexuality. In short, he was faced with a dilemma. Whilst erotic desire seems to be part of what stirs people to become interested in the world around them, that same force can become obsessed, and might just as easily eclipse any passion for wisdom, thereby smothering the love that may be pregnant with insight. If sexuality is part of eros, it might easily become the whole part. Plato's question is how is it possible to reduce those risks and so to love expansively and wisely?

This is where friendship comes in. Just how is revealed in another dialogue, the *Phaedrus*. The critical section comes in what is often called the Great Speech of Socrates. Here he imagines human individuals to be divided into three parts, and then pictures that as like a charioteer being pulled by two horses. The charioteer can be thought of as the voice of reason in the human soul. Of the two horses, Plato describes how one of them is powerful though obedient, and so drives the individual towards success in life. The other horse, however, is wild, and resists the wishes of the charioteer. All three parts are susceptible to love: in Plato's scheme, we all long for immortality, the beginnings of which is sexual desire. But trouble arises because, when the individual sees a beautiful youth, his two horses pull against each other, as it were. The wild one rears up in the compulsive desire for sex. It is all that the charioteer can do to muster his strength and bring the wild horse back under control. He must do so, though, if he is to unleash the higher powers of eros which the obedient horse represents.

This talk of chariots and wild horses is, of course, partly supposed to raise a smile. If it reminds you of Freud's division of the psyche into the sexually charged id, the morally upright superego and the embattled ego caught somewhere in between, that is no coincidence too: Freud was deliberating following in Plato's footsteps and tracing a path that the human individual might follow which is as potentially thrilling, and traumatic, as the one his forebear envisaged. The image of reigning in the wild horse of sexual desire conveys what Plato believes is necessary if someone is to love fully, and not merely give in to wanting to possess another human being. The implication is that it is only with some effort that it is possible to form relationships that are passionate and not sexually excessive, eclipsing the desire for more than merely having a great lover. Incidentally, if such discipline is lacking, Plato raises the possibility of another factor that can tame the wild horse, namely the passage of time. Time has the effect of making even the most exotic individual look familiar, of rendering even the greatest beauty less alluring. It provides an alternative mechanism for cooling the ardour. It too provides the space for a new element within eros to emerge.

That element is friendship. It is friendship that a couple win as their love leads to a mature relationship, full 'of bliss and shared understanding', as Plato puts it. The erotic element is sublimated into a wider love of life, which not only enjoys its connection with the beloved, but is freed to focus its energy on other things – perhaps by entering the stream of life in the business of having children, perhaps by looking upwards and gazing at the immortal stars. Those couples who do manage to create a mature relationship will have discovered one of life's chief blessings: the shared concern and understanding that is the basis of friendship, and very great friendship at that.

Platonic friendship

'Love is the attempt to form a friendship inspired by beauty', was one summary shared amongst the ancient Greeks. Plato describes it in an appealing way too: he says the young lover will be 'amazed by it as he realises that all the friendship he has from his other friends and relatives put together is nothing compared to that of this friend who is inspired by a god'. What Plato is arguing is that a friendship between lovers is not only possible but also can, via a mutual concern for the best things in life, make for very close friendship. This happens because the relationship comes to embody its passion in a certain way. The early fervour and erotic enthusiasm ceases to be primarily directed at the other lover, as is the case amongst new lovers, and can come to be directed towards the growing interests that emerge as the relationship develops too. It is a passion for the things that the couple, as friends, now enjoy together.

This movement from an erotic fixation on the beloved to a shared passion for life itself is well captured in an observation made by C. S. Lewis. He noted how lovers are typically depicted gazing into each others eyes, whereas friends portrayed together usually look straight ahead.

Nietzsche is another philosopher who pondered the move from lovers to friends. With Plato he saw it as something of a struggle. For example, in a deliberately provocative passage, he says that an obsessive love is actually the same as avarice – cupidity, we might say, noting the reference to the Roman god of love. It longs to possess the other at all costs:

> If one considers ... that to the lover himself the whole of the rest of the world appears indifferent, pale, and worthless, and he is prepared to make any sacrifice, to disturb any order, to

subordinate all other interests – then one comes to feel genuine amazement that this wild avarice and injustice of sexual love has been glorified and deified so much in all ages ...

However, when lovers become friends a new passion becomes possible. Again Nietzsche does not pull his punches:

Here and there on earth we may encounter a kind of continuation of love in which this possessive craving of two people for each other gives way to a new desire and lust for possession – a shared higher thirst for an ideal above them. But who knows such love? Who has experienced it? Its right name is friendship.

So, Plato's theory of love is that sexual attraction can, with a degree of will power, and the gift of time, be channelled into a passion for things that the lovers share beyond (though not

Figure 5: 'Friends have all things in common.' Plato (left) walking with Aristotle in Raphael's famous depiction.

necessarily excluding) their desire for each other's bodies. This in turn makes way for a particularly wonderful kind of friendship. In a way, all Plato is doing is deepening the truism that a sexual relationship will only continue to grow if friendship feeds or possibly supplants the early physical attraction. One way of putting this is to say that lovers must learn to love each other body and soul if they are to stay together. The Platonic conception is to focus on the passion: when two individuals share a passion for life, erotic love and friendship find their best synthesis.

So much for the theory. What of the practice? This brings us back to Aristotle, and his reflections on the links between love and friendship.

Practicalities

Aristotle was Plato's pupil, and he ventured into the same territory, taking a line which in certain respects can be thought of as building on that of his teacher. He is never so explicit about sex, at least in his surviving writings: 'As for the pleasure of sex, no one could have any thoughts when enjoying *that*', is one of his more memorable comments. However, if Plato has a theory as to how erotic love can lead to friendship, Aristotle is illuminating when it comes to the practicalities of the move.

In his *Nicomachean Ethics*, wellbeing is the chief concern. He assigns close friendship top place in the hierarchy of human relationships, regarding it as a key ingredient in any flourishing life. There's a place for 'friendly lovers' too, if lower down: they can hope for some contentment. They belong in his second category of friendship, the kind that form because of some mutual shared pleasure, in this case that being sex. A sexual friendship will thrive insofar as the pleasure it brings to both parties appeals and remains vigorous. However, if the erotic attraction dips or falls away, then the friendship is at risk: it hasn't got much else to go on, and like the work friends who drift apart when one moves job or office, the chances are that such a relationship will flounder. The two have failed to get to love each other for who they are in themselves.

Aristotle is clear, then, that a relationship based solely on erotic desire is compromised. Sexual pleasures vacillate. What individuals find sexually attractive changes over time, as does the sexual appeal of their partner. So, relationships that are heavily dependent upon a sexual component tend to be fickle. The more the sex counts, the more broken hearts, affairs and infidelities accompany them.

For lovers not so obsessed, though, Aristotle, like Plato, believed that friendship can flourish. It is all a matter of overcoming the hurdles. One problem Aristotle identifies is that relationships based predominantly upon sexual pleasures tend to form quickly. People can be attracted to one another after little more than a glance across a room, which makes for a speedy liaison, though with little need to disclose much of themselves – as in the *Last Tango in Paris*. As evidence, Aristotle cites young people who are particularly erotically inclined: 'hence they love and quickly stop loving, often changing in the course of the same day'. The problem with this is that their desire tends to colour their vision of everything else: their newfound lover looks uncompromisingly physically beautiful to them and appears beautiful in mind and spirit too. The danger, in turn, is that their vision becomes so clouded by swirls of emotion that they may know only very little about the person they claim to love so well. The illusion will fade sooner or later, and then the love needs to root itself more deeply in the beloved's true mental and spiritual character. Any potential for a long-term relationship rapidly disappears if nothing lovely is found there.

It is for this reason that when a love affair cools, the question of the lovers' future together is determined not by the intensity of their former passion, which may have been considerable, but by how deeply their passion has been transformed into the passion that can be shared as friends. And it is as friends, not lovers, that they know each other truly.

Young lovers have an advantage, though, Aristotle continues. They like to spend time together and if they are interested in a long-term relationship – that is, in becoming friends too – they should capitalise on the long hours they spend together. They might use some of the time to not only stare into each others' eyes, but talk, ideally about something other than themselves. Or they could go to the movies, and watch the film. Or an art gallery, or a walk in the countryside. The point is that when you're in love, everything looks lovely, if you care to look. Aristotle's advice is concise: choose the lover who you like the most, not only because the sex is great, but because it is easy to spend time with them. Then you will get to know them, and they you. And from that ground of affection, the world around you will start to look different as your eyes grow in the habit of catching sight of that which is good. The emerging friendship will shape the amorphous passions of romantic love and render it sustainable, along the lines Plato had suggested. What is more, a virtuous spiral will ascend carrying you higher, since if loving one another leads to knowing one another, knowing one another leads back to loving better too. Lovers might even have a head-start over people who become friends outside of any erotic affair, since they are more fully charged with love.

This sense that friendship lies at the heart of what it is to truly love someone, and not sexual attraction, is, I think, what John Bayley, husband of Iris Murdoch, calls a sympathy of understanding. It is wholly different from 'that intoxicating sense of the strangeness of another being which accompanies the excitements of falling in love', as he puts it in his memoir of his wife, *Iris*. He notices that after the heat of their courtship, and in the earliest days of their marriage, something new emerged in their relationship.

> Already we were beginning that strange and beneficent process ... by which a couple can, in the words of A. D. Hope the Australian poet, 'move closer and closer apart'. That apartness is a part of the closeness, perhaps a recognition of it: certainly a pledge of complete understanding. There is nothing threatening or supervisory about such an understanding, nothing of what couples really mean when they

say (or are alleged to say) to confidants or counsellors, 'the trouble is that my wife/ husband doesn't understand me'. This usually means that the couple, or one of them, understands the other all too well, and doesn't rejoice in the experience.

This is a friendship that thrives on the subtle process of growing, mutual understanding. Thus many a couple will confess that with increasing years together the companionship, the shared life, is as important as the sex, or more so. Their physical intimacy comes to turn on intimate trivia as much as anything else, becoming partners who know a lot about each other's physical likes, dislikes, needs and pleasures.

Further, just because lovers become friends does not mean that their relationship will loose its passion. This is the crux of the value of Plato's ideas about the friendship of lovers. It will include the humdrum, of course, for it is often on this level that friends like to share their lives together – 'some drink together, some play dice together, others train, or hunt, or philosophise together' was Aristotle's list of activities: it is at this level that friendship brings good and remedial things to life such as fun, wellbeing, satisfaction and companionship. However, inasmuch as their shared passion moves on from being focused exclusively on each other, so too the sexual element will evolve, becoming much more an expression of the friendship as opposed to pure eros – a sign of friendship's intimacies, securities, commitments and ardour. The ecstasy will arise from what is known of the other rather than what is unknown. The sexual intimacy of eros becomes the embodied knowing of sexual friendship, which in turn becomes the physical and spiritual coexistence of partnership. Passion in this sense 'feeds back'. Thus, folk in long term relationships may well say that he or she has become more attractive to me now than ever. Or they have the sense that their partner's body has almost become an extension of their own, which is why it is natural to hold hands whilst sitting together, or to fall asleep as spoons. That kind of physical intimacy may come to feel more substantial than the momentary peaks of genital sex.

Eventually sexuality ceases to be a threat to friendship altogether for the two loves learn to speak the same language. A synthesis of similarity and difference becomes possible: friendship speaks the language of the body as well as the mind, and sexuality becomes a manifestation of the friendship. Then the love called friendship need not think erotic love perilous. With passion widened, and the beloved well known, there is every reason to think that lovers might aspire to the best kind of friendships there are.

Better than sex?

Lucky lovers! But what of the case of friends who, although aware of a sexual frisson between them, resist the temptation, and never indulge it. And there are also the passionate friends for who there is no apparent desire to engage in any physical intimacy at all.

The latter case is easier to explain. Here, the erotic is spontaneously and uncomplicatedly sublimated in the friends' delight and enthusiasm for life together. Their passion exists only in the broader sense – Nietzsche's higher thirst or Plato's shared understanding. One can think of examples of this kind of friendship. It is what happens when intellectual friends share a passion in their studies, reading, insights or wisdom; or when artists seek friends who are motivated by the desire to create something beautiful or expressive; or when friends who are interested in science together delight in the wonder of nature or noetic entities – strange as that may seem. Further friendships may well form between, say, a philosopher and an artist, or a scientist and a musician, or a gardener and an actor, since each recognises the passion that their friend has for something which, in turn, encourages and fuels their own interest. Even someone who has a passion for making money can find friends with a similar passion for power – say a politician.

I've a sense of this passionate potential in friendship myself when I think about the dynamic between myself and a friend, Guy Reid, who is a sculptor. He has a great gift for carving human figures in wood that have the uncanny appearance of being almost alive. When I first met Guy I found this ability of his quite intimidating since any creativity I possessed seemed woefully pedestrian in comparison. It was a privilege just to write an occasional press release for him when he was having a show. But as our friendship developed, I allowed myself to be inspired to pursue my own more creative hopes in writing. Our friendship awoke that passion in me. I recall going to a literary festival to catch a whiff of the creative energy in writers I admired and at the festival being very conscious of my friendship with Guy. The friendship, I realised, was nurturing my desire to write.

When it comes to the case of friends struggling with sexual undercurrents in their relationship, the matter is, unsurprisingly, more complex. In fact, the question of sex may appear to hang in the balance almost indefinitely – even if the rational part of the mind knows that nothing sexual will or should ever happen. The complication that comes from such an unresolved sexual frisson is the suspense. Indeed, suspense is as much a cause of erotic frisson as any actual sexual attraction might be: people do not even need to fancy each other, just be conscious that they might. In Evelyn Waugh's phrase, even 'a thin bat's squeak of sexuality' can frighten people off or distract them from becoming friends. People can misunderstand their feelings too. In a culture in which sexual consummation is seen as the highest expression of love that two people can hope for, a fascination for someone is easy to mistake for falling in love, even when it is simultaneously obvious that a sexual relationship would be inappropriate, unsustainable and possibly ruinous of the friendship.

Of the three relationships with which this chapter opened, the friendship of Simon Callow and Peggy Ramsay is closest to this state of sexual possibility, at least when they first met. Callow has written about it honestly, insightfully and often colourfully in his book-length account of their friendship. It provides excellent material for philosophical reflection and a way of thinking through this set of sexual ambiguities.

He begins by noting that it was not so much a bat's squeak of sexuality that they had to confront as the squawk of love at first sight.

> At this first meeting we spurred each other on higher and higher with great thoughts and terrible truths until we finally fell silent, having completely exhausted ourselves. I got up to go and we shook hands, oddly, awkwardly. She sat at her desk, combing her hair and repairing her lipstick as I left the office. Going back through the reception area to pick up the script which I dimly remembered had been the occasion of my being there at all, I caught the eyes of the secretaries and blushed. It was as if Peggy and I had been making love.

Callow is, and was, well known as a gay man: when he met Ramsay he was in the middle of a love affair with a man called Aziz Yehia. However, partly because sexual orientation is rarely entirely clear cut, and partly because passion can be close to erotic feeling even in the most high-minded, the sexual suspense persisted between him and Ramsey, expressed in the passage above in the guise of the 'as if' they had been making love. This question had to be resolved if his friendship with Ramsay was to grow.

Callow describes the way the suspense was at least temporarily lifted a few days later as a result of Ramsay inviting him to an intimate, exotic dinner à deux. He reports how she shuddered when he kissed her on the cheek in greeting. She trembled when he said she was beautiful. She was, as Callow says, Tatiana receiving Onegin. But the bloody obvious was now clear even to our Tatiana; Callow did not desire her.

Luckily, that was not the end of the story, for it might have. The challenge now was to sustain 'that most beautiful and elusive thing, a passionate friendship'. At first, it did not look all that promising. Callow writes of a kind of uneasy ménage à trois that evolved: he loved Yehia and Yehia loved being loved by him; Ramsay loved Callow who in turn gained much from that love and returned it, though without consummation. But they survived a moment of truth, the first time they were all together, and after that Callow talks interestingly of how his friendship with Ramsay became more permanently established. They identified the areas they enjoyed talking about and educating each other on, notwithstanding the recognition that some things should be off limits. Later, for example, when they took to spending evenings together listening to records, he writes:

> Sometimes, as we listened, we would hold hands, but that was a little too explicit. Generally we sat in separate pools of emotion, as if contemplating some grief that was beyond physical or verbal expression, a grief that we both knew about but could not name.

What is arresting about those evenings is that although they did not touch, their mutual separateness was not experienced as aloneness but as the deepest moments of friendship. They were, it seems, ascending a spiral of love. Callow later recalls that those evenings were among the best evenings of his life.

How can we describe this friendship? Some might be tempted to say that the boundaries they had to enforce were the product of unresolved sexual tensions that persisted between them; their relationship was irreconcilably ambiguous, as if they were like tempestuous lovers endlessly delaying gratification, swinging from one emotion to the next and never finding a resting place. I think that Callow and Ramsay's friendship is much more than that. If they had been unable to redirect their passion to anything other than an unhealthy absorption with each other, Ramsay would not have awakened in Callow a talent that he now confesses to valuing even more than his acting, that of writing. He dedicates his first book to her as a monument to their friendship.

This is a crucial clue for understanding the thing that happened between them and is another example of the redirection of passion Plato encourages us to contemplate. Like a painting, that works with the mean materials of canvass and oil to conjure up a world that barely existed before, their friendship transformed the dollops of colourful passion which were given to them upon first meeting, and which might have been merely thrown together in an affair, so that with a kind of discipline and restraint, as well as a joyful enthusiasm, they could rework them into a life on an altogether higher plane. The celibacy that this involved is not supposed to evoke a prohibition or a stigmatisation of sexuality. Rather it is to point to a voluntary renunciation that emerges from within a relationship when friends of this sort sense that self-control in one area will make for a transformation of themselves as a whole. Friends like Callow and Ramsay have distinguished, and discarded, a physical kind of love in favour of the other person's intellect, creativity or soul. They do not seek a desire for close physical intimacy – though they simultaneously do not compromise the passion that fires their friendship.

A further example of how this can come about, and this time in a case when an affair was certainly on the cards, is beautifully portrayed in Sofia Coppola's film, *Lost in Translation*. Bill Murray plays Bob Harris, an old movie star, who when in Tokyo on a mindless trip to endorse a brand of whiskey, meets Charlotte, played by Scarlett Johansson, who is similarly stranded in the city while her husband, a photographer, is engaged on a shoot. The story is of their encounter, and what is striking is that whilst there is an erotic charge between the two from the start they do not embark upon an affair. Part of the film's brilliance stems from the way it toys with the audience's Hollywood assumptions that they will fall into bed, whilst simultaneously conveying the sense that something would be lost if they did. That something is the passion they have for their own lives. To become lovers would have been to lose that passion and the opportunity a friendship brings to quicken it. Instead, they would have experienced the loss of self that a sexual encounter revels in. Friendship, in contrast, gave them the gift of being able to return to their lives with a sense of new possibility.

Getting with friends

Callow's story raises a final set of complications, that of the ménage à trois of two lovers and a friend. The complexity here arises when a new lover finds an old friend threatening, or in Callow's case when a new friend troubles an old lover. Is it possible to have one person who is your committed lover and another who is your profoundly close friend? And what of the relationship between those two individuals, for is there not the possibility of threat again, should the lover ask what the friend gives that they cannot?

In such love triangles, those who suddenly find themselves playing third fiddle may find it difficult to deal with the intimacy of the other two. Unsurprisingly, in Callow's case, it was his partner, Yehia, who was intimidated by Ramsay. Callow writes when all three met together:

> It could have been the end of a number of things: my friendship with Peggy, but also, to my amazement, it seemed to threaten the continuation of my relationship with Aziz. Next to Peggy, everyone seemed less: less passionate, less perceptive, less brilliant, less honest, less absolute. And Aziz had seen, not only how important Peggy was in my life, but a side of me, fervent and wild, which was only brought forth by Peggy.

What Callow sensed was that his friendship with Ramsay somehow threatened his lover because his relationship with her was more passionate, though chaste. Clearly, on one level, the resulting sense of threat was groundless. Sexually speaking, Yehia had no competition in Callow's eyes. But Ramsay was a threat not because she might have become Callow's lover; that faint possibility had been pushed aside. Rather, the problem was that her passionate hold over him challenged the ideal of romantic love that was part of Callow and Yehia's relationship.

This, then, is the nub of the final issue to do with friends and lovers. In today's world, there is a myth of romantic love based upon the idea that two lovers become one flesh, a totalisation of life in the other, supremely enacted in sexual ecstasy which is symbolic of that union. The myth or ideal tends to exclude others, not because lovers do not want friends, but because it tells them that their friends are incidental – pleasant but non-essential adornments to the lover's life together. Although few people in real life believe the myth in its entirety, it is difficult to ignore entirely too. Thus, Yehia could not ignore the fact that Ramsay was essential to awakening Callow's passion for life, and this seemed to contravene the romantic awakening that 'should' have been exclusive to their relationship. It was as if there was a third person in the marriage; hence the sense of threat.

It is indeed a brave soul who would come between lovers. Think of the estrangement that can come about between friends after one of them marries another. What place for the friend is there, given that 'what God has joined together no-one should put asunder', as the old marriage service puts it. Or recall just how hard it can be to sustain a friendship when your friend started a new sexual relationship: the thrill of such attraction, and the collapse into the new lover's arms, will appear to eclipse all previous cares and affections. That said, there is definitely a place for the third party friend. After a period of time, the old friend can provide the lovers with a break from the burden of the romantic myth, with its dictatorial insistence on total, exclusive involvement.

Perhaps friendship should assert itself more strongly in our romance obsessed world. Perhaps friends should refuse the otherwise overwhelming pressures of the quixotic and declare the joys of their own kind of passion, though that would be a hard thing to do in a culture besotted with the power of erotic possessiveness. The thought provides us with a conclusion. For contra the myth, there is a love that does not desire to possess. It is called friendship. It loves the other, and wants them both to be free. Once friendship has come to be the determining force in a relationship, individuals are able to find themselves and nurture a passion for life, not merely lose themselves in starry-eyed love.

Faking It

'Most friendship is feigning.'

William Shakespeare

The sages of friendship are found in the most unlikely of places. Take Friedrich Nietzsche. This nineteenth-century philosopher spoke in the language of fire and ice, proclaimed the death of God, and created the character of Zarathustra who wanders alone in mountains and deserts. If people know one thing about Nietzsche's life, apart from the fact that he went mad, it might be that he fell out with his sometime mentor and friend Richard Wagner. The split was of operatic proportions. So to most, including those philosophers who have studied his work, he is not readily associated with the affectionate spirit of amity.

But contrast that image with this reality. On 19 November 1877 he wrote this to Paul Rée another philosopher:

> In my entire life I have not had as much pleasure as through our friendship during this year, not to speak of what I have learnt from you. When I hear of your studies, my mouth waters with the anticipation of your company; we have been created for an understanding of one another.

Alternatively, on 22 January 1875 he penned this to his sister Elizabeth:

> It is precisely we solitary ones that require love and companions in whose presence we may be open and simple, and the eternal struggle of silence and dissimulation can cease. Yes,

> I am glad that I can be myself, openly and honestly with you, for you are such a good friend and companion.

Even in the case of Wagner, for whom his antagonism was real, Nietzsche acknowledged his continuing debt to his former friend throughout his life.

Private lives do not automatically translate into public philosophy but Nietzsche also devoted many words to the subject of friendship in the books of his so-called middle period, words which because of his aphoristic style pack a punch that the word count alone only hints at. His deep concern with the nature of friendship was undoubtedly connected to the struggles with Wagner, as much as the strength of the friendships that he shared with others. The details of the friendship provide an illuminating introduction to his thoughts – and the nature of the split, for in Nietzsche's analysis friendship is never far from failing, and it's what he has to say about this ambiguity of friendship that is so valuable to us. 'Friendship is two knives,' novelist Patrick White wrote: 'They will sharpen each other when rubbed together, but often one of them will slip and slice off a thumb.'

Nietzsche and Wagner had met in 1868 and within 12 months he was a close friend of both the maestro and his mistress, Cosima, the daughter of Liszt, visiting them frequently on the calm shores of Lake Lucerne. Their affection revolved around an admiration for Wagner's music – Wagner was not given to modesty where greatness was concerned – and an enthusiasm for the philosophy of Schopenhauer. A philosophical pessimist, he believed that the world was an illusion, the emanation of a daemonic Will. The way people commonly experience this Will is sexually, a yearning which, Schopenhauer argued, leads to either frustration or excess. Not the best grounds for human happiness and friendship one would have thought, though his gospel of gloom found an audience at the time.

The reason Wagner and Nietzsche liked him was that he thought art was the only way out of the Will's bind because only the aesthetic is disinterested or 'unwilful', supremely so in the case of music. It provides a particularly direct means of transcending the human creature's animalistic lot. Wagner opened Nietzsche's mind to the possibility of that transcendence. And the depth of feeling that Nietzsche owed him in this early period of his development is shown in his book of the time, *The Birth of Tragedy*. It begins with nothing less than a 'Preface to Wagner' and includes material he had presented at Cosima's 33rd birthday celebration. The friendship flourished.

However, only a handful of years later, in what we now know as his middle period, Nietzsche had changed. The transitional book is *Untimely Meditations*. It includes another chapter on Wagner, entitled 'Richard Wagner in Bayreuth', and is interesting because it shows Nietzsche's affection for Wagner beginning to turn sour; he was moving on but could not yet leave Wagner behind.

A clean break itself came in 1876 at the first Bayreuth Festival. Wagner presented his latest masterpiece, and Nietzsche was revolted by it, along with the philistine crowds that he charged Wagner with wooing merely in order to pay the bills. The young philosopher fled to the countryside with blinding headaches. He should have seen it coming. If he loved Schopenhauer he would have known that the one form that Schopenhauer excepted in his praise for music was that of Grand Opera. It was an unmusical invention for unmusical minds. That said, Nietzsche's histrionic revulsion does not feel quite reason enough for what was to become a permanent break. It is as if Nietzsche used his disapproval of Bayreuth as an excuse for the friendship to falter. The question is why, and what does that tell us about friendship?

Petty factors, such as the extent to which Wagner's brilliance eclipsed Nietzsche's rather pathetic abilities as a composer, could have played a part, though these animosities again do not feel like reason enough and cannot have been the whole story. When the rift happened, Wagner was not aware of it for some time and when Nietzsche later offered another reason, that the cause had been his horror at Wagner's conversion to Christianity, that does not ring true either: Wagner's Christianity had been in evidence for some years before.

It seems that Nietzsche had come to the realisation that he had to remove himself from Wagner's sphere of influence if he was to make anything of his own life. That meant he had to manufacture a break, at least in his own mind. In other words, it was not that he came simply to loathe Wagner and everything he stood for, though he did represent a way of life that an evolving Nietzsche now wanted to critique strongly. It was that Nietzsche recognised the deep impact Wagner's friendship had had on him and would have continued to have had, so that, like a child who must violently leave the womb to be born, he too had not only to turn his back on Wagner but sever the cord as well. Paradoxically, the break was out of a respect for the power of such profound friendship, the kind that can shape and determine a life: only friends who have at one time identified closely may at a later time come to a definitive split. Mere friends will merely drift apart – or, to put it another way, if someone who you hardly know unexpectedly off-loads the secrets of their heart to you, you'll sense its inappropriateness. 'I hardly know them!', or 'too much information' you protest.

It is easy to see Nietzsche exploring the echoes of this complex matter in his philosophical reflections. He writes:

> The friend whose hopes one cannot satisfy one would rather have for an enemy.

And,

> If we have greatly transformed ourselves, those friends of ours who have not been transformed become like ghosts of our past: their voice comes across to us like the voice of a shade – as though we were hearing ourself, only younger, more severe, less mature.

Or,

> Just as in order to walk beside an abyss or cross a deep stream by a plank one needs a railing, not so as to hold on to it – for it

would at once collapse if one did that – but to give the eye a feeling of security, so as a youth one has need of people who without knowing it perform for us the service of a railing. It is true that, if we were really in great danger, they would not help us if we sought to rely on them, but they give us the quieting sensation that there is protection close at hand (for example fathers, teachers, friends, as all three usually are).

Conversely, perhaps he feared developing a habit in relation to Wagner that he saw in other people who disparage and diminish those that they know in order to maintain their own sense of self-respect:

> Many people mistreat even their friends out of vanity when there are witnesses present to whom they want to demonstrate their superiority: and others exaggerate the worth of their foes so as to be able to show with pride that they are worthy of such foes.

Friendship with a future

Another longer paragraph extends the theme and suggests a framework within which to flesh out Nietzsche's understanding of friendship and its tensions. He observes that amongst people who have a real gift for friendship – these are not people who are simply bad at friendship – two types predominate. Some are like ladders; others, circles.

Ladder-types are individuals who are in a continual state of ascent in their lives. Life for them is a journey of change, evolution and progress. At each stage of their development, these people find friends who aid and encourage them and who in turn they aid and encourage. One can imagine, say, the life of a politician whose career is dotted with such friendships. At college they hang out with malcontents who inspire them. During their twenties they are nurtured by mentors who discipline them. In their prime they befriend individuals who are interested in

77

power, which they want to exercise at this point in their careers too. And then, in their dotage, disillusioned with power, they reflect on the vanities of life with those who are wiser and less sure.

The trouble that ladder-types find with friendship is that through no fault of their own this succession of friends produces people who rarely get on with each other. The malcontents will despise the mentor, as complacent, who will critique the powerful, as crooked, who will be irritated by the wise, as corrupt. So, passing friendships are a consequence of the ladder-life that such individuals lead, with later phases of their careers inevitably abolishing or infringing upon the earlier, with friends ditched as a result. The ladder-type has a philosophy of friendship which says that it is a mistake to expect or to try to cultivate close, life-long relationships. Amity is sacrificed on the altar of progress.

The second type of individual who is good at friendship, the circle-like, is different. They also collect around them individuals with different characters, dispositions and talents but in a way that diffuses any awkwardness or antagonism. Typical of such a person might be the celebrity. They count amongst their friends people as diverse as their management team, their peers, a handful of journalists, their family, their favourite charity-workers and even some fans. The force of their charisma provides the focus for this circle of friendship, showering it with warmth, and so like the sun, powering it over long periods of time. To be a friend with the circle-type is like being known by the host of a party who greets you with smiles and small-talk, champagne and charm.

Nietzsche thought of himself as a ladder-type. The implication of his analogy is that not only do circle-types compromise themselves, by being all things to all people, but that their friendships tend to be shallower to boot. It's is an interesting point. In Nietzsche's book, longevity is not the determining measure of friendship. A short-lived friendship may nonetheless be the most important of your life. It's not that there is anything wrong with long-lived friends per se; it is rather that time can suck the authenticity out of friendship. Friendships that have gone on for too long become idle – the 'flabby friends' we mentioned above, that perhaps should be shed like surplus pounds. Such friends do not really share that much, beyond their association, and so wind away the hours talking about this and that, conspiring in indecision and perhaps in all honesty becoming nuisances to one another. 'It is prudent to form friendships only with the industrious', Nietzsche concludes. He also suspects that such relationships are untrustworthy because when the dynamism disappears from a friendship, but the individuals concerned cannot quite bring it to an end, they constantly strive to re-establish their intimacy with each other – by dwelling on the 'old times' or college days; the past, not the future. This is a sign that habit has become a substitute for any real affection or closeness.

Neitzsche is not saying that a shared past is not important to close friends. Rather, he's arguing it's not enough. His observation about the future orientation of the best friendships is an arresting one. It's so crucial because the quality that the future has, which the past does not, is newness. The future is a place of possibility and growth; to look to tomorrow is to step up into the not-yet and unknown. Conversely, the past is a place that can't change; it roots us but, without the future, constrains us too. We must gather the past into the present and be drawn into what lies ahead. Therein lies the vitality of life, for the future is that which we do not possess. That makes it frightening, though invigorating too – invigorating of the friendships that move into the morrow as well.

Moreover, seeing your friendships as future-orientated, as opposed to comfortingly shaped by the past, reflects an aspect that feeds friendship itself. Nietzsche was a philosopher who was convinced that on the whole we don't know ourselves, or our friends, very well – though it's part of the gift of friendship that with friends we can come to know ourselves, and them, better. There's a parallel here, then, for the future is unknown too. It is not yet disclosed to us, as we are not wholly disclosed to ourselves, and as our friends have not yet fully revealed themselves to us too. And yet, in close friendship – the kind that embraces the future – we implicitly commit to these individuals. We agree to move into the future together, in directions not always foreseen. We agree to take the risks of showing more of ourselves to each other, and thereby to ourselves. That should deepen our humanity, all being well. And it is that deepening – that brave turning to the truths of the human condition – which inspires Nietzsche, and with him those who love friendship as a way of life.

To put it another way, with friends, you become what you are. Though there's a warning implicit in that thought too: choose your friends well. You will walk the same path together.

Truth hurts

Friendships with a future, then, are probably formed by individuals who have a mix of the ladder-type and circle-type within them. They like to have friends around them, for it is good to have wide circles of friends. They figure that with most people it is better to be friendly even should you feel otherwise because, first, at a day-to-day level, it makes for a happier life; and, second, because to expose every friendship to the full force and struggle of personal change and revelation would be asking too much. That's only possible with the closest friends, and anyway, friendships thrive on fun too. 'He's a bit intense', we say of the mate who should lighten up.

But getting the mix right – finding a sustainable balance between the pleasures of the past and the exhilaration of the future – is tricky. It highlights another set of ambiguities. They are those of closeness and distance (what is appropriate and how do you redress the balance when someone 'invades your space'); honesty and dissimulation (how truthful can you be with a particular friend or is it often better to obfuscate, or even tell a small fib); loyalty and the need, sometimes, to make a break. In fact, when you start to look, it quickly becomes apparent that in a million little ways, as well as some large ones, friendship is often a matter of nothing less than faking it. Or, to use Shakespeare's phrase, 'most friendship is feigning'.

In saying this, I am not talking about the ways in which people emote and just blatantly lie in the *name* of friendship. The faux-friendliness of the call centre, the salesman and the chat show host is as nauseating, or amusing, as it is transparent. Rather I am talking about people who would count themselves as friends to greater or lesser degrees but nonetheless employ what might be called the 'kind vices' of half-truth, evasion, prevarication and pretence. The point is that they sense that the friendship would not bear the weight of the whole truth of what could be said. If that were voiced, 'the pebbles [would be] set rolling, the friendship would follow after, and fall apart', as Nietzsche put it.

The examples of such pretence are legion. Someone smiles rather than admit their malign thoughts about their best friend's new boyfriend. They scream inside rather than speak out on the disciplining of their friends' children. They conveniently forget the suggestion of holidaying together, realising that to go away for two weeks would be a whole different ballgame to merely having dinner every other week. Alternatively, people can behave almost as if they were different people with different friends, a schizophrenia that provokes great anxiety at the thought of, say, a birthday party at which you invite all your friends to come together: you look out at the room, full of everyone you know, and panic that they won't get on, that some will probably fall out. Then there is the competitive element to negotiate. If everyone confessed like Gore Vidal that 'whenever a friend succeeds, a little something in me dies', friendship would soon die too. (Incidentally, I recently heard Vidal remark that he made that comment as a joke; he didn't really mean it. Only, it is a comment that was remembered as if it were true, which actually underlines its veracity.)

Friends are also complicit in each others' feigning for fear, in Shakespeare's phrase, of appearing 'unlearned in the world's false subtleties'. Celebrities, again, are past masters at this. A newspaper profile of Donatella Versace noted that her room was littered with signed pictures of her famous friends. A silver-framed photograph of Catherine Zeta-Jones clutching her Oscar in a black Versace dress had written across it, 'Dearest Donatella, a friend to cherish, I love you, Catherine.' It was next to a signed picture of Madonna and her children. That said, and much to her credit, Donatella protested that her real friends in life were not famous. 'I go to parties for work', she retorted.

Nietzsche records friendship's feigning foibles in a series of aphorisms and comments that are sharp, often playful and should perhaps be read as if uttered by Woody Allen, excusing the Germanic constructions.

> In many people, the gift of having good friends is much greater than the gift of being a good friend.

> One should not talk about one's friends: otherwise one will talk away the feeling of friendship.

> The man had the great works but his companion had the great faith in these works. They were inseparable: but it was obvious that the former depended wholly on the latter.

> They were friends and have ceased to be, and they both severed their friendship at the same time: the one because he thought himself too much misunderstood, the other because he thought himself understood too well – and both were deceiving themselves! – for neither understood himself well enough.

All this is the art of friendship and a fine art it is too. Its method is appropriateness. Its message is, 'I know you know but we both know not to go there.' Its medium is often gossip, because what is not spoken to one friend is usually whispered to another: 'There will be few who, when they are in want of matter for conversation, do not reveal the more secret affairs of their friends', wrote Nietzsche. 'Life is not worth living unless one can be indiscrete to intimate friends', was how the intellectual Isaiah Berlin expressed it.

What are we to make of this plethora of dissimulation? In short, both little and much. Nietzsche again helps. He did not give the lie to friendship to disparage it. Rather, he understood that for the most part friendship is human, all too human. For this reason a degree of dissimulation is required on occasion in even the closest of friendships.

> There was a time in our lives when we were so close that nothing seemed to obstruct our friendship and brotherhood, and only a small footbridge separated us. Just as you were about to step on it, I asked you: 'Do you want to cross the footbridge to me?' – Immediately, you did not want to any more; and when I asked you again, you remained silent. Since then mountains and torrential rivers and whatever separates and alienates have been cast between us, and even if we wanted to get together, we couldn't. But when you now think of that little footbridge, words fail you and you sob and marvel.

He's saying that there is no such thing as *merely* picking the right moment. If too much is said at the wrong time the consequences can be disastrous. So with regards to the dissimulation, one should make little of it, in the sense that even if you agree that most friendship is feigning you should, nonetheless, carry on as usual with one's friends; and much of it, in the sense that to try always to be honest will for the most part be ruinous.

The issue at stake here is this one of not knowing ourselves and others that well. It raises two practical problems. First, even if we think we know someone well, our judgements about them are usually a little off the mark and so would warrant their vexation were they made known; it is better to avoid offence by forming little habits of evasion, rather than to cause irritation by always getting it slightly wrong. If I'm pondering whether to critique my friend for the poor discipline of her children, the chances are I don't know the half of it – how little Sebastian and Sophie are only picking up on the stresses that exist between their Mum and Dad, say. I'm better to remark that having kids must be totally exhausting.

Second, and more profoundly, there's the element in our critique of others which is actually a projection of our own dis-satisfaction with ourselves, stemming from not knowing ourselves very well. Maybe I can only cope with children in small doses because I've buried the memory of my own unhappy childhood; or I find kids annoying because I'm really rather impatient.

Nietzsche deploys an analogy of the self as a castle to describe this bit of human psychology. The thing about a castle is that it is a building that is both a fortress and a prison. The self is a bit like that too. Inside it is dark, full of shadowy corners and echoing chambers, though we find windows out of which we can gaze at the world. The windows allow us to see what's around us, perhaps to look across to another guarded self, another castle. What that reveals is the barriers and defences that those other people construct for themselves too. 'Man [sic] is very well defended against himself, against being reconnoitred and besieged by himself, he is usually able to perceive of himself only his outer walls', Nietzsche explains. What's tricky is seeing your own defences. Having the dark corridors of the mind brought into the light of day is not very pleasant. It is much more preferable to spot the weaknesses and breaches in the fortifications that others construct around themselves.

To put it another way, if we feign friendship with others, to cover up what we think of as their faults, that's probably only because we readily feign friendship with ourselves. The tough question to ask is this: would I be my friend if I knew myself well? Thus, in a million little ways, friends reach for the mask and the world is a friendlier place for it:

Through knowing ourselves, and regarding our own nature as a moving sphere of moods and opinions, and thus learning to despise ourselves a little, we restore to our proper equilibrium with others. It is true we have good reason to think little of each of our acquaintances, even the greatest of them; but equally good reason to direct this feeling back on to ourself. And so, since we can endure ourself, let us also endure other people.

Another self

But is the well meant but feigning goodwill we show others mostly little more than an implicit acknowledgement that we ourselves are not very nice people if truth be known and, for at least some of the time, our friends are not very nice too? The answer may be yes. The philosopher Immanuel Kant averred: 'For everyone has his weaknesses, and these must be kept hidden even from our friends ... so that humanity should not be offended thereby. Even to our best friend, we must not discover ourselves as we naturally are and know ourselves to be, for that would be a nasty business.' Kant adds that to see the 'crooked timber of humanity', with its rotten core, would be 'repulsive'.

But that negative image covers a more positive possibility. It's one that points to the future. For sometimes toleration and dissimulation can give way to truthfulness and personal insight. It may only be achievable with one or two friends between whom a profound trust exists, and it may only come about only a handful of times in life, when the moment is right. But when it does, friends can rise above the ambiguities of everyday interactions and enter a zone in which they speak to each other as truthfully and directly possible. That moment may offer nothing short of a revelation, and form the grounds for a better tomorrow.

In such moments, your friend becomes another self to you, someone who feels as close to you as you do to yourself. It's a rich and hopeful notion. Nearly all the great philosophers of friendship have recognised it as such, though in illuminatingly different ways. That a friend can be 'another self' is never meant solely in the trivial sense that friends share similar interests or pleasures, though friends may clearly both delight in football, fashion or food. Some philosophers use it in a romantic sense; the friend as another self implies that friends almost become one person, 'one soul in two bodies', as Montaigne put it. That is a appealing thought. People have such a sense when they say they were 'basking in reflected glory': something has happened to their friend, but it is almost as if it has happened to them too, such is the sense of connection they feel with their friend. It's as if our sense of who we are as autonomous individuals shifts a little, and relocates at some point in between ourselves and the friend, with whom we are one soul in two bodies. That points to Aristotle's third type of friendship, the soulmateship in which you love someone for who they are in themselves, and are loved in return, because you know someone for who they are in themselves, and are known.

But if the friend as another self can mean, first, something shared, and second, something overlapping, Aristotle pushes at a third sense too. He also implies that it is only in friendship that we can fully discover ourselves. What is meant by this was, perhaps, easier to convey in ancient Greek. This is because the language declines not only in the singular and plural but in the 'dual' too. The dual is used for things that come in twos or pairs, as in *to ophthalme* – the two eyes. Alternatively, when Plato describes two young friends laughing together in his dialogue the *Lysis*, he uses the dual when he writes 'they laughed'. For friends, there is no laughing alone. The dual suggests that ancient Greeks could conceive of activities performed together that are so particular and intimate that they require their own conjugation.

That connectedness comes up in other ways. The Athenian leader Perikles points to it when he uses the word idiot or *idiotes* in his famous *Funeral Oration*. The ancient meaning of 'idiot' was someone who believes they can live only for themselves, who thinks they do best on their own. Perikles argues that the idiot has no right to regard him- or herself as a citizen, since to be a citizen is to acknowledge your dependency upon the collective that is society. Only gods and beasts can live alone, Aristotle noted.

Put these two elements together, and what emerges from the idea of 'another self' is that two friends are, in a sense, one; like the two eyes, their operation is conjoined or dual. The philosopher, Giorgio Agamben, has drawn attention to the importance of this expression for Aristotle. He believes that Aristotle was arguing that friendship with another is constitutive of an individual's own subjectivity: someone comes to a full awareness of their existence only as they become aware of the existence of their close friend. Agamben explains, 'The friend is not another I, but an otherness immanent in self-ness, a becoming other of the self.' With such a friend, we find ourselves; and in general, we only become someone with another person.

This observation would also help to explain why losing a friend can be so painful: you lose part of yourself. And if you fall out with a friend, and lose them that way, the pain is doubled: you are implicitly saying to yourself, I do not like the person I have become, even as you say to your former friend, I do not like the person you are.

Such a dynamic puts friendship in primary place in any account of human flourishing. It's saying more than just that a close friend is a mirror of your own independent self, someone in whom you find personal resonances, thereby realising that though autonomous, you are not alone; there is someone quite like you. It's implying that a close friend is another part of you and that you can only fully become who you are in who they are too.

Nietzsche was rather nervous of these collapses of selfhood into another, even if a good friend. Perhaps it was his experience with Wagner that made him resistant; he did not want to 'confound the I and Thou'. So, for him, 'another self' must also carry the implication that friends are still 'other' to each other too. The friend who is 'an other self' is someone with whom individual goals, personal aspirations and private hopes coincide – at certain moments or over periods of time. The joy of the friendship is not the collapse of all boundaries between the individuals. Neither is it a like-mindedness that any group of people might feel. Rather, it is the realisation that they are headed in the same direction. There's the future element in that understanding of the expression again. Such are friends, as Ralph Emerson put it, who exclaim to each other: 'Do you see the same truth?' – first, with surprise and then, with delight. This connection becomes more than a happy coincidence or pleasant discovery but a great blessing. 'In loving their friend they love what is good for themselves,' Aristotle said. 'For the good person, in becoming a friend, becomes a good for the person to whom they become a friend.'

This is a subtle point which is worth dwelling upon and has unexpected consequences, not least of which is that the best of friends may be found in the most unlikely of places. The point is well illustrated in the story told in the Oscar-winning movie, *Gods and Monsters*, directed by Bill Condon. It relates the last days of the life of the Hollywood director James Whale, played by Ian McKellan, whose fame and fortune was made with his film *Frankenstein*. Long after, in his declining years, Whale formed a friendship with his gardener, Clayton Boone, played by Brendan Fraser. This set tongues wagging in Tinseltown since Whale was a known homosexual, a fact to which the heterosexual redneck Boone was at first oblivious, then horrified, and only latterly indifferent. It is that transformation which was the key to a relationship that led to the discovery of a most unlikely and penetratingly honest friendship.

In the movie, the relationship begins unpromisingly when Whale asks Boone to sit for him as a model, under the ruse that Boone has an artistically fascinating face. It is a gratuitous come-on though it provokes Boone into reflecting a little on himself and his life. Something deeper between them begins to emerge when, at a second sitting, they realise that, for all their differences, they have something in common; they are both originally from poor families. Whale has kept this hidden from his starry Hollywood 'friends', a dissimulation that he is awakened to in the openness of Boone's face 'that makes me want to tell the truth'. Trust grows, and they confess their greatest secrets to each other: Whale relives the painful story of the great love of his life and Boone reveals his shame that he never saw action as a Marine. This latter revelation is important not only because of the confession itself but also because up to that point Boone thinks that, unlike Whale, he has no interesting stories to tell about his life and indeed could not even tell them if he had. That is a very good story, Whale says tenderly; one to match his own. Their relationship has become a friendship because in the telling of stories they not only find an equal and mutual respect for each other – many friendships get there – but because they have been able to be completely honest with one another.

In the final scenes, the film cuts to several years later. Boone is watching a repeat of one of the Frankenstein movies on television with his son and he remembers his friendship with Whale. The monster is heard wailing, 'Alone bad. Friend good.' The movie ends, and Boone shows his son a pencil sketch which Whale made of his original idea for Frankenstein, saying that he knew the man who made the movie. On the back is written, 'For Clayton, friend?' The question mark is wonderfully indicative of the ambiguity of honest friendship. His son retorts, 'Is that just another one of your stories, Dad?' It highlights the legacy of Whale's friendship and the good thing which now characterises his relationship with his son. Boone has overcome the limitations of his origins in a new ability with and love of stories. In a sense, Whale the storyteller lives on in Boone: they've become other selves to each other.

It's a way, then, that a friend can be said to be another self; they nurture what we might think of as a side we never knew we had. It is in such friendship that people find the courage and humility to overcome the stalemate of the little lies or ignorances in which most friendships inevitable trade to a degree, and turn to work on themselves and achieve the good things which as individuals alone, in isolation, would be beyond them. Is it not the rare, close friend who shares the intimacy of faults that can speak gently and with precision to our own? The book of *Proverbs* captures it well: 'As iron sharpens iron, so one man sharpens another.'

The story of Whale and Boone's friendship illustrates two further paradoxes in the friendship of another self. First, it is the

Figure 6: 'When the ways of friends converge, the whole world looks like home for an hour.' (Hermann Hesse)

differences between them that eventually count – what is unknown or unsettling – rather than the safe, familiar similarity that typically brings people together. What is strange challenges the friends to widen their horizons, search their souls and strive to speak honestly. 'It is not in how one soul approaches another but in how it distances itself from it that I recognise their affinity and relatedness,' says Nietzsche.

This issue has a bearing upon the business of making friends. The agony aunt might advise looking for people with whom you share something in common, perhaps a hobby or a concern. 'Like with like together strike,' it is said. And that is quite likely to be an easy way to open up conversation. Who knows, friendship may follow. But then again, perhaps it is the differences between people that generate deeper friendships. People complement one another, discover something new in life, are exposed to their shadow in their dissimilar friend. As the dry desert longs for wet rain, so we too can be drawn to those who embody something we feel we lack. Don't be closed to that possibility too.

Second, if the key to this kind of friendship is its challenge, its honesty can also be uncomfortable. To bear such frankness requires the right combination of timing and humility. In fact, in

Whale and Boone's case, Whale comes to see his predicament as a lonely old man perhaps too clearly for, though there is a certain catharsis in the act, he ends up killing himself. This is why such friendship is relatively rare and most of the time friends opt for at least a degree of feigning. Nietzsche provocatively suggests that someone who seeks a true appraisal from their friends might do better to turn to their foes, since enemies have the virtue of being honest and not counting the cost. Kant was alert to this too, and noted that people often prefer to tell their secrets to their doctor than to a friend, and hear the worst from the medic too.

Foes as friends in any literal sense is, of course, nonsense. But when the ultimate test of friendship is the ability to challenge one another, someone who might for a while be regarded as a bad friend could prove themselves a good friend in the longer term. Like a difficult book, the difficult friend may teach us something; affront at an initial presumption of unfriendliness may turn into gratitude for speaking the truth over time. Discernment is key. (Someone who is *simply* evil or unjust, impulsive or unsteady, will never be a good friend.)

Nietzsche is not the only philosopher to have thought that such genuinely challenging friendships are scarce and that the moments of truth they offer are fleeting in any individual's life. According to Plato, Socrates was aware of it too. In his dialogue on friendship, the *Lysis*, Socrates not only confesses that he has not been able to discover what friendship is really all about, but also that he wants a true friend more than anything else. The reason Socrates doubts whether he will ever find such a friend stems from his life as a philosopher. When he was young, the oracle at Delphi had told him that no one was wiser than he. This idea frightened him and so he took to wandering the streets of Athens in search of someone who would prove the oracle wrong. He was not able to. What is more his conversations with people increasingly revealed how little he knew. As a result he came to the conclusion that what the oracle must have meant was that no one else realised as profoundly as he did how little they knew. His wisdom was being wise to his ignorance.

This left him in a quandary with regards to friendship. On the one hand, he could not shake off a lingering sense of loneliness, because no one he met shared this profound sense of ignorance in the way he did and so could be another self to him. On the other hand, talking to people all day long meant that he enjoyed wide circles of (admittedly) lesser friends. This is the paradox of putting a high value of honesty on friendship. Given that you have the capacity to be honest with yourself, many people will not be up to it themselves. But since placing a high value on friendship means that friends will be keenly sought, it is likely that such a life will be nonetheless lived within circles of friends.

Plato provides an account of one particular occasion when these tensions came to a head for Socrates, in his relationship with an individual called Crito. Crito is an important friend of Socrates as far as history is concerned because he was present at Socrates' death. The occasion on which their friendship was put to the test was on the day of Socrates' execution, an encounter that Plato reconstructs in his dialogue called the *Crito*. The dialogue opens with Crito coming to Socrates in prison to tell him that the state galley is returning from Delos, a significant event because it marks the end of the religious festival during which Socrates, although condemned, could not be executed; with the return of the galley, his reprieve is over and it seems he must die.

Crito makes one last effort to persuade Socrates to allow his friends to pay off his jailers and secrete him into exile. Socrates refuses. He wants to drink the hemlock and die rather than flee the city and live. Therein lies the quandary he faces in friendship. It is not that Socrates does not care about Crito. Quite the reverse; apart from the intimate nature of their conversation, one reason why Socrates cannot escape is that to do so would implicate his friends who could then themselves face exile or injury. And more seriously as far as his beliefs about friendship are concerned, Socrates also knows that he must hold fast to what he holds to be true. Alongside the realisation of his wise ignorance, this includes the conviction that he should not be afraid of death. To run from the law would betray that conviction, though it is a burden he must ask his friend Crito to share with him. To go against his philosophy would be to go against his high ideal of friendship; his way of life as a philosopher and his search for true friendship – for another self – go hand in hand. Such is the price of honest friendship.

Other ways of honesty

Now, there are a number of objections that can be raised against such high ideals of friendship. For example, is it not too unfeeling, harsh, and perhaps suspiciously drawn to a kind of flagellatory ambition to be called friendship? For some, perhaps the answer is yes. However, to see it only in this light would be to misunderstand its undoubtedly strong character. For one thing, not all friendships are asked to rise to this level of intensity, only those who would be friends of the deepest kind. And, it is important to remember the comments made by Nietzsche about bearing other people's faults because they bear your own: the harsher ideals that friendship might demand are offset by the humane and compassionate behaviour that friendliness requires too.

Alternatively, consider another comment Nietzsche makes: 'Fellow rejoicing, not fellow suffering, makes the friend.' Nietzsche's point is that given that it is natural to want to respond to a friend's distress in some way, it is better to respond positively. Create something, Nietzsche says, 'that the other can behold with pleasure: a beautiful, restful, self-enclosed garden perhaps, with high walls against storms and the dust of the doorway but also a hospital gate'. He connects this more joyful approach to previous times in history when the paucity of medical science meant that much suffering was unavoidable, in response to which people developed an ethic of rejoicing. They put their efforts into a culture of celebration rather than amelioration; happiness rather than pain. This idealisation of history can readily be questioned, of course: who wants to go to a party with toothache? But considering the dominance of reality TV, chat shows and agony columns, Nietzsche is surely right to point out that these theatres of cruelty have proliferated in the modern world for the very reason that the spectacle of others suffering, and the opportunity it provides for us to show pity, distracts us from, and relieves us of responsibility for, facing the truth of our own pain.

Another objection might be that even if such high ideals of friendship are not as harsh as they first seem, because they appeal to a more genuine kind of compassion, are they still worth it? Are there not other ways to discover the truth of ourselves that do not require drawing others into the sometimes brutal truths of life? Or perhaps the effort that high friendship's penetrating honesty demands would be better placed elsewhere?

Some people have indeed concluded that truth is best sought not in friends but in substitutes for friends. Christina Rossetti, for one, wrote a poem about a tree, entitled with the ironic double entendre, 'A Dumb Friend'. One verse reads:

> So often have I watched it, till mine eyes
> Have filled with tears and I have ceased to see,
> That now it seems a very friend to me,
> In all my secrets wise.

More commonly, many might say that drowning the sorrow of their secrets in beer or wine is better and easier than bothering others; the alcohol seems like a good friend because it reflects their mood back to them.

More idiosyncratically, the Victorian art critic John Ruskin confessed that pictures were his only friends because they were the only things with which he could form honest attachments.

Or what of the case of a book as a friend? If 'the novelist lives in his work', as Joseph Conrad put it, then is not a book a friendship with a person, formed through its pages? Perhaps that's rather like the relationship expressed by Anne Frank. She famously called her diary Kitty, explaining that in the long hours of her hiding from the Nazis it was in a way a better friend than any person could be since 'paper is more patient than man'. In fact, a book appears to provide a good alternative to friendship proper because what a book shares with someone is the potential to impart objective self-understanding. For example, when we say we know a book well, because we have returned to it several times, there is the implication that it resonates with our own experience, throws light upon it, and constantly reveals things to us about ourselves. Supreme examples would be religious books like the Bible or the Koran. Stanley Cavell, a philosopher who has written widely on friendship, goes one step further and uses reading a book as itself an analogy for friendship itself, pointing out that in friendship one is able to 'read' the other and one allows oneself to be 'read'.

So, one can easily question whether a bottle of wine is really a good friend, unless you are an alcoholic. And the perpetual tree hugger is likely to be unbalanced. However, the case of the book is less easily resolved. Perhaps unexpectedly, Marcel Proust is someone who makes a strong case in its favour. He believed not just that friendship with people was unbearable unless individuals wear masks of good manners, a necessity that makes any real friendship very difficult if not impossible, but, more devastatingly still, he thought that people can never provide the opportunity for any real honesty anyway. In friendship, the greatest honesty that can be hoped for is a kindly acknowledgement that the request for friendship can never truly be given nor received. All friends can say to each other is, 'I'd love to be your friend.'

Books, however, overcome the limitations with which individuals find themselves encumbered when relating to one another. Proust invites us to consider the fact that friendship depends on conversation. The trouble with conversation, he implied, is that it is flawed: people get sidetracked, exchange only commonplaces, cannot communicate considered positions, or respect each other's self-delusion without challenging it. Novels, though, as means of communication are everything that conversation is not. They are focused, innovative, considered and disinterested.

Because of that, he concluded that there is a purity in reading to which friendship can never aspire; books have no false amiability.

When you are finished with a book, you shelve it without offence, something that is impossible with a friend. Proust even went so far as to misquote Aristotle and say that a book is another self, and better than a friend, since it is not susceptible to social habits, pressures or vices.

However, I think this is precisely why books will not, ultimately, do as friends. They may appear to be substitutes for friendship inasmuch as a spirit of honesty drives the desire to write and be read. But although books may be the product of another self, they are not 'an other self' as the adage implies in its deepest sense. For example, the control someone has over books may prevent false feeling but it indulges narcissism, the great enemy of self-honesty: a book is shelved with impunity when one does not like it because there is no obligation to respect it, like one must another person. Or, a book may open someone's eyes to difference, but difference only fully confronts us and challenges us to change in an encounter with another human being. It is the irreducibility of these human elements that makes for the powerful, if troubling, experience of deep friendship. And if conversation, though drenched in goodwill, is hardly ever entirely authentic, it is irreplaceable in conjuring up those rare moments of truth. Friendship of the honest sort may need the months and years of accommodation and propriety to produce it.

Solitude

A different kind of response to the ambiguities of honesty in friendship is to turn from it entirely. Most scholars would probably say that this is what Nietzsche did in the last years of his life. In the books of his final period, the few comments he makes on friendship appear to advocate increasingly adversarial relationships that precipitate ever more courageous acts of overcoming, with the result that mere circles of friends come to be seen as a dangerous hindrance: 'every person is a prison, also a nook and a corner'.

Nonetheless, if we look at the sayings of the character Zarathustra whom he creates in *Thus Spoke Zarathustra*, a more subtle position emerges than merely a rejection of friends. It is one that reveals another perhaps surprising dimension to this theme of truthfulness in friendship.

Nietzsche's Zarathustra is a prophet named after the founder of the ancient Persian religion Zoroastrianism. Nietzsche thought the original Zarathustra remarkable because he had struggled in his times with how to speak truthfully, how to pierce the smoke and mirrors of verisimilitude, how 'to shoot well with arrows'. In other words, he personifies a spirit of honesty. He first appears in Nietzsche's book coming out of solitude in the mountains as a prophet. He then utters a series of soliloquies to whoever will listen, one of which is entitled 'Of the Friend'. What is striking about it is that Zarathustra speaks as a hermit who longs for friendship. This is clearly a paradoxical state of affairs. How can someone who wants to be alone also want company?

The answer is that the hermit does not really want to be alone for isolation's sake, but rather that he seeks a retreat in order to achieve the state of mind that is rid of the clutter of life and allows him to see clearly. The difficulty Zarathustra's hermit has got himself into is that his isolation has caused him to turn in on himself. Rather than finding clarity of mind, he finds himself having a conversation between the 'I and Me' in his mind that only leads to him 'sinking to the depths'.

This is where his desire for a friend comes in. The good friend is someone who can save the hermit from his downward spiral without destroying the tranquillity of mind that much human interaction brings and from which the hermit longs to be free. More colloquially, we might say that one can be alone with a friend. Such an experience would point to Aristotle's third kind of friendship again, the closest sort. With such good friends, it doesn't matter what you are doing together, and you may well be doing nothing, just sitting silently; and there is no embarrassment. You are able simply to be together. No talking is required, no distractions.

(There is another sense in which solitude can be good for friendship, namely, taking some time out to think about it!

97

Reading or writing a book on friendship, activities that are mostly done in silence and alone, might provide a good case in point.)

Nietzsche's advocacy of solitude, then, has two senses. First, it implies a solitary solidarity of friendship between those who are other selves to one another. If the friend knows the individual better than themselves, then honest friendship is an opportunity to be alone together with the truth about one another. Second, I think Nietzsche is also pointing to a role friendship can play not only at a personal level but also at a social one. Solitude, in this case, is an isolation of a different sort: it is a mental separation from a world which loathes rest and reflection and has what is more mundanely called the wrong work/life balance. Nietzsche puts it like this:

> One thinks with a watch in one's hand, even as one eats one's midday meal while reading the latest news of the stock market; one lives as if one always 'might miss out on something'. 'Rather do anything than nothing': this principle, too, is merely a string to throttle all culture and good taste ... Living in a constant chase after gain compels people to expend their spirit to the point of exhaustion in continual pretence and over-reaching and anticipating others. Virtue has come to consist of doing something in less time than someone else. Hours in which honesty is permitted have become rare, and when they arrive one is tired and does not only want to 'let oneself go' but actually wishes to stretch out as long and wide and ungainly as one happens to be.

This way of life erodes the attention that is necessary for truthfulness. It is also strangely suspicious of joy for joy's sake. Instead, everything must be instrumental, including friendship. Nietzsche notes, that in the modern world when people are caught doing something pleasurable, like walking in the country, they excuse it as necessary for their health. I've read reports commending friendship, not because it's a good thing, but because it's good for your health too. This damages the capacity for deep friendship: 'Soon we may well reach the point where people can no longer give in to the desire for a *vita contemplativa* (that is, taking a walk with ideas and friends) without self-contempt and a bad conscience.' The concern is partly that friendship may come to be determined by utility, as we saw in the workplace. And partly that if honest friendship acts as a counter-cultural force to the multiple, frequently inauthentic ways that people have of interacting with each other, then other virtues like character or spiritual insight will come to an end too.

Solitude with a friend is the antidote. Though, again, it is no easy option. The psyche is a complex entity and a cosy solitude can easily lead to a smug presumptuousness, on the one hand, or moroseness, on the other. Friends together may also go the way of the isolated hermit, turning in on each other:

> If we live together with another person too closely, what happens is similar to when we repeatedly handle a good engraving with our bare hands: one day all we have left is a piece of dirty paper. The soul of a human being too can finally become tattered by being handled too continually.

Truthfulness and honesty, not self-justification and self-indulgence, are the test.

Ending friendship

His fear of being handled too close by Wagner is arguably what led to Nietzsche making a break. There was no solitude together to be had with the musician. Everyone around him was, instead, cast in his shade. So there is always the possibility that friendships may come to an end, not just because people 'trivially' fall out, but because sometimes it may be implicit in the dynamic of the relationship itself. What then on ending friendship?

Friendship can come under threat when people find themselves skating on thin ice: cracks of honesty that open onto icy water can destroy the surface on which the friendship relied. Add to this risk the fact that friendship is a game that is usually played out with many people at once. A new friend, for example, may give the game away because they have underestimated the subtlety of the rules by which the older friends are playing; the faux pas is easier to utter than the bon mot because it stems from ignorance not knowledge.

The closest of friends are not immune from the damage that can be caused by feelings of envy, distrust or betrayal too. In Shakespeare's *The Winter's Tale* two childhood friends, Leontes and Polixenes, fall out when Leontes suspects that Polixenes is having an affair with his wife, Hermione. 'Now my sworn friend and then mine enemy', breathes Leontes: the friends who were yoked together in love are now yoked by that which 'did betray the Best'. It turns out that Leontes is mistaken. But before he realises that, his son has died as, apparently, have his wife and daughter. The perception of disloyalty and deception can be as damaging to friendship as any actual deception itself.

As serious are the difficulties that arise when someone changes or moves, finds happiness or success. Prejudices that have been hidden since the foundation of the friendship can suddenly find themselves bursting at the seams – a double blow since it may well be that the friendship itself has opened up the new vista, as Nietzsche again laments:

> The best of them are lenient with us and wait patiently for us soon to find our way back to the 'right path' – they know, it seems, what the right path is! The others resort to mockery and act as though one had become temporarily insane, or they make spiteful allusions to the person they suppose to have misled us. The more malicious declare us to be vain fools and seek to blacken our motives, while the worst former friend of all sees in us his worst enemy and one thirsting for revenge for a protracted dependence – and is afraid of us.

However, in all these cases there are steps that can be taken before the end of the friendship is signed and sealed. Nietzsche's advice is

a conciliatory approach: at the first sign of mockery or malicious-
ness offer the friend a year's amnesty during which they can reform
their attitude. There's a practical suggestion: have a 12 month
cooling off period.

But what happens when an amnesty is not enough? Or, more
generally, how should one treat a friendship when it breaks up
whether by deliberate action or unavoidable accident?

Aristotle was alert to the pain and difficulty of ending friendships and devoted some thought to it. He noted that the problem is particularly intense when someone thinks they are liked
because of their character, for who they are in themselves, and it
turns out that this was feigned and they were really only liked
because of their wallet or their wit. Worse still, when the usefulness ends or the pleasure the friends shared dries up, it is also
easy for the one who has changed to feel duplicitous for having
feigned the friendship to start with. 'Quarrels between friends
occur more than anything when there is a difference between
what they think the basis of the friendship is and what it actually
is,' Aristotle wisely observes. In such cases, when very great
offence is taken, there is little possibility of a good ending.

Figure 7: 'Let us believe in our star friendship even if we should be
compelled to be earth enemies.' (Friedrich Nietzsche)

Another possibility Aristotle considers is whether friendships should be dissolved when one friend changes for the worst, to avoid the pretence that they are as likeable as they have always been? This perhaps happens more than we would care to admit: principled character can be eroded by money or success; warm natures can become embittered by experience. With these changes the thing that was good about the friend, and that formed the basis of the friendship, goes too. Consequently, if the unchanged friend feels they can do little about it, the friendship will fade as faking it becomes too much. Sadly but honourably one might retain a memory of the intimacy that was shared in the past, Aristotle adds, and remember the former friend in a kindly way.

A third possibility arises from Nietzsche's concept of ladder-types. These friendships will feel under threat because although one or both friends have changed, and probably for the better, they will now be on different paths that may take them a long way apart. They have no future together. This, surely, is how he came to see his friendship with Wagner. And 'star friendship' is Nietzsche's poetic way of describing this end to friendship:

> We were friends and have become estranged. But this was right, and we do not want to conceal and obscure it from ourselves as if we had reason to feel ashamed. We are two ships each of which has its goal and course ... and then the good ships rested so quietly in one harbour and one sunshine that it may have looked as if they had reached their goal and as if they had one goal. But then the almighty force of our tasks drove us apart again into different seas and sunny zone, and perhaps we shall never see each other again ... Let us then *believe* in our star friendship even if we should be compelled to be earth enemies.

The picture he draws is of a star in the heavens that memorialises the friendship, as it were, and which we might see if we look up. It can be appreciated there, for although it shines like the things that were shared, it no longer casts a shadow over the former friends' lives as they are now. Creating a star friendship out of a friendship that has turned bad will take a long time. Jealousy, envy and hatred don't dissolve overnight. It seems they never did in the case of Nietzsche and Wagner. Moreover, if the friend has been another self, then you are not just losing someone who was in your life but was a part of you. And if you are losing a part of yourself in anger or bitterness, then you are rejecting part of yourself too. Such wounds take time to heal, if ever they do.

However, the idea of star friendship can still help: it provides a sense of direction, the place you would like to end up, should you be able to get rid of all the bad feeling. It's where you'd like to be in relation to the old friendship, free of it now, and remembering it well for what it was.

There is, then, such a thing as a good and a bad break in friendship. The good break is a consequence of the positive thing that the friendship gave, the new path or insight, that then took the friends apart. The bad break is a consequence of negative change. Perhaps, in most breaks there is a mixture of both, like the split between Nietzsche and Wagner. Whatever; past friendships should lend themselves to future graciousness, for, even if it was a gift wrapped in thorns, or less of a gift than it first seemed, friendship is a gift nonetheless. For that, they are well remembered.

Friending Online

'Garbage in, garbage out.'

IT department saying

If friendships at work can be tricky, friendship with lovers complicated, and trusting friends more risky than first meets the eye, then online friendships appear to be inducing something of a panic. For social networking sites have put many social commentators in a spin.

Websites like Second Life, Facebook, Bebo and Twitter have gathered users at astonishing rates. Millions are spending hours at a time pursuing friendships that, previously, they would have presumably conducted in the playground or pub, or not at all. The anxiety stems from whether the virtual world is a good, safe and honest world in which to get to know and be known by another – or at least whether it is good, safe and honest enough. Panic is associated with the uncertainty that surrounds this question, and the fact that there appears to be evidence for thinking it is not.

Take online bullying, one aspect of virtual culture that regularly grabs a headline, and the even nastier phenomenon of online grooming. These are clearly threats faced by children of the information age, and not just children. Teachers are being bullied too. In one poll for YouGov, ten per cent of teachers confessed that they'd been bombarded by instant messages and emails. Whilst it was happening, their life was a misery.

What you might call the internet's tendency to abuse relationships can be a subtle thing too. Most people will have had an email that, written in a hurry, struck them more forcefully than was intended. These short messages, which now rule millions of lives, are misunderstandings waiting to happen. Surely, it is no overreaction to wonder whether the world has become a little less humane when bosses would send notices of dismissal, and lovers would send notices of rejection, via such memos, simply on the grounds of efficiency. A letter was personalised by its hand-writing; a telephone call by the voice.

Alternatively, there is a question of trust. David Holmes, a psychologist, has estimated that up to 40 per cent of the information displayed on social networking sites might be fabricated. It's easy to understand why people post false details about themselves: they want to protect their privacy, and screens are very good at screening. However, the same safe practice simultaneously undermines trust. No one can tell whether you're a dog online. When you're sharing with someone via a website, you often have little means of determining their truthfulness or not.

Thinking of friendship in particular, it seems to be much easier to terminate virtual friends than those rooted in real life. Holmes believes that may be causing widespread upset and depression. The difficulty is that you can be pouring your heart out into a chat, whilst the individual on the other side of the screen is yawning with boredom, gossiping with someone else, or suddenly decides to switch off. Your apparent soulmate disappears without warning, leaving you in the lurch. This might all be called the casual callousness of the internet. In the real world it is mitigated since people have more signs that they can read from a face – signs that tell them much earlier whether an interlocutor is really interested or would rather be somewhere else. Online, though, people plunge in. That forces a rejection: it is harder to let someone down gently, so you become a brute, perhaps against your better nature, and routinely mete out the virtual cold shoulder.

The sociologist Sherry Turkle has explored a different source of concern. Her fear is that we are being deskilled by life online: by being able to leap into virtual space at any time of day or night, and there find an inexhaustible supply of mates and stuff to distract us, we erode our capacity to be alone. She believes that solitariness is an important skill since it is then that we learn to manage and contain our emotions. Turkle's worry is that the internet is transforming human psychology, creating

105

what she calls a 'tethered self' – one that is dependent upon being wired, and feels most intimate when relationships are mediated by machines. Similarly, she's written about how online conversation is different from engaging with someone face to face. Then you are able to look them in the eye, and have to make the effort of being in the same physical place, as opposed to doing nothing more arduous than clicking on a hyperlink. Hence, online chat is mostly about gossip, bullet-point profiles, and instant reactions, whereas conversation grips the whole individual, nurtures a natural sense of reserve, and requires a deeper commitment to each other.

To put it another way, whilst the internet opens gateways of community, it does not of itself teach us how to make connections or deal with complexity: it is a medium, not a culture. Or, as has been said, it is a tremendous mechanism for the accumulation of facts, but from that rainstorm of bits, knowledge, let alone wisdom, does not automatically flow. There is the added problem that the information itself can easily be wrong. All this distracts from self-reflection. It nurtures quick, ill-considered responses. This is what would alter people's psychology.

As if that were not enough, some highly respected scientists have gone so far as to raise the spectre of social networking scrambling the mind like eggs in a pan. Professor Susan Greenfield, the head of the Royal Institution of Great Britain, is one. A series of articles and press interviews have generated headlines from 'Social websites harm children's brains' to 'Do you have Facebook flab?' Apart from the sedentary lifestyle that virtual living necessitates – it would make couch potatoes of us all – she suggests that time online changes the very structure of your brain, a conclusion that would appear to follow from the fact that the billions of nerves and connections inside your head are now known to be highly plastic. That does sound alarming coming from a leading neuroscientist, though being a scientist she does qualify the speculation. However, maybe it is the case that if you train your brain by occupying it in imaginary space, or by clicking from one site to the next like as many TV channels, than that could lead to anything from inattention at school to a psychotic disregard for others.

The panic can be fuelled by semantic considerations too. Consider the language deployed to describe the business of forging friendship online. A couple of years back, users of MySpace created a new verb, 'to friend'. It means 'to link to', differing from befriending which involves getting to know someone too.

Some researchers have interpreted the new language positively. Talking about 'friending', rather than befriending, draws a distinction between just connecting and properly knowing someone else. That implies individuals understand that forging virtual links with someone is not the same as forging real links with them. Similarly, no one could confuse actually meeting someone with the software tools that will just 'friend' for you, the applications that seek out individuals with whom you have something in common and add them to your burgeoning list of buddies. (There are also viruses and worms that will multiply the number of contacts you have without the burden of human intervention: it sounds like attending the cocktail party from hell, and is perhaps another reason why such bugs are referred to as 'malign'.) 'Friending really appeals to the ego, where friendships appeal to the conscience,' writes Michael Bugeja, author of *Interpersonal Divide: The Search for Community in a Technological Age*. To put it another way, to friend is a quantitative activity: more is more. To befriend is qualitative, a case in which fewer friends may well mean deeper friendships. Everyone, presumably, understands the difference.

Or do they? 'Acquisition of friends is like any other fix but it's competitive,' comments David Smallwood, an expert in addiction from the Priory health clinic. He believes that like any addiction, compulsive friending could be defined precisely by an inability to tell the difference between more and better. 'You judge yourself by how many friends you have online. You go out of your way to amass friends and that means people bend out of shape and become something they are not.' He is quite clear that such internet addictions are real. The parallel is with the shopaholic: social networking sites are friendship's equivalent of a credit card. In the same way that someone might load their flexible friend with the debt required to buy more things, a Facebook account is the means by which to load up on friends.

The panic is such that the matter is being discussed in academic journals. *The American Journal of Psychiatry* published one article by Jerald Block. You can count yourself an addict if you answer 'yes' to five of more of these questions:

1. Do you feel preoccupied with the internet?
2. Do you need increasing amounts of time on the net?
3. Have you repeatedly made unsuccessful efforts to cut internet use?
4. Do you feel restless, moody, depressed, or irritable about that?
5. Do you stay online longer than originally intended?
6. Have you jeopardised anything that really mattered because of the internet?
7. Have you lied to others about your use of the internet?
8. Do you use it to escape from problems?

Worried yet? Well, you've company. In South Korea, probably the most connected country on the planet, the number of people who have died from blood clots caused by sitting too long at a terminal is now counted in the dozens, and it is reckoned that 210,000 children have an addiction problem. In China, which never does anything by halves, it is reckoned there are ten million addicts.

The sociologist, Zigmunt Bauman, believes that a consumer culture is precisely one that confuses quantity with quality, and struggles to tell the difference between measuring something and assessing its meaning: in preferring the prolific to the profound it takes the prolific to be profound. There is, therefore, a risk of seeking to compensate for a lack of depth in friendship by simply searching for more friends. 'While unable to put our suspicions to rest and stop sniffing out treachery and fearing frustration, we seek – compulsively and passionately – wider "networks" of friends and friendship; indeed, as wide a "network" as we can manage to squeeze into the mobile phone directory that, obligingly, grows more capacious with every new generation of mobiles,' he writes in *Liquid Fear*.

Webs of concern

And yet, all that said, there are very good reasons for looking opti-mistically at what the internet has to offer friendship. One way into this different perspective is to recall Aristotle's different kinds of friendship. He noted the difference between friendships based on doing something together, such as work, and friendships based on knowing and loving someone for whom they are in themselves – the close friend with whom you can be doing absolutely nothing and have no sense of embarrassment or awkwardness. This obser-vation leads to a reflection on the quality of time you need to spend with someone in order to become close friends, namely that you must have time with them when you aren't doing anything very much – what might be called non-instrumental time. Con-versely, instrumental time is highly structured – it's time for things, be that going to the match, doing the shopping, picking up the kids, getting the job done. Non-instrumental time is for nothing, and for that very reason is very good for close friendships.

The internet can, then, provide quite a lot of time that is 'for nothing', as when individuals might say they are hanging-out online. Thereby, it is arguably good for the cultivation of closer relationships. Such a possibility has been found in practice. A group of researchers from the University of California inter-viewed 800 young people, and monitored their activity online. Many were nearly always online, constantly communicating with their friends by messaging, phoning or using social networking sites. And it turned out that the majority of these people used new media just to hang out. Their primary goal was not to pursue interests, or to do anything in particular. It was merely to extend the time they could spend with their friends.

That would seem to be good for closer friendship, as it is not instrumentally driven. It might well create the time necessary for the kind of affection based on knowing someone for who they are in themselves. Moreover, these people spent this online, non-instrumental time with friends they had made first in the real world. That the online activity is mostly driven by their offline realities would support a positive conclusion: it reduces the fear that people are attempting to get to know each other via the one dimensional medium of the screen, and are instead able to draw on what they know of their friends face-to-face.

Another example of how the internet can be a great good is when it brings together people with common interests and shared concerns. I have a friend who discovered this when she had twins. Lisa used to be a self-confessed technophobe. She would tease her husband at his excitement over the new technologies. Then began their quest to have a baby.

It resulted in many dark days of infertility investigations and treatments, during which it was hard to find people to talk to about the heartache. Other friends were falling pregnant and having babies. With the best will in the world, such friends could only partially share in their hopes and disappointments.

It was at this point that Lisa turned to the internet. She discovered the world of infertility message boards and found that, perhaps bizarrely, it was hugely comforting to connect – albeit anonymously – with people who were going through what they were. That support continued when, having become pregnant, with twins, there were complications. She went online again, and joined a twins club, sending out messages with subject lines like: 'Can anyone help with advice re twin pregnancy and growth restriction?' Within hours, she had dozens of reassuring replies. Though it was not only the reassurance that touched Lisa: it was also the fact that complete strangers had taken the time to be a virtual shoulder cry on.

When the babies were safely born, the online advice reaped benefits again: people had suggested visiting the neonatal unit before the birth so as not to be shocked by the tubes and wires, and that helped. Again, when the babies came home, the internet provided a lifeline: it provided people to talk to whilst Lisa was otherwise stranded in the house. She is quite convinced that she stayed sane throughout the whole process because of the rich interactions – the friendships – she enjoyed in cyberspace.

So what can be made of this mix of good news and bad? Is the panic justified? If there are undoubtedly positive possibilities that come with the internet, are there new dangers emerging too?

Life in cyberspace

We are in the midst of the revolution, if revolution is what it is, so any conclusions will be provisional: there seems little doubt that the boundaries between being on- and offline will continue to be eroded, we will spend more and more of our time in what some philosophers call the infosphere. Time will be the best judge of online amity. However, it is not too early to make some suggestions about how to do friendship well in the virtual world. And the truth, I suspect, is in fact relatively prosaic. In order to show why, consider two theories that put the question of online friendship into a wider frame.

The first challenges the suggestion that there is something inherently different about the medium of the infosphere. It suggests that we are really only in the midst of pre-existing shifts in our sense of what it is to be human, shifts that we sum up in the word 'modernity'. Think of it this way. At the beginning of the sixteenth century, on the eve of modernity, Copernicus showed some friends a little notebook. In it he had sketched out his reasons for thinking that the Earth was not at the fixed centre of the universe but rather that it revolves around the Sun. This heliocentrism sparked a radical shift in thought, the one for which Galileo famously paid a price when the Pope sentenced him to house arrest for subsequently lending his support to Copernicus' work. Today, this change in thinking is typically taken as emblematic of scientific progress, which it is. But it has another facet too, one that might have a bearing upon internet friendship.

Figure 8: A Copernican sketch of the cosmos

Part of the reason for the anxiety then was that, after Copernicus, our planetary home had no significant place in the cosmos. We now know that it moves continually and randomly through space. This freedom of the Earth to move amongst the stars, as it were, can be seen as a model for the modern sense of liberation. Thus, being tied to a particular place seems unbearably constraining to the contemporary individual; being forced to follow an allotted course in life dangerously undemocratic. Instead, the ability to change has come to seem as synonymous with freedom, and enjoying plenty of choice crucial to being human.

Life online might be thought of as another manifestation of such a way of life. This infinity of virtual space is one where innovations are routinely heralded as 'liberating' and 'freeing'; as Web 2.0 unfurls – from Friends Reunited, through Facebook, to Twitter – a story is told of power being placed in the hands of people. Never mind that secretly those same people will confess that they can no more make sense of what's coming at them than they can see into a black hole. We just feel freer as a result. This contemporary celebration of de-centredness is a quintessentially post-

Copernican response. It would have been inconceivable before the birth of modernity.

The link with online friendship can be made by considering how some of the great writers about friendship have depicted their soulmates and kindred spirits in those same modern times. Typically, close friends are presented as a refuge against the alienation that so much freedom may bring; amity has become a consolation in the face of cosmic isolation. 'When the ways of friends converge, the whole world looks like home for an hour', wrote the novelist Hermann Hesse. 'It is not wrong to want to be happy, but it is wrong to want to be happy all alone', judged the existentialist Albert Camus of the modern condition. 'I hate the prostitutions of the name of friendship to signify modish and worldly alliances', opined Ralph Waldo Emerson on the shallowness of mere networking.

This, I think, is what the wired generation has to learn – and quite possibly is learning – all over again. If the silicon universe is not to leave one as lonely as Major Tom, it may be necessary to realise that the primary context for real friendship is not within this infinite, shapeless medium. Rather, online friendships are but reflections of the close intimacy of embodied exchange. ('I have a body too,' reads one virtual bumper sticker.) We can of course be friendly online, showing courtesy and kindness to the many individuals we stumble across. We can also be callous. Like chatting in the corner shop or smiling on the bus, human benevolence makes on- and offline worlds much better places. Nevertheless, there is as big a gap between friendliness and friendship as there is between cooperation and love; we forget the difference at our peril.

That's one theory. Here's a second. It was penned by the evolutionist and priest Pierre Teilhard de Chardin in his 1955 posthumous publication, *The Phenomenon of Man*. It is not a straightforward book, verging from the tangible to the mystical, from facts to dreams, as he himself admitted. And yet, it seems to capture something of what is now said of the internet.

Teilhard presents a visionary account of evolution on a grand scale. In a first stage, humanity spreads itself around the Earth,

113

so that it comes to cover the globe. That phase takes place over centuries. But then a second stage begins, one with origins in the twentieth century. Now, human beings spin a tapestry of ideas across the planet, so that intellectual and imaginative energies merge and connect in a great web. As it converges, it unifies. He calls it a 'super-arrangement'. It is like 'some great body which is being born – with its limbs, its nervous system, its perceptive organs, its memory – the body in fact of that great living Thing which has to come to fulfil the ambitions aroused in the reflective being by the newly acquired consciousness.' This 'thing' he also calls the 'noosphere', from the Greek *nous* for mind. Though Teilhard undoubtedly conceived that the noosphere would have more than just a material manifestation, it is easy to relate his vision to the internet and the human energy it transmits.

There is a link to friendship here since he also thought this process of organisation would accelerate. A new consciousness would be achieved, which he called the 'Omega Point'. It encapsulated his idea of human freedom – that being quite the opposite of the liberty of the Copernican view. Instead of floating freely as individuals, Teilhard imagines our freedom as being found at the point where individuality meets universality. 'We can only find our person by uniting together,' he wrote. It is a description of cosmic friendship.

There are, of course, all sorts of reasons to be sceptical of this philosophy. The mystical element may turn you off. The totalitarian ethic of unification may do so too. However, it can perhaps serve as a heuristic model through which to interpret the meaning of web-enabled human networks. On the one hand, there is this hope that they nurture the compassionate side of humanity, that by being more exposed to one another we plummet the depths of what we have in common. But on the other hand, Teilhard was fully aware of the evils connectivity can nurture too. 'As things are now going it will not be long before we run full tilt into one another,' he continued. 'Something will explode if we persist in trying to squeeze into our old tumble-down huts the material and spiritual forces that are henceforth on the scale of the world.' He added: 'Evil may be growing alongside good, and it too may attain its paroxysm at the end in some specifically new form.' Whether or not the ills the internet transmits have taken on new forms, it certainly amplifies those that exist already. There is ample evidence of that.

The shock of the old

So once again, the internet looks like a prism through which pre-existing trends come to be seen in primary colours. And so, when great claims are made for the internet, be they for good or ill, it is always worth asking whether the real issue at stake is really not novelty but an intensification of human experience.

Consider this case. There are today occasions on which an individual meets a stranger who is really no stranger at all. This is because the two concerned have already developed a relationship online. In a reversal of the normal pattern of friendship, they meet after they have got to know each other, not before. Indeed, it is because they sense that they have enough in common, and would like to take the relationship to a new level, that they arranged a coffee or drink. Granted, it is an anxious experience, because for all the ease with which words flowed on the screen, there is no guarantee they will flow in the flesh. We are embodied creatures, and there is nothing so alarming, and alluring, as being physically present with someone. Only then can you answer the question of whether you really know them. Therein lies the frisson and fear. But is this not new?

It seems not. People in previous centuries formed friendships via writing letters, and then might subsequently meet. Take the poet Emily Dickinson, who exchanged many missives with Thomas Wentworth Higginson over several years. Brenda Wineapple has written about it in her book, *White Heat*. Their communication is not just similar to the internet friends of today, but arguably has something to teach us too.

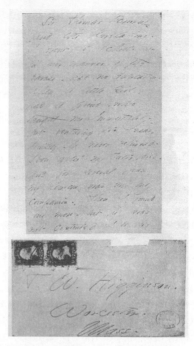

Figure 9: Manuscript letter and envelope that Dickinson sent to Higginson, in which the poet talks about love.

Wineapple describes how their friendship was 'based on absence, geographic distance, and the written word [and yet] somehow these two people created out of words a nearness we today do not entirely grasp'. In one letter, Higginson writes: 'I cannot reach you, but only rejoice in the rare sparkles of light'. Though in another he confessed, 'I am glad not to live near her'; he perceived that she drained his 'power'. Interestingly, she refused to send a picture of herself when one was requested and instead describes herself: 'small, like the Wren, and my Hair is bold, like the Chestnut Bur, and my eyes, like the Sherry in the Glass, that the Guest leaves.' Doesn't that say more than a jpeg? Perhaps next time someone asks for a picture, you might try a description instead.

According to Wineapple, the friendship of Dickinson and Higginson thrived because it was a tie that 'neither of them expected or wanted ... to lead anywhere specific'. As Aristotle might have analysed, they had learned to love each other for who each was in themselves, and who they became together – in spite of, or maybe because of, the distance.

Togetherness and distance. If it is right to think of the web as a network of communication around the world, then it is but a particularly sharp reflection of the processes of urbanisation and globalisation that has long being taking place in other spheres. There too, good accompanies bad. In particular, there appears to be a causal link between urbanisation and individualisation – which paradoxically may well run in tandem with a sense of collectivity too.

For example, there are many polls which suggest we are losing friends. And typically, urban life is blamed, of which wired, mobile living is a part. One suggests that in London, over two-fifths of people drift away from their close friends. Urban lifestyle and work brings individuals within the orbit of a wide range of amiable people. Witness the crowded pubs after work. But they are good only as acquaintances; they leave one stranded when it comes to real intimacy.

On the other side of the Atlantic, some sociologists are tracking similar trends. *The American Sociological Review* has carried research showing that the average American now has only two close friends, and a quarter don't have any at all. The number of people who say they have no one with whom to discuss important matters has risen in the years since the turn of the millennium – that is, during the years in which the internet has blossomed. Similarly, both Save the Children and The Children's Society are increasingly worried that technology is damaging young people's ability to socialise, often leaving them lonely, disruptive and prone to bullying.

But worrying as that may be, it is also not hard to find research which implies the opposite. Another study, conducted by Hua Wang and Barry Wellman, explicitly addresses what the authors call 'the social panic in the United States about a possible decline in social connectivity'. And they find the panic is unjustified. Friendships continue to be abundant among adult Americans and, they report, appear to have grown from 2002 to 2007. The internet makes no difference to this result: it is the same amongst non-users, light users, moderate users, and heavy users. In fact, heavy users have the most friends both on- and offline. Could it be that the internet, far from undermining friendship, is reawakening our desire for it?

Taking a step back from the figures, such confusion is surely only to be expected. Cities have long brought people together with mixed results. It seems likely that before long, more people will live in cities than live outside of them, as will be the case with being online. That sounds good for community, were it not that cities simultaneously create a sense of isolation. This is because their size affords people an anonymity that is just not possible in small populations. Their diversity also means that people live in parallel worlds: neighbours physically located on the same street may never meet because their work or interests or commitments are so different. Or again, whilst at one level cities can be seen as great organisms – much as the web can been seen as a 'super-arrangement' – the paradox is that different elements in that organism may know nothing of each other, for all that they work together: a hand has no conception of what it is like to be an eye, hair looks utterly unlike skin, for all that they are positioned so closely together. Thus, urban centres, like the leading websites of the internet, are places in which strangers gather, and if they are aware of each other's presence at all, they are more conscious of their differences than their dependencies. As the saying goes, the loneliest place is in the middle of the crowd.

Cheerleaders and doom mongers

I think that this kind of analysis helps to explain why the internet generates hope as well as panic, why online friendship has as many cheerleaders as prophets of doom. In a sense, both are right, for whenever human beings come together it precipitates loneliness and belonging in equal measure, and heightens both. We should only expect that for every positive story of virtual amity, there is a negative story of virtual animosity too.

So, the internet certainly extends incidences of friendship, or at least friendliness. If you read something that moves you on a blog, you can leave a kindly message there and then. If you want to offer an author a constructive critique, email makes it easy to be in touch, and so the engagement is more likely to happen.

Conversely, vitriol is easier to exchange online too. Ill-tempered comments that would previously have been contained in a private letter can be beamed like searchlights across virtual space. In Second Life, there is the phenomenon of 'griefing', a kind of virtual happy-slapping: individuals instruct their avatars to assault the avatars of another and in so doing fail to see their target as the representation of a real human being. It's not nice, but then again, happy-slappers on the streets of our towns and cities don't see their victims as human beings either.

Another unpleasant invention is 'comment swarming', when interest groups, gathered around some public figure or point of view, launch a virtual attack on, say, an opinion contrary to theirs published on a website. The remarks they leave are clearly neither friendly, nor intended to be. But once more: hate mail has existed for as long as people with quills have found parchment to write on. So, in both the positive and negative cases, there is nothing strictly new occurring. There is, at best – or worst – an intensification of the friendliness or animosity that was already well known to those who lived before, or still live without, the worldwide web.

Incidentally, it must be for similar reasons that the more utopian claims made for the internet, and its potential effect in human affairs, are overblown. Some have suggested that the internet might transform human affairs by allowing individuals from different sides of disputes to communicate on neutral terrain. The Israeli and the Palestinian will be able to talk regardless of any dividing wall. Those of the right will meet those of the left, though they'd never pass each other on the street because they live on opposite sides of town. Websites will provide a level playing field, the optimistic view goes, on which everyone can hear the complaints of their opponents, and simultaneously feel they have been more clearly heard.

This may happen in some cases: anyone can stumble across a blog expressing opinions contrary to their own and discover that they've learned something about a perceived enemy. However, at the same time, the internet surely operates to bolster prejudice too. As people buy newspapers that reflect their own views, or as they go to a church that teaches them more or less what they already believed, so online behaviour sees individuals congregating around the sites to which they feel they belong. The medium of exchange may be different, but human nature remains the same. On the whole, we prefer to feel we're amongst friends.

The conclusion to draw, then, would be this. It seems right to be wary of claims that the internet is introducing something radically new into the human experience of friendship. It may well be that today we have wider circles of friends because of the internet. And that might be a boon. But beware: there is nothing more ruinous of relationships than thinking they are something they are not – and friendship may be particularly prone to such blind spots as it is something people rarely analyse. It is still quality, not quantity that counts. Even on the internet, this is something that most people understand quite intuitively.

Research conducted by Ray Pahl, into the way people use Blackberrys, seems to capture the heart of it well. His evidence suggests that even the most wired and technophilic of individuals use PDAs to sustain a small core of really good friends, perhaps a dozen at most; and simultaneously use the technology to manage their wider circle of acquaintances – sometimes keeping them at bay, sometimes drawing them in closer.

To put it another way, the online age is like any other in this respect: it needs a good understanding of the philosophy of friendship, of its rules and limitations, as well as its promise. A good lesson to learn would be that the internet is not so much a new forum for friendship, though it certainly brings more people within our orbit; rather it's best application for amity is as a tool for sustaining friendship. Virtuality may feel liberating, as free as a planet whirling through space. But we are persons, and embodied persons too. Intimacy ultimately depends for its flourishing on contact in the real world, face-to-face.

Unconditional Love

> 'Because they love no one, they imagine that they love God.'
>
> Thomas Keneally

In 375 CE, Augustine of Hippo – Saint Augustine – returned from the splendour of the Roman University at Carthage to his hometown of Thagaste, an outpost of farmers now called Souk Ahras in Algeria. A few years earlier, he had left as a pagan. He came back now a Manichean. This illegal sect that believed in the radical separation of good and evil was almost bound to appeal to the sometime student, now young teacher. It brought him not only philosophical certainty but also the fellowship of a cultivated group of friends. As he settled down to teaching in Thagaste he quickly found a new set of Manichean friends and established for himself a way of life that was a model of classical friendship – something we know about from the record he provides of it in his autobiographical *Confessions*:

> All kinds of things rejoiced my soul in their company – to talk and laugh, and to do each other kindnesses; to read pleasant books together; to pass from lightest jesting to talk of the deepest things and back again: to differ without rancour, as a man might differ with himself, and when, most rarely, dissension arose, to find our normal agreement all the sweeter for it; to teach each other and to learn from each other; to be impatient for the return of the absent, and to welcome them with joy on their homecoming; these, and such-like things, proceeding from our hearts as we gave affection and received it back, and shown by face, by voice, by the eyes, and by a thousand other pleasing ways, kindles a

flame which fused our very souls together, and, of many, made us one.

Aristotle could not have described this happy life more accurately himself: 'Friendship is a kind of excellence and furthermore is very necessary for living,' he said. Augustine even had a friend of the very best sort, someone who was another self, sweeter to him than all the other joys of life.

Ancient philosophy was never far from Augustine's mind, so it is not surprising that he interprets his experience of friendship using ancient Greek ideas. And it was not just in relation to understanding friendship that he turned to Athens. For example, the youthful prayer for which he is now well known, 'Lord give me chastity and continence: but not now', is a troubled response to Cicero's description of the pleasures of the body as 'snares and the source of all ills': Augustine kept a lover, unlike many of his Manichean friends, and he worried a little – though obviously not enough – about the impact of this sensual indulgence upon the powers of his intellect.

Then, within a year of his return to Thagaste, calamity struck. His best friend developed a fever. The young man lost consciousness and, fearing for his life, he was baptised by his Christian family, though he was a Manichean. Augustine thought little of it at the time, believing that his friend would laugh at the ceremony when he revived. However, when his friend did rally, and the matter was raised, he turned on Augustine and warned him not to mock: Augustine must accept his new faith or become his deadly enemy, he said.

Augustine was stunned. He tried to comfort himself with the thought that his friend's belligerence was an after-effect of the illness, though the altercation disturbed him enough to end his round the clock vigil at the sickbed. So, when his friend's fever returned a few days later, Augustine was not there. Neither was Augustine there when the friend died.

Augustine was entirely overcome:

> My own country became a torment and my own home a
> grotesque abode of misery. All that we had done together
> was now a grim ordeal. My eyes searched everywhere for
> him, but he was not there to be seen. I hated all the places
> we had known together, because he was not in them and
> they could no longer whisper to me 'Here he comes!' as they
> would have done had he been alive but absent for a while.

He was also shocked by the extent of the grief itself. It seemed
to undo all his of former confidence. He told himself to wait for
God's help but his soul refused to be comforted; he became
afraid of death and was haunted by fantasies of other friends
dying.

And then the horrible nub of it became clear to him. He
realised that he loved the friend he had lost more than he had
ever loved God, and, worse still, that he loved himself even more
than that. If he depended so utterly upon himself, a thing that
could so easily pass away, was not his self-sufficiency a terrible
conceit? 'What madness, to love a man as something more than
human!' he cried.

Augustine lost faith in everything; we would say he had a breakdown. He could find no peace in people, books or poetry. He tired
of himself. 'The god I worshipped was my own delusion, and if
I tried to find in it a place to rest my burden, there was nothing
there to uphold it.' Even the soil beneath his feet became synonymous with death and, much against the advice of his elders, he
took his leave of Thagaste and left.

Back in Carthage, Manicheism provided some comfort and he
took to writing a book on beauty as if by the effort he could
restore his faith in the world. Time did heal the wounds of his
immediate loss – but not those of the more profound crisis. The
vertiginous and very modern-sounding fear of having to rely on
himself was to haunt him for 11 more years, until he became a
Christian.

Figure 10: 'What madness, to love a man as something more than human!' (Augustine)

Conversion transformed him. It saved him from himself, installing in place of his own divided will, faith in Jesus Christ. He was overjoyed. However, the self-renunciation becoming a Christian entailed had serious implications for his belief in friendship. He started to look back on those early years with his Manichean friends and thought them vainglorious: 'In public we were cocksure, in private superstitious, and everywhere void and empty.' He came to the conclusion that they were all as deluded as each other and, because the things they loved were false, their friendship was false too. 'Ours was not the friendship which should be between true friends ... for though they cling together, no friends are true friends unless you, my God, bind them fast to one another through that love which is sown in our hearts by the Holy Ghost.'

This thought explained why the death of his friend had been so overwhelming: it was not only that he had relied too much on his friend's love, but also that the friendship was really just a mirror

125

of his love of himself. Thus, to lose the friend had been to lose himself. Now, though, his Christian faith, in contrast, taught him something very different: when people love God and renounce their love of themselves, they can then love others with confidence. Their love is then primarily located in God and so unconditioned by the vagaries of life: 'They alone will never lose those who are dear to them, for they love them in one who is never lost, in God.' True friendship, Augustine believed he was discovering, is triangulated: two human friends must be linked by a third, divine connection. Friendship must be seen from the viewpoint of divine love, its security and ultimate end.

This 'friendship-in-God' ethos has cast a shadow over subsequent interpretations of friendship, for in the same way that Augustine once turned to the ancient Greeks to understand his experience of friendship, the western tradition since has often turned to Augustine. At one level, all Augustine wanted to do was recast the vicissitudes of human love within the steadfast love of God. However, the upshot was, I think, that Augustine never quite recovered his faith in actual friendships again. For one thing, he came to see the death of his friend as an act of God's vengeance for his earlier false faith; it was a crucial moment in breaking the spell of his youthful, Manichean delusion. But, more profoundly, if the painful end of a friendship started him on his journey to his true home, the Christian understanding of eternity – 'which does not fall because we are away' – friendship itself was never going to seem quite the same again. Thereafter, Augustine learns again to celebrate friendship, but only insofar as friends assist him in his higher calling, to love God. Hence nearly forty years later, when he came to write *The City of God*, he cast friendship in a distinctly doubtful light. It can never be carefree, he said, because life is too full of dangers. Friends will die or be parted from you, a tragedy and sadness the likelihood of which increases with the more friends one has. Worse, friends will betray you, in matters of state or affairs of the heart. Indeed, there is a part of Augustine that now rejoices when he hears of a friend's death for the very reason that such dreadful possibilities have ceased. As his modern biographer Peter Brown has put it:

> The man who had once thought that he could reach an ideal of perfection fixed for him by the philosophical culture of his age, in the company of friends of recognizable quality, unambiguously marked out for the higher life by education and serious intentions, becomes filled with Romantic longings for states he would never achieve in this life, for friends he would never entirely know.

The loss of faith in friendship became, as Brown describes it, 'the silent tragedy' of his Christian life.

From loss of faith to rejection

Augustine's story marks a pivotal moment in the history of the philosophy of friendship. Many of the things that he wrestled with in friendship, such as its fragility and its relationship to love of self, were familiar to ancient philosophers including Aristotle and Plato. The fragility of friendship is arguably the defining feature of Plato's portrayal of friendship in the *Lysis* where Socrates confesses he does not have a true friend and does not even really know what real friendship is. Aristotle examined the apparent contradiction of the second issue, that loving another depends on loving oneself. He concluded that the paradox is in fact unobjectionable: self-love and other-love are intertwined because unless someone can befriend themselves they are hardly likely to be able to form any deep friendships with others. What people need to cultivate is the good self-love that enables them to overcome themselves, to be at ease with themselves, to be free to pay close attention to others. This kind of self-love is still good. What they need to avoid is the bad self-love that is narcissistic, self-obsessed and solipsistic.

Where Augustine is different – and where he injects radically new Christian ideas into our understanding of friendship – is in his response to these features of amity: he reaches very different conclusions. First, friendship's fragility is not to be simply embraced but, he thinks, must be underwritten by the unconditionally reliable love of God. Friends must love each other through and in what his faith teaches him is the only true and firm foundation. Second, he concludes that friendship's inherent self-love should not be the springboard of other-love, but that it should be renounced. The individual who thinks that they can learn to love others by first learning to love themselves, as Aristotle suggested, is in fact inculcating a dangerous state of mind, a dependency upon themselves and love as it is found in this world. Friendship in this mode, he believes, is bound to fail in betrayals and partings, moments when the friend, no matter how well-meaning, chooses or succumbs to something else. However, if this love of self is renounced entirely, a new way of loving opens up that depends not on the weak will of the individuals concerned, but on the constant will of a loving God.

It is important to stress how alien both these moves would have seemed to Plato and Aristotle. The idea that self-renunciation is the key to the good life would have been antithetical to Aristotle's self-perfected man; he would have thought of self-renunciation as indistinguishable from self-abnegation. The right approach for him was to find a middle path between that extreme, self-denial, and its opposite, self-conceit. With the right balance an individual can cultivate a good kind of selfishness – wanting to become the best kind of person they can in ways that are in turn of benefit to others. For Augustine, such a hope might seem admirable but it wildly underestimates the treacherous nature of human love and the tragedies with which life assails us.

When it comes to Augustine's second move, the triangulation by which individuals come to rely on the love of God, the ancients would have been equally uncomprehending. They tended to think that although people rightly worship gods and honour them for the qualities they possess, to associate friendship with the divine is a mistake. Aristotle argued that one could no more be friends with a god than one could with a king: both are superior to mere mortals, and friendship flounders when the would-be friends are unequal in status, power and capacities.

It is for these reasons that the Augustinian intervention in ideas about friendship has such a significant effect on the way friendship has since been assessed and valued. Christianity appears not to have been suspicious of friendship from the outset: Jesus himself is reported to have had a disciple who was a particular friend, 'the disciple whom Jesus loved', as he is called in John's gospel. In the same gospel is also found the moving comment about there being no greater love than to lay down one's life for a friend: scholars have speculated that as this must refer to early Christian martyrdoms, so it could be that amongst the other words by which they were first known, Christians were called Friends.

However, Augustine unleashes a new train of thought. His response was not to seek philosophical resolutions to the ambivalences inherent in the concept, as the ancients had, but was to question the very virtuousness of friendship itself. Further, if self-betterment is replaced by self-renunciation, as Augustine argues, then friendship is inevitably downgraded in the hierarchy of values. Or again, if the chief characteristics of friendship – that it is particular and linked to self-love – are subsumed within the defining characteristic of Christian love, which is universal and selfless, it is easy to dismiss friendship outright.

That may seem a bit extreme but it is a logical outcome of Augustine's anxieties about friendship and is a position that has been advocated by many Christians thinkers since. Perhaps the clearest case in point is found in the writings of the philosopher and theologian Søren Kierkegaard. This nineteenth-century Dane, whose surname means 'graveyard', once said that he wrote to make life more difficult for people. He certainly throws down the gauntlet for any writer on friendship, crystallising the essence of the Augustinian problem with friendship to such a degree that it becomes an outright rejection of friendship as such.

In his *Works of Love*, he begins by asking what friendship is in its purest form. The answer, he says, is that it is a passion whose ideal is as exclusive as erotic love; whilst friendliness may be offered to many, friendship's finest image of itself is a love that makes two, and only two, one. From this preference that friends show one another all the other manifestations of its selfishness follow. Choosing you, the friend says, is *my* choice (Kierkegaard does not buy the Aristotelian reading of the friend as 'another self'. For him, the relationship is not I–Other, it is I–other–I). In support of his thesis, Kierkegaard points out that friendship is as prone to jealousy as erotic love and similarly cannot bear to be rejected. This only goes to show that to have one's affection unrequited is to be confronted with one's narcissism and the possibility that one is not lovely. Alternatively, he notes that friendship, like erotic love, arises spontaneously from an individual's affection – it 'selfignites' – and is not a voluntarily act of will; people arbitrarily 'fall in friendship' as much as they randomly fall in love. And then friendship gets caught up in all kinds of little acts of pride in the way that people congratulate themselves on the friends they have; they admire themselves for being so clever as to have such admirable friends, and so on. Friendship is a Vanity Fair.

Given this negative assessment of friendship, the question arises as to the correct way for Christians to love one another as, after all, God's law requires. The answer, Kierkegaard says, is the diametric opposite of friendship, namely, to love your *neighbour*. Neighbour-love is wholly different from friendship because it is unconditional and selfless: 'Christian love teaches love of all men, unconditionally all', and any exception to this unconditionality is a compromise. This means that there is no way, according to Kierkegaard, to integrate a notion of friendship into neighbour-love. It may be thought that loving one's neighbour begins with loving one's friends. Wrong, says Kierkegaard, because to love one's friend is to practise selfishness not selflessness. Or some Christians might claim that Christian love is like classical love but for the fact that it is stronger, loving unto death. Wrong, says Kierkegaard; there are endless examples of this so-called perfection of love in ancient Greek culture.

Another question that comes to mind is who is your neighbour if they are not your friends? Kierkegaard comes up with an disarmingly simple answer. The first person you meet as you step out of your front door. The next human. In fact, and not without some wit, Kierkegaard argues that neighbour-love is a blessed release from the burden of having to find someone to befriend. It does not require you to admire other human beings, or like them. Neither does loving your neighbour depend in any way on being able to love yourself. Rather it depends on renouncing yourself. (Neither should neighbour-love be thought of as a higher form of friendship. Neighbour-love abhors the idea that individuals can be united in a single self on the basis that they are the same, or indeed different. They love each other simply because they are equal before God who loves all equally and unconditionally. There is no continuity between the two; neither unconditionality can be reconciled to particularity, nor selflessness to selfishness.)

If someone protests that this does not sound like love at all, since it is passionless, Kierkegaard says they are mistaken too. The selfish passion of friendship gives way to the selfless passion to obey God, to fulfil the obligation of eternal love. 'Christian love is self-renunciation's love and therefore trusts in this *shall*.' And finally if someone else thinks that such a position is extreme to the point of ridiculousness and only causes offence, not least against the 'obvious' value of friendship, Kierkegaard retorts that what might be a stumbling block to some is the heart of the blessedness of Christianity to others. If you want to overcome the tragic disappointments of friendship then make that leap of faith! True to his name, Mr Kierkegaard does his best to bury friendship.

But what does one philosopher's rant, let alone another theologian's loss of faith 1500 years ago, matter to us in the so-called secular world today? It matters because Kierkegaard's stance is not the only product of the long shadow that Augustine's tragedy cast across friendship. Much secular thought is similarly wary of friendship too – and sometimes as out-rightly antagonistic. Indeed, far from dissipating over the intervening years, the shadow could be argued to have intensified because when cut loose of the Christianity that gave birth to it, a framework that at least places great value on love of certain kinds, the antipathy can take on a life of its own. This is a big claim but it is one that can be seen to hold water if we cut to another seminal figure in the story, Immanuel Kant.

Christian secularism

Beyond his enormous influence, not least of the reasons for looking at what Kant has to say about friendship is that he is one of the rare philosophers since the Enlightenment to address the subject at all. If you turn to Descartes, Hobbes, Spinoza, Hume, Rousseau, Bentham, Mill, Hegel or Marx you will simply not find enough to go on. Kant though included sections explicitly on friendship in one of his books, *Metaphysics of Morals*, and he also gave a lecture on friendship as part of the course he taught at the University of Königsberg from 1775 to 1780. It provides a neat summary of secular modernity's equivocal attitude towards friendship.

The lecture begins by addressing what he sees as the familiar crux of the problem. Human beings are driven by two imperatives; their self-love and their love of others. Kant has a problem with self-love that refines the Christian concern. It worries him because although selfish acts may not break any moral laws (i.e. they can be of benefit to others), neither can they be said to have any moral merit of their own (because they are motivated by selfishness). Contrast that with selfless acts, which explicitly seek to promote the happiness of others and can rightly be thought virtuous.

This analysis is bad news for humanity because, Kant thinks, it is quite clear that most people, most of the time, act out of their own self-interest, that is, amorally. So what is to be done? How can human beings aspire to be moral? Kant's answer is his famous categorical imperative. He accepts that people will act in their self-interest but points out that it is also in your self-interest to have others acting in your self-interest too. The upshot is that in order that everyone's self-interests are taken care of, each person must do for others as they would have things done for themselves. Or, to put it another way: act only in such ways as would conform to a universal law – that is, make no exceptions for yourself, else others will do the same, and your own self-interest will be threatened. Kant has, in effect, reinvented the Golden Rule (though he himself did not like the comparison).

The problem for friendship is how it is to be understood within this frame. For example, Kant continues, if someone tries to act for the happiness of their friend, it is highly likely that they will have to subordinate their own happiness, a situation which would not seem to make for very happy friendships. Conversely, if they decide to prioritise their selfish desires and look after their own happiness first and foremost, then it is very likely that they will ride roughshod over the happiness of others, and that too seems counterproductive.

Maybe there is a way out of this conundrum, Kant wonders. Perhaps someone can look after the happiness of their friend without worrying about their own happiness, because their friend will be doing exactly the same for them? In other words, friendship is presented as a pact in which individuals apparently put their selfish motives to one side because they secretly know that their self-interests will be foremost in the mind of their friend, and vice versa. This, Kant says, is the ideal in friendship; a self-love that is 'superseded by a generous reciprocity of love'.

Now, this is again a neat logical trick. But it does not really absolve friendship of its selfishness; it just puts it at one step removed. Kant's reinterpretation of the Aristotelian idea of a friend as another self reveals the underlying calculation in this reading of friendship and its associated moral duplicity. He says that the friend is another self not in the sense that they are similar or share goals, but in the sense that they love another as if that person were themselves, literally: friends are, in effect, really just loving themselves. So even on his best account, Kant cannot shake off the suspicion that friendship is selfish. It might lead someone to act for another but only, if paradoxically, for almost wholly selfish reasons.

The dubious moral worth of friendship is compounded by the fact that this so-called 'generous reciprocity of love' only takes place in the ideal case. In practice, Kant believes, no one can look after their own happiness better than they can themselves, and should someone surrender their happiness entirely to another in the hope of complete reciprocity, the friendship would inevitably fail. This is why in life people never actually call on their friends in the way that they call on themselves; rather than make such demands on others they will usually revert to doing things for themselves. Similarly, people may have one or two friends with whom they feel they can be completely open, but in reality they always hold things back in order not to disturb the illusion of friendship – another manifestation of feigning it and amicable dissimulation. This is also why to demand proof of friendship is the best way of ending it, Kant reflects, though he adds that the disposition of goodwill encouraged by friendliness, even when fake, improves life in its own way.

Friendship's suspect nature is revealed in other ways. He observes that people may form circles of friends on the basis that they share the same beliefs, interests or identity. But again these gestures are morally suspect because they tend to harden the heart against those outside the charmed circle.

Kant hints that the effort to make oneself deserving of friendship may be of some moral worth as a result of a strange twist of the obligations imposed by the categorical imperative: it implies that it is a person's duty to respect other people's friends because that is what they would hope for in return, lest their own illusions about friendship are shattered. 'Friendship develops the minor virtues of life,' he concludes, damning it with faint praise. All in all, the morally ambiguous status of friendship is really left unchallenged.

In ethical no-man's-land

So much for Kant. But then Kant is arguably the most tortuous of that tortured species of humanity: rationalist philosophers.

They take themselves too seriously, for surely most people don't worry so much about the dark undercurrents of friendship. They just get on with it – and discover the joys of friendship, and even the virtues it encourages, as a result.

However, Kant is onto something that even the most carefree will find alarmingly familiar. Think of the following simple scenario. Suppose someone lives in a boarding house with fellow tenants whom they do not know. This boarding house has a shared bathroom. The cohabiting strangers have good reason to leave the bathroom clean and tidy after washing because only then can they hope, with impunity, that the others in the house will do the same as well. In other words, there is good reason for the housemates to be equally bound by an unwritten rule of 'bathroom cleanliness'.

Now consider someone else who lives in a shared house, though not with a group of strangers, but with a group of friends. Their relationship to each other is entirely different. They do not treat each other impersonally but as individuals whom they know. This may cause them to act selflessly sometimes – when, for example, they clean the bathroom after their inveterately messy friend. But it may also cause them to act selfishly if, for example, that same messy friend happens to leave the bathroom dirty one too many times and the cleaner friend becomes annoyed.

The point is that in the first case, of cohabiting strangers, there is a universalisable law governing bathroom cleaning, whereas in the latter case, of cohabiting friends, there is not. The reason? Friendship. It makes individuals behave inconsistently. Sometimes they won't mind that the bathroom is messy, and will clean up after their friend. Other times the grime around the sink, and the hair against the porcelain, will drive them up the wall.

The general point is that modern, secular ethics also finds it hard to cope with friendship because if everyone acted as they do with friends, there could be no universalisable moral laws. For similar reasons, friendship sits uneasily alongside moral theories that work on the basis that it is best to act so as to maximise other people's welfare, the other approach to ethics that many contemporary philosophers take. This so-called utilitarian approach means that a good action is one that achieves the greatest happiness for the greatest number. But friendship can play little part in this moral scheme because, as friends, friends are interested predominantly in each other, not in the general happiness of all.

The net result is that friendship occupies a moral no-man's-land today. Because it is at best wrestling with selfishness, and at worst positively encouraging it, amity gets pushed to the margins of moral behaviour. In fact, Kant was so uneasy about the place of friendship in his moral universe that he speculated upon a time when friendship will cease. He wonders if human society will advance to such a stage of luxury that people will stop having needs and so similarly stop having need of friends. This will be a time in which people have a broader set of goals than the mere satisfaction of desires, since all their desires will be met. It is a kind of heaven on earth that insofar as it is heavenly will have transcended the need for friendship. He summarises: 'Friendship is not of heaven but of the earth; the complete moral perfection of heaven must be universal; but friendship is not universal.'

All in all, what Kant achieves is a reinvention of the reactionary attitude to friendship that originates in Augustinian Christianity, reinvigorated for the modern, secular world. For a full-blown belief in heaven he substitutes an ideal of perfection; for sinfulness, selfishness; for unconditional love, universal obligation. This new 'religious' language of universal duty and categorical imperatives simply does not know what to do with friendship, and tends to think that it is suspect and perhaps better done away with. 'It is no wonder that friendship has been relegated to private life and thereby weakened in comparison to what it once was,' reflects the moral philosopher Alasdair MacIntyre.

So, contemporary ethical discourses adopt an attitude towards friendship that is as detrimental to it as any Christian one. Why is it that if someone promotes someone with whom they are friendly to a higher place in the office, it is invariably branded as nepotism, with no thought given to whether they are up to the job or not? Sometimes the favouritism of friendship almost certainly leads to abuse, as when, for example, George Bush nominated Harriet Miers, his own lawyer, for a seat on the Supreme Court in the United States, only to find her name withdrawn later when it had become clear she was ill-qualified for the post. But is such a judgement automatically the case? Could there not be situations in which it is better to appoint a friend, other things being equal, since at least you know what you are getting?

Or why is it that modern society has no public means of recognising the bonds formed between friends, a fact that is in stark contrast to the family, which is celebrated as the very basis of community? Surely friendship plays a vital part in that too. This is a complex issue to which we shall return, but is the hiatus – the blind-spot when it comes to friendship – not in part because friendship is treated as a selfish concern: unlike the family which gives something to society, friends are thought to be mostly interested in themselves, so society is hesitant in supporting it?

The plot thickens. Consider the impact on friendship of the value assigned to egalitarianism in the modern world – the idea that everyone should be treated the same. It lies at the heart of democracy: in theory at least, everyone has equality before the law and, say, the right to one, and only one, vote. The power of the rhetoric of human rights rests on its claim to be unconditional too: either rights are universal or they are nothing at all. 'This equality absolutely every man has, and he has it absolutely.' (That quote is not from The Universal Declaration of Human Rights but is from Kierkegaard on neighbour-love, though it significantly works equally well in both places).

Of course, this kind of unconditionality can be hugely valuable and underpins many great goods. However, the trouble for friendship is that amity is not unconditional, but partial – one would do something for a friend and not for others. Thus, friendship is routinely treated as if it were questionable. The contrast with the family again provides a ready case in point. It is not just that friendship is not recognised in society, whereas family is, but that the particularity of friendship can often be regarded as a threat to the unconditional love that is supposed to reign within the family too. Why else do individuals some- how feel they must renegotiate a long-term friendship when their friend gets married? Or, to put it another way: is there not a steely strand in the ethic of modern marriage which repels anything that compromises the unconditional commitment of husband and wife – 'forsaking *all others*', as the service says? Close friendship can count as infidelity quite as much as a fling or affair.

This is a deeply unsatisfactory state of affairs. For all Kant may wish it, and ethical discourse may ignore it, friendship will not cease. Aristotle's intuition is right: it has to do with self-love, and it is certainly partial, but it is also undoubtedly necessary for a happy life. Moreover, if friendship is rising back up the agenda of people's personal commitments, as marriage reforms and other institutions of belonging become less reliable, then an ethical dis- course that takes friendship seriously is needed, not least to provide some structure for people who want to make the most of it. Friendship will always be full of ambiguities. We've estab- lished that by now. But that does not mean it is not possible to think through them and welcome friendship as a key, if com- plicated, facet of life – which, after all, is only complicated itself.

It turns out that a resurrection has been attempted before. A number of more friendship-friendly theologians have sought to find a place for it that reconciles it to the principles that would otherwise damn it. One attempt stands out: that of Thomas Aquinas. He is first among equals with Augustine as a doctor of the Church and has also been called one of the greatest inter- preters of Aristotle, an accolade that might give us hope that he thought highly of friendship. He is also important because his thought led to a distinction that is critical if modern, secular attitudes towards friendship are to be revivified – the distinction between egoistic and altruistic love. (He did not use these terms himself, but the origins of egoism and altruism are found in the distinctions he draws and are convenient for unpacking what he says.) So another step, from modern secularism back to medieval Christianity, and the resources that lie for us there.

Reaffirming friendship

Thomas – he is known as Thomas and his philosophy as Thomism because Aquinas is a place not a name – was born in 1225 at a seminal moment in the history of western ideas. For most of the Middle Ages, ancient Roman philosophy, including the works of Cicero and Seneca, had formed the staple diet of an education in Latin, and Greek philosophy was in large part unknown. Then during the twelfth century a handful of Aristotelian texts in Latin translation began to find their way into the universities of Europe from the Islamic world, and by the end of the thirteenth century, Thomas's century, virtually all Aristotle's surviving works were in circulation. A major figure in this undertaking was a Dominican colleague of Thomas, William of Moerbeke, who tackled not only Aristotle's vast corpus but also ancient commentaries on him too, 'by dint of great toil and much mental tedium', he writes in one place. An important translation of the *Nicomachean Ethics* containing Aristotle's reflections on friendship was completed in 1247 by an English philosopher who went by the name of Grosseteste. And by the time Thomas became a professor of theology in Paris at the age of 30, Aristotle was so dominant that he was commonly known simply as 'the Philosopher'.

Aristotle's leading interpreter at the time was the Muslim philosopher Ibn Rushd also called Averroes, and correspondingly 'the Commentator'. It was the Commentator who determined Thomas's life's work: the Christianisation of the Philosopher.

Averroes had made two observations that unless challenged were fatal to Aristotle's reception in the Church. First, he said that the Philosopher believed the world was eternal and, second, that he thought individual souls were mortal. Christianity teaches precisely the opposite on both counts: heaven is eternal, not the world; and souls are immortal and go to heaven. As a consequence, Aristotle aroused great suspicion in ecclesiastical circles, even provoking a series of papal bulls that on occasion went so far as to ban him from the lecture halls of Paris and Oxford. Thomas's great achievement was to find an accommodation between these incendiary doctrines and the tenets of Christianity, an accommodation that secured Aristotle's fundamental place in western thought to this day.

Thomas's philosophy of friendship is ingenious too. It is found in his *Summa Theologiae* whose second part is modelled on the *Nicomachean Ethics,* a choice which makes the Augustinian problem with the love called friendship unavoidable, the difficulties raised by Aristotle's focus on the idea that friendship is particular and stems from a kind of self-love. Thomas changes the focus of the debate by arguing two things. First, although friendship can be for oneself or for another, that does not mean that it is not of benefit to both parties in both cases too. For example, friendship based on utility or pleasure is primarily for oneself but can also contain elements that the friend benefits from too. This kind of friendship, says Thomas, may not be especially virtuous but neither is it necessarily evil; in essence it is no better or worse than the desire to eat or to own something. Conversely, friendship that is explicitly for another is a love that although primarily for the other person and their sake also benefits the individual offering the friendship. It is a friendship that is disinterested in what can be gained from the relationship but which gains nonetheless. In short, friendship is always a question of give and take, and even when the taking is more in evident than the giving, it can be regarded positively to a degree, for it is never just on the take – or at least, if it is, it is already ceasing to be friendship.

Thomas's second point follows on from this. Given that friendship always benefits both parties, if to varying degrees, the real question is the extent to which the friendship on offer is possessive or not. Love always wants something. Indeed, Thomas thought that everything humans do is done out of some kind of love, some kind of want or lack. The thing that determines whether

Figure 11: 'An honest answer is the sign of true friendship.' (Proverbs) Thomas Aquinas, pictured here, saw friendship as a school of love.

love is good and godly is the extent to which it is primarily focused on the good of the other person: love that is solely other oriented is what we now call altruistic love; love that is solely self-oriented is what we now call egoistic love. But in reality, love is probably a mixture of both. It is the nature of the mixture that interested Thomas.

Friendship reveals itself as either altruistic or egoistic in several ways. For example, an altruistic friendship is one in which if something happens to one friend – say that something is said against them – then the other person in the relationship feels it as if they are themselves being hurt or maligned; they will oppose anything that might harm their friend as if it were harming themselves. It's friendship as another self. In an egoistic friendship, however, someone will only go out on a limb when they are directly threatened themselves. Friendship in this case is not with another self, but flourishes only insofar as it benefits the dominant individual.

141

A related test concerns how someone relates to the friends of their friend. When characterised by altruism, a person will be friendly to the friend of their friend for the sake of their friend, even if their friendliness is not readily returned. Conversely, the egoistic individual will make little effort with the friend of a friend, and in all likelihood unpleasantness with this third party will cause the original friendship problems too.

Another key indicator is provided by the way altruistic friendship looks differently from egoistic friendship. With altruistic friends, the depth of the mutual feeling is paramount and self-evident, this feeling that someone else has become part of you due to 'indwelling', as Thomas calls it. To onlookers this kind of friendship is not just appealing, but it looks more like a habit that the two friends have formed. The friends come to routinely act for each other. They speak almost as one. Their lives become ones 'styled by friendship', as Alexander Nehamas pointed out in his 2008 Gifford Lectures on friendship, adding that what such friendship admits is that whilst I might maintain my own self-interest, I allow you, my friend, a stake in my self-interest too. And vice versa: you allow me a say – perhaps a large say – in your life. Hence, the orientation of self-interest develops a new perspective, towards another.

When it comes to how they relate to others, generosity and kind-heartedness become similarly overarching principles in the lives of such friends, a quality of relating that characterises everything they do. Those who only befriend in egoistic ways, in contrast, will not experience such an expansion of love to anything like this degree. They may be friendly, but mostly because it benefits themselves.

Thomas explains that altruistic friendship forms between people who are alike or equal in what they have or are, whereas egoistic friendship tends to dominate when one person has something that the other ardently desires. Think, for example, of a friendship between someone who is famous and someone else who is not. Fame is so alluring that it is hard for the friends of the famous not to want at least some of the glory. This means that such friendships are likely to be egoistically coloured, and friendship will only flourish in the altruistic sense if both parties are in large part indifferent to the benefits that come with celebrity.

However, this fluidity – this sense that even egoistic friendships contain elements of goodness – means that there is the possibility that even the most selfish friendships need not be thought irredeemably tainted, so long as the relationship clings onto being worthy of the name to some degree. Traces of altruism can still flourish, if only like a light that flickers shadows, though it's always possible that the light will drive the darkness away. Consider an individual who forms a friendship with another who seems at peace with themselves for the reason that they long for peace too. That might be thought to make it egoistic. But since longing for peace is the first step to gaining it, and peace is itself a virtue that tends to be generous to others, the individuals who are otherwise unequal in their peacefulness, as it were, can find common ground between them that makes for an increasing altruistic friendship.

Thomas can similarly recognise that friendship has mixed motives and is based upon loving the complex particularities of another individual who also has egoistic and altruistic intentions. It is the details of anyone's life that counts for a friendship to form, be it their virtues, interests or needs, things that will always be expressed altruistically and egoistically. This is another a reflection of the commonsensical assumption that one good person will not automatically be friends with another solely because they are both good. Further, he sees that it is only natural that an individual will be closer to some people than they are to others, and that a particular intimacy does not necessarily negate more distant relationships. Indeed, he goes a step further again and explicitly points out that it is only natural for someone to love themselves more than their neighbour, at least in their best parts, since they are a unity and so 'closer to themselves' than anyone else. This is his reading of Aristotle's good self-love, making the point that an introverted love of oneself can still have an altruistic dimension. If, for example, I followed a wholly selfless commandment to love my neighbour, I might take that to include an act like pushing them off a cliff if they sincerely wanted it. However, if I have a love of myself too, that might prevent the assisted suicide inasmuch as I would be deterred by having to live with the consequences – a selfish consideration that would lead to someone else's good.

The general point for Thomas is that people may love others to greater or lesser degrees but it is not quantity but quality that counts. Loving less is still loving. In fact, because friendship can become an over-arching principle in someone's life, an experience of close friendship is likely to make someone love others more, even when those others are barely known to them.

Thomas was writing on friendship nearly six hundred years before Kierkegaard and in most respects they are theologically even further apart. However, he does provide a remarkably full response to Kierkegaard's hatchet job. Where Kierkegaard says that friendship is selfish, Thomas says don't overlook the altruistic dimension to friendship that is a selfless love for another. Where Kierkegaard says that the union friends seek is inherently exclusive, Thomas says don't forget that the closer altruistic friends become the more they will seek to act lovingly to their friend's friends even when they receive animosity in return. Where Kierkegaard says that love should be unconditional and friendship is always partial, Thomas says it is wrong to think that partial friendship cannot lead to a more universal love because altruistic friendship nurtures natural affection, not undermines it. Where Kierkegaard says that friendship is just like erotic love in its desire solely to possess, Thomas says it is in fact different precisely at that point. Where Kierkegaard says the Christian should act unconditionally and without distinction to all, Thomas points out that there is a difference between benevolence, which is the intention to do good, and beneficence, which is the act of doing good and is bound to be compromised, even in a saint. Where Kierkegaard says the Christian should act out of obligation, a leap of faith in response to God's commandment that 'you shall love your neighbour', Thomas says the Christian acts in response to God's love which is itself a supreme kind of altruistic friendship.

In fact, Thomas notes that whereas in the New Testament the commandment refers to neighbour, in the Old Testament the Levitical code says you shall love your *friend* as yourself. (In fairness to Kierkegaard, this is a contentious point. The old Greek and Latin bibles that Thomas knew did use a word for friend, as did the fourteenth-century vernacular translation by Wycliffe. However, by the Tyndale and King James versions, the word 'friend' had been replaced by neighbour, though not least because of the problems that loving friends evokes.)

In summary, what Thomas would point out to Kierkegaard is that he has not considered the subtleties of the movement between altruistic and egoistic love deeply enough. He might also gently say to Augustine that the former Manichean too saw his friendship mostly in terms of its egoistic elements, perhaps something that was inevitable following the shock of his friend's death when he was left with only himself to think of.

Thomas, then, goes a long way towards rehabilitating friendship in the Christian tradition. He even finds a partial reconciliation between the Christian idea of friendship with God and the classical view that such a thing is impossible. If God is taken as a principle of love, then locating friendship in God can be reinterpreted as a process by which the friends and their friendship is transformed by that divine principle. On that reading, this is not so different from Aristotle's idea that the best kind of friendships are those in which the friends' lives are transformed by the good life.

In more recent times, Thomas' understanding of friendship was expressed by the Victorian cleric, John Henry Newman. He once preached a sermon, in which he attacked the downgrading of friendship. His critique, in short, was that unless you can love one person in particular, you are hardly likely to be able to love everyone equally, as the Christian ideal demands. Friendship is a school of love: it both teaches you how to love and provides a tangible locus within which to practice loving. This perhaps explains why

those who say they love everyone equally, and no one in particular, are often deeply unpleasant people to know. They love only
in the abstract, which in a way is no love. Moreover, what is
human love if not a lifelong effort and practice, for human beings
are flawed. It even seems to have been the strategy that Jesus
adopted, the man who had a disciple distinguished by being
known as the one 'whom Jesus loved'. Here's part of what
Newman said, from the pulpit of the University Church of St Mary
the Virgin, in Oxford:

> There have been men before now, who have supposed Christian
> love was so diffusive as not to admit of concentration upon
> individuals; so that we ought to love all men equally ... Now I
> shall maintain here, in opposition to such notions of Christian
> love, and with our Saviour's pattern before me, that the best
> preparation for loving the world at large, and loving it duly and
> wisely, is to cultivate an intimate friendship and affection
> towards those who are immediately about us.

These are crucial points. But for a secular account of friendship,
Thomas only takes us half way. He provides the first step that
links the classical world of Aristotle with the Christian world of
the Middle Ages. We must now try to forge another step to span
the gulf that exists between the Middle Ages and modernity,
and ask whether Thomas provides the kind of resources that
can challenge the negative attitudes towards friendship found
in secular ethics.

Against atomism and absolutes

To do this, take a second look at the moves Thomas makes. His
rehabilitation of friendship was achieved by questioning the
grounds on which it was thought morally dubious: he unpicks
the knot of selfish particularity tied round it. Hence, he pointed
out that because people love those to whom they are close, it is
only natural for them to love themselves to whom they are

closest. But that does not necessarily mean they love others less. Look at the mutual indwelling of friendship, the friend as another self, and the altruistic zeal that one friend can feel for another.

At a deeper level, what this argument suggests to the modern mind is that individuals are inherently connected to one another. Thomas is able to say that selfless acts can emerge from self-love, and that altruism and egoism are not opposing opposites, because his idea of individuality is blurred at the edges. This contrasts with the atomistic, autonomous Kantian individual who is more or less bound to go about the world worrying over their selfish desires to excess. It is also distinct from the mentality of the modern individual who, as Alexis de Tocqueville characterised him or her, has become rich enough, and educated enough, to feel they can supply their own needs. 'Such folk owe no man anything and hardly expect anything from anyone,' he writes in *Democracy in America*. 'They form the habit of thinking of themselves in isolation and image that their whole destiny is in their own hands.' Modern ethics likewise tends to see people as billiard balls, smashing into one another as each tries to maintain their separate course. Thus, reconciling one individual's happiness to another's is treated as a problem – as is friendship.

But perhaps human beings are more like creatures of clay who are formed and moulded by mutual contact and even, on occasion, become attached. In fact, a number of concerns are encouraging such a renewed notion of connectedness in contemporary moral debates, from global environmental calamity to the problems of social alienation. In that case, the choice between one person's happiness and another's does not seem so stark: my happiness is your happiness, the friend says; if I care for you, I care for myself, and vice versa. Alternatively, such connectedness can be thought of in relation to the question of utility and friendship. If someone feels blatantly used, as they too often do in the workplace, then the selfish aspect dominates and stymies friendship. If, in contrast, someone relies on a friend, they may still be using them to a degree but with an appreciative need that is also an opportunity to give. In the generosity of that kind of non-calculating exchange – when people are as glad to give as receive – the individuals draw closer and the friendship can flourish.

The second aspect of Thomas's move was to develop the inclusive character of divine love. In effect, he does not allow the idea that the unconditional is best to become the enemy of the particular, which is good. Rather, he argued that the love of someone in particular can be seen as a gift through which someone learns of wider concepts of love. He went so far as to conclude that God represents friendship – prompting another reflection that he might offer to his forbear, Augustine: your experience of the death of your friend was, in a sense, an experience of a loss of God. That is why it was so shocking, not because you didn't love God but for the very opposite reason. You loved God in your friend and despaired when he was gone.

The challenge is to translate the scholastic and theistic arguments into a modern and non-theistic frame. This is hard to do because there are certain beliefs that are key to Thomas's re-affirmation of friendship and simply incommensurate with modern times. For example, he makes claims that are impossible for an atheist to embrace, such as the idea that God is friendship. Even for many theists such a notion may seem strange.

However, Thomas also refers to God as a 'principle of love', an ethical as opposed to theological notion, and that perhaps helps us find a way around the problem. It is even possible to go a step further and substitute the idea of God with that of the good, agreeing with Iris Murdoch: 'Good is the magnetic centre towards which love naturally moves.'

With that move, it is possible to follow Thomas's argument in this way. The idea of the good becomes one that helps transform friendship in practice. Rather than condemning friendship as conditioned and partial, it offers a principle of love that can operate as a kind of steer in all sorts of morally ambiguous situations. Hence, we can use Thomas's tests to assess when a particular friendship is headed in a more altruistic, or more egoistic direction. If I won't tolerate your friends, though you are my friend, I will be acting too selfishly. If I feel the pain you are suffering almost as if I were suffering it myself, then this is a sign of friendship's selfless dimension.

This principle of the good is less vertical, more horizontal; less universal, more applicable; less absolute, more conditioned. To be fair to Kant, he sees the ideal of friendship a bit like this too: '[friendship] is employed as a measure of lesser qualities'. The trouble is that his is a measure that invariably finds actual friendship wanting. An alternative ethic of good friendship would substitute such unforgiving abstractions with more humane sentiments; the governing standard should be principled direction not tyrannical rule. Friendship as a school of love.

Another way to translate the theological aspects of Thomas's thought is to understand that his ethics tell a complete story of human life. For him, it is the individual's journey to God that provides the overall frame. For us, it can be a conception of the ethical life that aims at human flourishing. Within philosophy, the school of thought that promotes this way of thinking is virtue ethics. The idea is that instead of thinking of moral philosophy as a series of problems that need to be solved by sets of rules or decisions, one thinks of moral philosophy as nurturing a way of life organised around certain virtues that nurture human potential. This is, in fact, very much in the Aristotelian way of things. His *Nicomachean Ethics* includes friendship amongst a list of virtues that the individual should foster in order to have a happy life. Such an approach does not mean that all the ambiguities associated with friendship are automatically resolved. Indeed, most of Aristotle's discussion of friendship is about them. But because friendship is placed high on the list of things that are necessary for a fulfilled life right at the outset of his moral philosophy, it does prevent friendship being marginalised in favour of more easily handled, though less humanly valuable, qualities – like, I would argue, neighbour-love.

Trust in friendship

Clearly, there is a lot more that could be said about this – indeed that *needs* to be said about it, given the compromised status of

friendship in modern, secular ethics. However, by way of conclud-
ing this chapter, I want to draw attention to another facet of
Thomas's rehabilitation of friendship that is, I think, at least
as important. For apart from engaging with the ethics of friendship on rational grounds, he also seeks to address the fundamental
difficulty raised by Augustine's tragic experience of it. The author
of the *Confessions* lost faith in friendship. Thomas seeks to restore
it. A restoration of trust in friendship is also vital today.

Briefly, consider Thomas's approach one more time. In challenging the assumption that friendship is purely selfish, he does not
only untangle the issue intellectually but also tries to restore some
faith in the complexities of human motivation by pointing out
that selfish desires can include selfless intentions. The best does
not have to be the enemy of the good.

Alternatively, one of the things he achieves in calling God a
friend is to unsettle the assumption that God's love is distant and
transcendent. This simultaneously questions the related ethical
assumption that unconditional universality is preferable to conditional particularity. In a post-Kantian idiom, the equivalent
would be to point out that it is a mistake to think that all morally
important imperatives are categorical. Rather it is worth trusting
compromised situations, like those in which friendship is operating, whilst exercising powers of discernment, because clearly good
behaviour may arise from equivocal and mixed motives.

In other words, contemporary ethics needs to re-incorporate a
dimension of trust into its account of friendship, not in the
sense of acknowledging that friends trust each other but in the
sense that moral philosophy itself needs to trust friendship as a
way of life and guide to action. It is at this level that friendship
has been most deeply damaged. Secularism's distrust of friendship
has stymied the ethical climate within which it might thrive as
successfully as any Christian patriarch's declaration that it is sinful
and offends God. The contemporary reliance on the ethics of
rights and egalitarianism, and the ugly associations that accrue
to nepotism and cronyism, is proof enough: friendship is thought
to offend absolute ideals.

Trust is about making a judgement: will I place or refuse to place my trust in someone or something? If the place of friendship is to be restored, this is the decision that moral philosophy needs to make, namely, to trust friendship again. It needs to recognise that its motivations may be complex but they are not psychopathic; its affection may focus on just a few individuals but it need not be perniciously exclusive. What is more, if someone says they love humankind when they have no good friends it is right to think something is out of balance.

Politics of Friendship

'There is little of friendship in tyrannies but more in democracies.'

Aristotle

If our exploration so far has grappled with one thing, it is that friendship faces pressures in many parts of modern life. The good friend is someone who can manage – and to some extend transcend – the pressures that work, sexuality, dissimulation, an online culture and the ethical demands that democratic values exert on it. That explains why friendship is an art not a science, and whilst friends frequently find themselves challenged, there are also ample opportunities for deepening relationships.

With work, the threat comes from being used. In a utilitarian culture, such as obtains in many parts of our world, the problem is that people tend to be valued for what they do, not who they are; they tend to be thought of as means to ends, and when treated as such become, in Adam Smith's word, 'unlovely'. And yet, when people do things together – share a common project or strive for goals – there is an opportunity of friendship. The key is to get to know your colleagues and peers for who they are in themselves, so that when the work or utility disappears the friendship does not.

With sexuality, the competition between the urges of erotic love and the gentler affections of friendship can trouble relationships and, if it does, eros often seems to win out. But if a passionate, as opposed to a merely sexual element in a relationship gains the upper hand, and the desire to get to know the other person in mind and spirit takes root and grows, then the possessiveness of lovers can give way to the wider aspirations of friends.

With the third issue, dissimulation, the nub of the problem is that often friendship rests on feigning. Most friends, consciously or not, know that there are no-go areas in their relationships, and they don't go there for the sake of the friendship: you put up with my disagreeable foibles, opinions or weaknesses, and I put up with yours. In fact, in practice, friends generally rub along rather well and trouble only arises when goodwill and accommodation are perceived as fake or false. Moreover friendship can, on occasion, rise above our flaws, and in rather wonderful ways. A moment of frankness and receptive humility comes about and the friend who is another self can speak words of truth to me, words that might even transform my life.

Next we considered the online environment of the internet, though I suggested that when it comes to friendship, its challenge is not quite so novel as some make out. There is undoubtedly lots of nastiness online, but then there's lots of nastiness in pubs and playgrounds. There is also lots of kindness, and the internet can be a lifeline for many seeking companionship and compassion. The full impact that the internet will make on our lives has yet to reach maturity, for the technology is still improving, though to date it seems that there are plenty of offline analogues by which to interpret the vicissitudes of friending online. Again, the philosophy of friendship has the resources to act as a wise guide.

Finally, there are the ambiguities of the Christian legacy on friendship. In the extreme case, Christianity – like democracy – fosters a veritable tyranny of unconditional love, manifest in so-called secular times as the requirement that we treat each and everyone equally. Hence, the partial and excluding affections of friendship can be found seriously wanting. Linked to this is the suspicion that friendship, unlike family, is essentially selfish and therefore morally dodgy. But then again, the democratic world is a free world, and freedom and friendship are deeply linked.

Each of these sets of ambiguity – the perils to friendship, and the related promise – are set in a broader context, namely, contemporary society. And it is to that I think we should turn next. For, it seems clear to many that we live in times that exhibit a breakdown of trust. Many of the old institutions upon which community is based – rooted in religion, education and politics – are changing fast, and not infrequently failing in the process. Inner cities are pockmarked by no-go areas. The gap between rich and poor has never been greater, and we've become very conscious of the threat of economic collapse as those at the top of the pile cause the financial system to become unbalanced, even as they cream off the profits.

Friendship has a part to play in all this, and it might matter to us personally too. The quality of our attachments to those with whom we share our towns and cities will have a direct bearing upon how pleasant those places are to inhabit, on the one hand, and on the other, the quality of our personal relationships is, in no small part, shaped by the environments in which we try to forge them, as we've already seen in relationship to the workplace, to a sexualised culture, and to a society going online. There is a word for all this: politics. Aristotle knew that friendship played a key part in any political philosophy. He saw that the vibrancy of a city, and the feel of the place, grew out of the vitality shared by its inhabitants – the care that individuals, families and households have for each other. If you can get those microcosms of friendship right, then friendship might come to characterise the feel of the city as a whole – a mood or attitude towards others that once learnt at the hearth spreads out like the warmth of embers. Conversely, a thriving city is a good place to live because the energy it generates itself nurtures the friendships of those who live in it.

In short, our personal friendships cannot be divorced from the politics of friendship, the way we live together. So here's a question: might we learn anything from the politics of the past, not by way of return, which would be impossible, but by way of expanding our own relational imaginations? The thought here is neither that there might have been periods in the past in which people enjoyed a depth of friendship that we can barely conceive: such a suggestion would be to indulge in a kind of illusory nostalgia. Nor is it to suggest that former times were friendlier because friendship somehow burst out all over. In fact, if more friendship-friendly times did exist in ages gone by, we would expect them to be characterised by outbreaks of animosity too, such are the ambiguities of friendship: to claim someone as a friend is not much different from declaring someone else as an enemy. But we can still ask whether there may have been societies and cultures whose ethical norms, social institutions and political frameworks were better placed to negotiate the perils to friendship – the pressures associated with utility, sexuality, dissimulation and so on – because friendship was more clearly recognised as a key personal and political concern.

This is a possibility worth pursuing for what it might say about today. And at a cursory level there is prima facie evidence to support it. For one thing, the great philosophers of friendship appear in distinctly historical clusters. Plato, Aristotle and Epicurus wrote within two or three generations of each other, and the later Romans Cicero and Seneca, who also paid attention to the subject, did so to recover what they thought was being lost in relation to the Greek take on things. Why is it that not since the Greeks has friendship been thought a problem worthy of a solution, Nietzsche wondered? Perhaps friendship was high on their agenda because it was high up on their list of social goods, in a way that it is not today, for all that we tell ourselves friendship matters.

A second age of writing on friendship, perhaps more silver than golden, occurs in the Middle Ages. It produced the philosophies of Thomas Aquinas, Aelred of Rievaulx and Anselm. The rare philosopher of friendship after them, notably Montaigne, writes rather like Cicero and Seneca, in a mood that laments the present and tries to look back. Evidence of another sort is found if one considers the tales and legends of famous friends: the greatest are again located and promoted in the same periods of history. The myths of Orestes and Pylades, Achilles and Patroclus, and Aristogiton and Harmodius were celebrated in classical times. The tales of Amys and Amylion, Bewick and Graham, and Abelard and Heloise are medieval.

So, given that the weighty reflections on friendship have come from certain periods in history, let us consider the classical era and then the medieval to see whether these were exceptional times, and if so, what they reveal about the politics of friendship today. We turn, first, to Athens.

Tyrant slayers

When Pausanias, author of the best-selling *Guide to Greece*, visited Athens in the second century CE he saw a remarkable statue. Erected in the centre of the marketplace, it depicted two friends, Harmodius and Aristogiton. They stood next to each other, striding forward with arms raised and hands clutching daggers. At the political heart of their city, the Athenians had erected neither a sitting president in a temple, like Lincoln, nor a solitary admiral on a column, like Nelson. Rather, they had an image of a friendship.

At the time these friends had lived, six centuries earlier, Athens was ruled by a dynastic tyranny. It had been established by a man called Pisistratus, and he had passed it onto his sons, Hippias and Hipparchus. The beginning of the end for the younger dictators came when Aristogiton, one of the figures in the statue, slew Hipparchus, one of the brothers. It was this act the Athenians commemorated. But why the two friends, and not just the one who'd ridded the city of the tyrant? In fact, the tyrant-slaying friends were probably motivated more by personal passion than revolutionary fervour. According to Thucydides, one of the tyrants was in love with Harmodius and was close to forcing Harmodius to return that love. When he insulted Harmodius' sister instead, the friends decided to act together and kill the other ruler, Hippias.

The date they chose was the feast of the Panathenasa in July 514 BCE since on that day citizens could bear arms in the city without rousing suspicion. They told a few collaborators about the plan, asking them to foment a more general revolt in the chaos that would follow the deed. But then the friends saw one of their fellow conspirators talking to Hippias. They panicked, thinking that they were betrayed. Full of fury, they switched targets and rushed off to find Hipparchus, whom they killed. One of the friends, Harmodius, died in the fight and Aristogiton was captured, tortured and then executed. The tyrannicides had apparently failed, though as it turned out they had destabilised Hippias' hold on power. Four years later the dictatorship fell and Athens was free.

The statue was remarkable because the original, made by the master sculptor Antenor, was the first public monument in Athens commemorating mortals, not gods. This anthropocentric shift was prompted by the high esteem which Harmodius and Aristogiton rapidly assumed; they came to be regarded as the founding heroes of Athenian democracy. Legend quickly mixed with the historical event itself. Herodotus records how Hipparchus had been warned of his doom in a dream. He'd seen a tall and beautiful man standing over his bed who murmured: 'O lion, endure the unendurable with enduring heart; No man does wrong and shall not pay the penalty.'

Later, Athens was sacked by the Persians, and Xerxes carried the original statue off to Susa. But as soon as the Athenians took repossession of their city, they commissioned a replacement. It was as if they didn't believe they were secure unless the city was decorated with this emblem of liberty. 'Truly a great light shone in Athens when Aristogiton and Harmodius slew Hippias,' sang Simonides of Ceos, getting his history slightly wrong. The two were symbolically embraced in the songs that were sung at symposia. Indeed, the friends were celebrated more than Cleisthenes, the man whose reforms, in truth, played a greater part in securing Athenian democracy than anything they did.

To enquire into the form and function of classical friendship is to enter contested territory. Scholars of the highest calibre radically disagree. Statues aside, the bulk of the evidence rests on surviving texts which immediately raises a problem. The Greek for friend, *philos*, has at least as wide a range of associations as its English equivalent. It can be applied to fellow-citizens as in the Shakespearean invocation, 'Friends, Romans, Countrymen'. Equally it could refer to a friendship of the most intimate kind: 'But if the while I think on thee, dear friend, All losses are restored and sorrows end' (Sonnet 30) So it is hard to discern whether the use of the word 'friend' in the political sphere denotes merely a kind of patronage or something more personal and intimate. Context alone can decide.

However, context allows us to imagine that one of the reasons why an image of friendship resonated so strongly with the Athenian taste for freedom was that the experience of being a citizen was closely interwoven with the experience of being a friend. To be an ancient Athenian was to be a citizen and to be a citizen was to take part actively in the collective life of the city, to the extent that an Athenian's political wellbeing was for the most part more important to him than his economic wellbeing. Of course, a man had slaves and women to attend to his domestic affairs when he was away exercising the right to vote, sitting on juries or attending important events like the games and the festivals of plays. But taking part in the life of the polis was a way to build social standing that neither wealth nor family could match, not least because wealth and family were inherited, whereas networks of friends could be built up. Little wonder Democritus describes citizens becoming physically ill when absent from public life. Or, as the contemporary historian Christian Meier sums it up: 'Where we today introduce our economic and other interests into politics, the citizens of Cleisthenes' era politicised their own persons.'

Friendship of various sorts therefore assumed a prominent role in public life. One factor to bear in mind is that friendship would have played a key element in political activity simply because the number of people involved in politics was relatively small, certainly by today's standards. To take part in ancient democracy, a citizen could not avoid personal considerations, for good or ill. More substantially, friends provided support and expected support in return. Xenophon credits Socrates with such a utility-based account of friendship in his *Memoirs of Socrates*: although good friends are to be judged superior to any other possession someone might have, it is in relation to what they give that they are valued, he says. Similarly, public shows of loyalty were an important characteristic of those one would call friends. The tale of Orestes and Pylades is an extreme case in point. Orestes, the story goes, was contemplating killing his mother to avenge his father. Pylades demonstrated his close friendship with the disgruntled son by offering unequivocal, public support for the act: 'Embrace the enmity of mankind/Rather than be false to the word of heaven,' he advises according to Aeschylus. It's within a similar context that aphorisms of the time make sense: 'Gold can be put to the proof by fire, but goodwill among friends is tested by circumstance', and, 'Reversals test friends'. A friend could become a foe if they failed to stand by you.

All in all, it is quite natural for Aristotle to include a couple of chapters on politics in his discussion of friendship, an inclusion that to the modern mind might be something of a non sequitur. As there are three kinds of friendship, he says, so there are three kinds of politics – in descending order: kingship, aristocracy and timocracy (or rule by the wealthy). Friendship provides a model from which political arrangements take a lead. In the best case, the just and good king thinks of his subjects in the same way that the just and good friend thinks of his companions. In an aristocracy and timocracy, social goods are assigned according to position or property respectively, in a way that is parallel to the hierarchical organisation of the workplace, and with similar effects on friendships. Conversely, these political arrangements can all collapse, into tyranny, oligarchy and democracy respectively. (Note that for Aristotle, democracy was unlike our own form of *representative* democracy, in which the masses elect politicians, as it was simply rule by the masses.) Again, these types of politics can be thought of in a way that is analogous to friendship. A tyrant is like a friend who only considers their own interests not the interests of others. An oligarchy operates as a cabal, that is as a closed circle of friends. A democracy is the most conducive to friendship of the three, though it also has its flaws since majority rule inevitably alienates the minorities who do not agree. Further, like gangs of friends, democracy can be subject to the whims of the crowd.

It was for such reasons that Aristotle believed that if you cared about your community or society you need to care about the virtue of civic affection too. And vice versa: the kind of community you live in will have a bearing upon the friendships you enjoy. After all, he argues, mutual concern is the best reason that people have for wanting to live together anyway, and a happy city-state will be one in which people do more than merely associate with each other for commercial reasons or mutual defence. He wants citizens to have a concern for their fellows' character too, in order that they might not only live, but live well. He would want citizens to be proud of their fellow nationals who are exemplars in some way, perhaps having won a race at the Olympics. And citizens should be dismayed at the unethical behaviour of others, not just because of the injustice, corruption or exploitation involved, but because it does, in a sense, diminish everyone. When a country successfully hosts the Olympics, any citizen of that country might enjoy the credit. Whilst a country heads up the league table of carbon producers, any citizen of that country might sense the collective shame.

This quality of civic connectedness is different to, say, the concern for the human rights of others important though those are: it's not about rights but affections. And it is deeper than, say, the groundswells of sentiment evoked by the media when a personal tragedy, like the death of a rock star, sweeps around the world. The goodwill Aristotle wants people to embrace looks to a citizen's spiritual wellbeing.

The ancient Greek institution of the symposium is fascinating in this respect. *Symposium* literally means 'drinking together', though these dinner parties were more than occasions when individuals met to feast. Food, drink and entertainment were vehicles that provided common ground for the main purpose of the evening, namely, quality conversation. The alcohol was consumed ritually, in order to steer the participants along the fine line between enough alcohol to loosen the tongue and crack personal reserve, and not too much alcohol, which reduces conversation to abuse or incoherence. Fine wine was not the only thing that encouraged the right intimacy. The layout of the rooms in which symposia were hosted did so too, with couches facing inwards so that sight-lines crossed. The participants also drank out of the same cup, a shared act with religious overtones, enforcing a sense of reci-procity: the drinking vessel was sometimes referred to as the *philotesia* which could be translated as the 'cup of friendship', a phase that we still have today. Songs were sung, not least those referring to Harmodius and Aristogiton. 'He who does not betray a man who is his friend has great honour among mortals and gods', goes another one, if losing its metre in translation.

The symposium was a place in which friendships, alliances, soli-darities and comradeship could be forged and fed. Its political dimension was found in the bridge it provided between what we would now think of as the public and private arena. It took place in the privacy of the host's house; to be invited was to be wel-comed into his personal life, perhaps for friendship. The gesture is not wholly unlike the difference between going out for dinner with someone, or meeting them at a reception, and inviting them to a dinner party at home. The latter carries overtones that the cocktail party does not.

Not that the symposium was necessarily friendly. Enemies could find themselves at the same do too. This was the case at the sym-posium about which we know more than any other, the one Plato creates in his eponymous dialogue, the *Symposium*. The host was Agathon, life-long friend and probably lover to Pausanias, another person who was also there. Two other old friends present were Eryximachus and Phaedrus. Their presence is worth noting since, a year after the date on which Plato sets the *Symposium*, they were exiled for the religious crimes of profaning the Eleusian Mysteries and mutilating Herms: they were friends and conspira-tors. Next to Agathon lay Socrates and during the dinner the philo-sopher rather belittles his host, perhaps because he had also invited Socrates' archenemy, Aristophanes, though at least they talk on this occasion. The last person to make an appearance, later on, was Socrates' sometime love interest and sparring partner, Alcibiades. He arrives drunk and then drinks more, showing that the propriety of even a symposium could be broken.

161

What we might say is that ancient friendship appears to have been neither wholly private nor wholly public. Quasi-institutions of friendship, like the symposium, linked the political with the personal. Political philosophers, like Aristotle, advocated a kind of civic affection on top of the rights and responsibilities of which political rhetoric is largely composed today. Thus, if today, the remarkable thing about democracy is that it is a way of life voluntarily shared by strangers, in ancient Athens, friendship played a widespread, if sometimes compromised, role in the life of citizens. It was not always easy. Often it made enemies. But because politics was assumed to be close to friendship, when functioning at its best, philosophers like Aristotle sought to articulate just what conditions might sustain and support the link between the two. This effort is not something that many muse on today. Our relationships as citizens are mediated between by impersonal institutions, like the law, possibly with detrimental effects on our affections for one another as a result.

Garden friendship

The political dimension that friendship enjoyed in classical times did not pass without comment. It had its critics, one of the most prominent of which was Epicurus, a philosopher who lived a few years after Plato and Aristotle. For him, the city was far from being the place in which people could live well. Instead, he regarded politics as antithetical to friendship, a point well summarised by his later follower, Philodemus of Gadara:

> If a man were to undertake a systematic enquiry to find out what is most destructive of friendship and most productive of enmity, he would find it in the regime of the polis.

It was the shenanigans of the human 'political animal', meant in the pejorative sense, that worried Epicurus. By the time he was writing, the somewhat idealised imagine of things described by Aristotle had ceased to be viable. Athens had fallen to Alexander the Great, whose domain extended across the known world and integrated it to a degree that had not been seen before. The local nature of political life was undone, and with it much of the old-style affection. Individuals like Epicurus tended to regard themselves as citizens of the world, though with perhaps no place they could call home, and few compatriots they might call friends. The situation was more like our own.

Epicureanism was in part an attempt to forge a new sense of identity, and when it came to friendship, Epicurus preached a retreat from 'the prison of affairs and politics'. He might have sympathised with Ronald Reagan's comment: 'Politics is supposed to be the second oldest profession. I have come to realize that it bears a very close resemblance to the first.' Hence, unlike Socrates who taught in the marketplace, and Aristotle who taught in the city, Epicurus established his philosophical school in a place he called the Garden, a deliberate antonym to 'city', and although we know relatively little about it, he clearly cultivated a way of life founded on the friendships that he believed could only flourish in that context.

Another critique of the politics of friendship comes from Plato. In the *Republic*, which can be thought of as an extended exercise in fantasy politics rather like Thomas More's *Utopia*, he excludes friendship as a political force. Instead, personal relationships of a different sort come to the fore, namely, those of family. Plato suggests that citizens, and certainly the ruling classes, should think of themselves as belonging to one big family, to such a degree that they share partners and children and think in exactly the same way on any issues that confront them. The advantage of such an extreme sense of mutual identity is that the city will be protected from its worst fate, being divided and torn apart. On this criterion, friendship does not fair well since its exclusive nature can readily nurture division and dissent.

He takes a different stance on friendship in the city again when he broaches the subject in the *Laws*. This work is generally taken to be an attempt at an applied political philosophy, as opposed to an idealised one. The description of friendship it presents seems to resonate closely with the way friendship probably functioned in ancient Athens. For example, in the *Laws* friendship is regarded as a valuable, not dangerous, social force since it makes for the happiness of citizens. Legislators are urged to keep 'friendship in view' in the decisions they make and to make allowances for it. Citizens are similarly encouraged to value the services of their friends, an attitude conducive to civic affection.

The *Laws* also sounds notes of realism. Plato advises that friendship between a master and a slave is inherently flawed, no matter the intentions either may have. In a similar vein, he deals with ambiguous aspects of friendship. Friends know each other well, he observes: this means that a good friend might testify to another's virtuous conduct; but it also means that someone will know enough to reveal the weakness of their 'friend' should that be necessary, say, for the sake of justice.

One might ask how Plato can espouse these views and the apparently opposite attitude he has towards friendship elsewhere, not least in the *Symposium*. It is most likely that he is deliberately exploring different ways of looking at things. And this seems to be the way the ancient Athenians treated the matter as a whole: if you are going to make friendship central to your politics, you had better consider the risks as well as the rewards.

The end of an age

If we leap forward three centuries and into the Italy of the late Roman republic, it seems that friendship again had a more public role than today, and again, that had an upside and a downside. The aristocratic classes participated extensively in politics, not least because many public offices – the equivalents of representatives and councilors – were held for only short periods of time, and thus required a large supply of candidates. Thus, though differently from Athenian democracy, late Roman republicanism was highly participatory for the ruling classes and encouraged circles of what the Romans usually referred to as 'clients', again a category within which friendship would inevitably exist and thereby gain public standing.

Coupled to this, the great political events of the day, such as battles in court, were publicly staged and could attract widespread attention. A defendant would call on friends as witnesses, and on clients to side with him in the crowd. Of course, these public displays of amity did not necessarily mean that the individuals concerned were bosom buddies. An opponent with bigger pockets, greater charisma, or other winning ways could conjure up 'friends' as needs required. Cicero, for example, remarked more than once that he longed to see the individual he regarded as his true friend, Atticus, because he was sick to the back teeth of the cloying affection of 'these politicking and powdered-up friendships'. However although Romans could be sceptical about political friendship, they were not merely cynical about it in the way Disraeli implied when he commented that there are no permanent friends in politics, only permanent interests. In fact, public abuses of friendship could have serious repercussions for someone's political standing to an extent that is, again, hard to imagine given the private nature of friendship today: to be accused of being a poor friend, and bad at friendship, was to lose public standing.

A good example of this is Cicero's *Second Philippic*, a defence of himself against the accusation that he had violated the friendship of Mark Anthony, lover of Cleopatra. After the death of Julius Caesar, Anthony had plans to seize power, which the republican Cicero resisted in a speech to the senate on 2nd September 44 BCE. A furious Anthony counter-attacked a couple of weeks later, casting aspersions upon Cicero's friendship. Cicero replied by writing a pamphlet – the *Second Philippic* – though on the advice of Atticus it was not published until after his death.

The argument is complex but basically turns Anthony's accusation around: he counter-accuses Anthony of betraying their friendship, having calculated that no one would support his claim to be Caesar's successor unless he had publicly become Cicero's enemy. To support his case, Cicero lists other ways in which Anthony was a flawed friend. He says Anthony had read out loud the private letters that Cicero had sent him. Not that any goodwill exists now: Cicero is quite willing to fling mud at his erstwhile friend, accusing Anthony of winning people's loyalty by inviting them into his bedroom, among other things. Such was the mire into which late republican politics descended. However, even then, the obligations of friendship carried weight in public discourse and breaches of friendship could still count severely against someone at a social level. What is more, if an individual was accused of such a betrayal, they would not brush it off as tittle-tattle, or leave it to the diary pages. Like Cicero, they would go to great lengths to restore their virtue even when the original affection was clearly long gone; even, in Cicero's case, posthumously.

It was in this environment that the philosophers celebrated friendship, and puzzled over it. It was because friendship was so important that the effort was deemed worthwhile. It was not that they lived in a perfectly friendly society: far from it. However, they did aspire to something nobler than typically they managed to exercise in practice. And they held onto that nobler vision of a friendly politics. It is perhaps like the great Italian cities of the Renaissance: they were often bloody places, but they were animated by a humanistic spirit that encouraged them to strive for what at times seemed beyond them – witnessed to by the legacy of their great works of art.

If Cicero had trouble with Mark Anthony, which was eventually his undoing, his more aspirational side left a dignified and constructive legacy for the philosophy of friendship too. He wrote a dialogue, with a main speaker imagined as one Gaius Laelius, a Stoic philosopher born a hundred years before him – a literary device which perhaps signals that although Cicero knew he was no great exemplar when it came to ideal friendship, he knew the ideal needed rehearsing in his own time for individuals aspiring to a higher life. And this rehearsal of good friendship he at least did well:

Friendship is ... complete sympathy in all matters of importance, plus goodwill and affection, and I am inclined to think that with the exception of wisdom, the gods have given nothing finer to men than this.

I have heard this longer quote from Cicero's dialogue being used as a reading in a service celebrating the commitment of two friends:

> As for myself, I can only exhort you to look on friendship as the most valuable of all human possessions, no other being equally suited to the moral nature of man, or so applicable to every state and circumstance, whether of prosperity or adversity, in which he can possibly be placed ...
>
> Whoever is in possession of a true friend sees the exact counterpart of his own soul. In consequence of this moral resemblance between them, they are so intimately one that no advantage can attend either which does not equally communicate itself to both; they are strong in the strength, rich in the opulence, and powerful in the power of each other. They can scarcely, indeed, be considered in any respect as separate individuals, and wherever the one appears the other is virtually present.
>
> I will venture even a bolder assertion, and affirm that in despite of death they must both continue to exist so long as either of them shall remain alive; for the deceased may, in a certain sense, be said still to live whose memory is preserved with the highest veneration and the most tender regret in the bosom of the survivor, a circumstance which renders the former happy in death, and the latter honoured in life.

Cicero believes friendship springs from nature rather than need, citing the association of animals as proof, nature's counterpart of human life in the city, though he also suggests that people who enjoy good friendships must not be too needy. He clearly has the ambiguities of friendship in mind – 'in friendship there can be no element of show or pretence; everything in it is honest and spontaneous' – and the ambiguities of political friendships which are examined in some depth:

> The most important thing in friendship is the preservation of a right attitude toward our inferiors.

> It is incumbent upon those who are the superiors among friends or relatives to avoid making any invidious distinctions between themselves and their inferiors ... similarly it is incumbent upon the inferiors not to take umbrage at the fact that others surpass them in natural endowments, fortune or rank.

That Cicero dwells on relationships between individuals of different social standing is more proof, first, that these relationships counted for something in Roman life and, second, that Cicero was alarmed at the way political amity could be eroded. Hence throughout his dialogue there is the sense that friendship is under threat because of events as much as because it demands fine balances. That his argument is set in the past, recalling a 'truly remarkable friendship' between Laelius and Publius Scipio, is another indicator. As is Laelius' talk of 'deadly perils' overhanging friendship. It is ironic that the tyrannicidal atmosphere of Cicero's day placed such stresses upon public friendships, whereas one of the most enduring public images of friendship for the Greeks was of two tyrannicides.

Cicero was right to be concerned. Soon after he died, the horizontal politics of the republic were replaced by the vertical government of empire and with the rise of imperial Rome came the demise of these forms of political friendship. Roman society became highly stratified under the emperor, obliterating aristocratic participation in governance on a large scale along with the matrix of friends, clients and enemies that overlaid it. Public relationships were clouded by the tensions between the senate and the emperors, with sincerity compromised by deference, goodwill by distrust, and loyalty by obsequiousness. The political virtues of friendship, and its value for life in the community, ceased to carry

Figure 12: 'I hope I'd have the courage to choose my friend over my country,' said E. M. Forster, implying that friendship and citizenship had become opposing concerns.

their praiseworthy value; individual interests became permanent. So, although one should be wary of summarising these changes and their impact in a few lines, it does seem right to highlight a certain privatisation of friendship in the new Roman empire.

Evidence for this is found in two epistles that Seneca, the tutor of Nero, wrote in 63–65 CE just over a hundred years after Cicero. One, entitled, 'On Grief for Lost Friends', pretty much speaks for itself. Seneca himself was well acquainted with grief: he was nearly executed by Caligula, banished by Claudius, and finally ordered to commit suicide by Nero. In the letter he argues that grief for a friend is either self-indulgent, a kind of phoney proof to ourselves or others that we truly loved the deceased, or, more sadly and perhaps more appositely for Seneca, it is a sign that someone has no other friends left, or no candidates for new ones. The pervading politics directly affects the opportunities for friendship.

In the second epistle, 'On Philosophy and Friendship', he picks up on Cicero's belief that people have friends out of nature not need but takes this self-sufficiency to extremes that again seem to reflect the animosity of his times. First, he argues that the virtuous person can do without friends, though he may not wish to, the implication being that many have to nonetheless. Second, he says that friends offer a way of exercising noble qualities; again, the implication is that ignoble times do not afford many opportunities for public displays of friendship. Third, he adds that friendships which are made for their own sake, and not for an individual's advantage, insulate people from the full effects of bad fortune. And again, it is in bad times that such a reflection makes most sense. Moreover, Seneca argues that winning friends is a matter of will not luck. 'Just as Phidias, if he loses a statue, can straightway carve another, even so our master in the art of making friendships can fill the place of a friend he has lost.' One does wonder what quality of friendship is possible under such circumstances? The golden age of friendship, such as it was, is well and truly over by Seneca's time.

Every cloud has a silver lining, and there is a more positive side to the retreat of friendship from the public. For example, when operating mainly in the private sphere, the range of individuals one might count as friends seems to have been extended. In another letter, Seneca compliments one Lucilius for living on friendly terms with his slaves. They are unpretentious friends, Seneca says, fellow-slaves as far as fortune is concerned:

> That is why I smile at those who think it degrading for a man to dine with his slave. But why should they think it degrading? It is only because purse-proud etiquette surrounds a householder at his dinner with a mob of standing slaves.

Aristotle would have been astonished at this: if amity can shape social expectations, so can social expectations shape the friendships it is thought fit to have. We see as much to this day, inasmuch as friendships across social classes and ethnic divides are relatively rare.

Another more positive outcome of the changing times was the gradual emergence of friendships between men and women, so much so that it became possible to think that husbands and wives might routinely think of themselves as friends as well as lovers. Hence Plutarch, writing about the same time as Seneca, outlines three forms of marriage in his *Marriage Precepts*. The first is purely sexual. The second purely contractual. However, the third and best type is one of total unity between husband and wife who are bound together by love: their marriage is like 'a rope of intertwining strands'. Plutarch still implies that such a relationship has less value than friendship between men, but it is clear that the combination of warmth and strength that his ideal of marriage implies must be embedded in a reciprocal friendship.

Again, Aristotle would have been surprised. For him, the ideal relationship between husband and wife is one marked by affection, but it is determined by the 'natural' superiority of the man over the woman. He likens it to the relationship between rulers and subjects in an aristocratic constitution. The man rules and only gives over to his wife those parts of life that are 'fitting' for her, parts of life that seem pretty limited. If a women should happen to rule over the household because she has inherited it, for example, Aristotle says that the situation is like the degenerate form of aristocratic constitution, an oligarchy not based on excellence but power. Aristotle cannot be our wise guide on all matters of amity.

Public kisses

So much for what we can learn about friendship and community from the ancient Greeks and Romans. What of the second period in which there is a marked interest in friendship, namely, the 'silver age' of the Middle Ages? Something different is going on here, I think. Friendship was important at a social and political level as a result of two factors. First, certain activities like eating and sleeping, that are today carried out in private, then had a distinctly public dimension. This leant a corresponding degree of social significance to the friendships that could accrue around doing these things together, and hence friendship became a matter of discussion. Second, a strain of religious piety that put a high value on friendship developed during the Middle Ages, simultaneously raising questions about friendship. This religious piety never quite gained the status of theological orthodoxy, though it got close in the work of Thomas Aquinas. However, at a popular level it informed an attitude towards friendship, and even semi-institutionalised 'marriages of friendship', that are remarkable when compared with the status friendship has today.

It is the work of the late historian, Alan Bray, that has brought much of this otherwise forgotten history to light. His posthumous book, entitled *The Friend,* may well prove to be one of the most important books on the subject for many years, and certainly does much to expand our imaginations as to what we might make of friendship again today. He identifies a tipping point for the move from the medieval to the modern social attitudes towards friendship in the second half of the seventeenth century. And he tells a story, recorded in the memoirs of Sir Anthony Weldon.

In his memoir, Weldon describes a farewell. It was between the King, James I, and the Earl of Somerset, Robert Carr, and took place on the staircase of the King's hunting lodge at Royston, Hertfordshire, in the autumn of 1615. The farewell was marked by an apparently deep display of affection. Weldon records the Earl kissing the King's hand and the King hanging about his neck 'slabbering his cheeks' and saying 'For God's sake when shall I see thee again? On my soul, I shall neither eat nor sleep until you come again.' In fact, the exchange was particularly noted by Weldon because he thought the King's farewell a charade: it turns out that Carr fell out of favour at court almost as soon as the two apparent friends had parted. However, this is precisely what makes the incident so interesting for us.

Given that the King's farewell was an act, it is wrong to interpret the exchange as that of two friends lost in the spontaneous signs and sentiments of overwhelming affection: public embraces and declarations that eating and sleeping will cease until reunited again were not indicative of some nascent sexual ambiguity or excess of affection, as we who now show reserve with public kisses, let alone sleeping together, might imagine. Rather the King was performing gestures of social patronage, protection and loyalty. Carr, and those who looked on, would have taken them as signs of the King's connection with him, though not necessarily affection for him. The physical intimacies of kissing and eating and sleeping together were symbolic of what we might call social capital; Francis Bacon called it 'countenance' and others 'honour'.

Now, although countenance and honour did not primarily depend on personal friendship, they did not exclude it either. Between James I and Robert Carr it seems there was little love in the autumn of 1615. However, when people were friends too, such practices could indeed be tokens of affection. This is the opportunity for friendship: it could then gain social, as opposed to purely personal, standing.

Consider the significance of these signs in their own right. The kiss is perhaps the most demonstrative but it is not primarily a kiss of affection, as we might exchange kisses on cheeks today. Rather, it needs to be seen in the light of the kiss of peace at the Eucharist. This was a sacramental part of the Mass. When the priest 'shared the peace' with the people, they greeted one another with a kiss as a sign of the union of the Trinity that Christian people sacramentally participated in too. This same kiss in the social setting expressed a reality that says 'we are united even as God is united'. It may or may not express a narrower sentiment and add 'I am fond of you'.

Eating and sleeping together were similarly signs of social connection, and not mere emotion. Take the eating. The dining table was placed at the symbolic heart of the medieval household. It was a place in which everyone from lord to serf ate, each in an allotted place that reflected their relationship, and its obligations, with superiors and inferiors. The great halls and high tables of university colleges today are the legacy of that tradition though they do not quite capture the full significance of the sign. Eating together was not just a representation of pre-existing social relationships. Communal eating constituted those relationships in the same way that the food which was eaten changed into the bodies of those who ate it. To be called up higher was to be called into a deeper connection. And if that included friendship, that relationship was given a corresponding boost in its social standing too.

Similarly with sleeping together. People used to share the same (very large) beds or sleep on pallets in the same room, whence the origins of the epithet 'bedfellow', which means ally or associate. To do so was a sign of social proximity. John Evelyn, the seventeenth-century diarist friendly with Margaret Godolphin, celebrates the time that he had 'a private audience with his Majesty in his bed-chamber': it was the pinnacle of his countenance at Court. But once again, being bedfellows might not be just a sign of social standing. If it also included friendship, that friendship then carried the social weight 'of the bed', as it were. So, the seventeenth-century Archbishop of Canterbury, William Laud, dreamt of again sharing his bed with the Duke of Buckingham because he longed for his friendship. They were presumably not lovers.

Clearly, this symbolic world is long gone. In fact, it disappeared rather quickly – hence the tipping point in the second half of the seventeenth century identified by Alan Bray. The question he poses is why it disintegrated to such a degree that the meaning of kissing, eating and sleeping together became unintelligible, even scandalous, just a hundred or so years later? Moreover, what have we lost in the process?

It's possible that the cause was a growing fear of homosexuality. We've already raised the possibility that homophobia can distort friendships, particularly between men. However, although 'sodomites' did come to be persecuted with a vengeance around this time, that was probably a product of the change rather than a cause: as these signs lost their social intelligibility, the idea spread that anyone might be a pervert, whereas before the sodomite had been a strange, alien creature, and certainly nothing to do with unabashed signs of affection and connection. However, we can suggest that that is, arguably, one thing we have lost, at least in the west: the public expression of affection by men towards one another.

Another possible cause might be as prosaic as the changes that took place in the layout of houses. This had the effect of moving what had taken place in public spaces into private quarters: servants moved off pallets and into dormitories; grand staircases became back stairs; great halls in which gentlemen served food to all became private dining rooms attended on by servants. These changes were certainly noticed. Visitors to Britain from abroad, where the changes had yet to take place, such as François de la Rochefoucauld, were surprised by them since they had not yet been seen on the European continent. Similarly, the French writer and popular orator, the Comte de Mirabeau, expressed astonishment that Englishmen had ceased to greet each other with a kiss and used instead a strange shaking of the hand. But again, these are products of change not causes of change.

Bray believes that the fundamental cause is to be located in the way the life of the body itself changed. A whole range of bodily activities including eating, drinking, toilet and sleeping stopped taking place inside what might broadly be called the space of the extended household and started taking place within the much narrower confines of what might be called the 'marital space'. As a result, bodily intimacy ceased to be an instrument that could be used to carry wider social meanings, including friendship, and came to be associated primarily with the more limited concerns of married couples.

In other words, public institutions of friendship were replaced by the private institution of the family. In the seventeenth century and before, people lived in a multiplicity of networks and fraternities according to their status, their age, their work or their luck. It is important to remember the high rates of death in childbirth too, which meant that husbands might often marry several times and that children could be routinely raised by a number of different people including stepparents, relations or friends. These various connections were held together by the fundamental unit of society, the extended household, which in turn created lots of space for friendship to play an important social role.

One gets another feel for these lost times in the work of another contemporary historian, John Bossy. He has also charted the changes in the west over this period and notes, for example, that in the latter Middle Ages, fraternities were hugely popular, the product of a widespread desire to enjoy formalised friendships that went beyond the limitations of kinship and the hierarchical strictures of feudalism. Celebratory meals and affectionate greetings did not only allow individuals to bond alongside family and fiefdom but also served to mitigate the civil unrest that was an ever present threat, particularly when the hand of the law could be quite distant.

It is also within this context that the relationship between John Evelyn and Margaret Godolphin can be understood. These two Restoration figures had an extraordinary passionate and chaste friendship in spite of the fact that Evelyn was married. John, Margaret and his wife Mary did on occasion experience jealousies, as the quote from her letter at the start of Chapter 2 shows. But to the modern mind it is remarkable that, first, John and Margaret could associate so freely in and around London without rousing suspicion and, second, that Mary could come to count Margaret as her friend too and write the following to her husband:

> She is now yours in spirit and the bond of friendship as she is mine, and how can I be happier? ... you both want something of each other, and I of you both, and I hope in God we shall all be the better for one another, and that this three-fold cord shall never be broken.

What happened in the seventeenth century is that these notions of the extended household collapsed. Social ties and solidarities were replaced by marital bonds and the boundaries of the family; the threefold cord was replaced with a tie, for two. Physical intimacies that were part of the public, symbolic world of friendship – in particular kissing and sleeping together – came to be seen as the prerogative of husband and wife, excluding friendship in the process. This, then, explains the rise of homophobia. The meaning of affectionate connection between men was undone and, if subsequently displayed, was left hanging undecided. The world had changed and with it a public space within which friendship could flourish largely disappeared too: it was relegated to the strictly private. Though it is easy to think that the modern world is one in which there are more opportunities for freer relationships, it is quite possible that the medieval mind would see our world as more constrained, at least in this respect.

Another way of looking at this is to consider how the meaning of the word 'society' changed over the same period. The older meaning is simply 'being together'. To say, 'I enjoy your society' was to say 'I enjoy being with you.' Friendship was, therefore, a form of society. But during the seventeenth century, society came to carry structural and organisational overtones too, as in civil society or industrial society, meanings that eventually became dominant and marginalised the dimensions of friendship. The philosopher John Locke is seminal in this evolution of the word. His 1690 publication, *Essay concerning the True Original, Extent, and End of Civil Government,* is instructive. In chapter VII, 'Of Political or Civil Society', he discusses what he takes to be the origins of what he calls civil society: 'The first society was between man and wife, which gave beginning to that between parents and children, to which, in time, that between master and servant came to be added.' In other words, he takes what he sees as the first society of Adam and Eve, in the Bible, and uses that as a model for civil society as a whole.

Note the binary structure – man and wife, parents and children, master and servant. One can clearly see the priority being given to what we now call the nuclear family, and the nuclear family as the basis of society to boot. However, that is not the only thing to notice. In turning the 'first society' into a model for 'civil society', he changes the sense of the word society: the first society was company; political society is organisational. It evolves from being something that tangibly exists in the company or companionship of two or more individuals to being an abstraction or framework within which upright individuals will find a sense of who they are and where they belong. In short, instead of people *having* society, they think of themselves as *in* a society. Again, lost opportunities for nurturing friendship is arguably the result.

The changes to the marriage laws are a tangible example of the difference. Before Locke, marriages were fixed rather informally between individuals, again part of the pre-modern culture of flexible kinships and friendships. Afterwards, though, marriage changed and could only be contracted after the bureaucratic rituals of reading banns and signing registers, and in the presence of a clergyman, also called a Clerk in Holy Orders. He was the official representative of the new form of society within which the marriage was explicitly located. So the Lockean move can be thought of as doubly detrimental to friendship. First, it makes a binary notion of family the basis of society, excluding friendship. And second, that society is conceived of as an ominously bureaucratic entity that has few means of understanding, let alone nurturing, friendship.

Sworn brothers

The story does not stop there. The most recent research of historians like Bray is showing that something else was lost in these changes too. It seems that the political standing, and social nurturing, which friendship could gain was only part of it. Within the same milieu, friendship did not just piggy-back on certain symbolic practices but was semi-institutionalised in its own right. This brings us to the second factor that had a bearing on friendship in the Middle Ages, namely, the 'marriages of friendship'. Once more, the history is quite a discovery, not least since it was a widespread religious piety that underpinned it.

Bray's lead into this unexpected dimension of medieval friendship is his research into shared graves. Shared graves, as opposed to common graves, are those in which two people are buried together as an explicit demonstration of the friendship that they shared in life. Once you start looking for them, Bray found, they start appearing everywhere – in churchyards, crypts, cathedrals and chapels.

Consider the fourteenth-century monument above the tomb of Sir William Neville and Sir John Clanvowe: it could not be missed in the church of the Dominicans in Constantinople were it was located. These two English knights died in 1391 and what is remarkable about their funerary monument is the way that their shields, which are carved on it, incline towards each other. Similarly, the crowns of their helmets meet as if in a kiss. These heraldic arms show that Sir William and Sir John were in life what was known as 'sworn brothers', a voluntary form of kinship based upon an exchanged promise of committed friendship.

These kind of sworn brotherhoods were afforded great respect in pre-modern Europe. They existed alongside marriage – there is no evidence that they were exclusive relationships – and were even tacitly sanctioned by the Church: the kiss of the helmets shown in Constantinople is like the kiss of peace from the Mass, the sign of divinely sanctioned connection. In the west, the kiss of peace exchanged before receiving communion together was in fact the action that sealed the sworn brotherhood, that gave it social standing. Sir William and Sir John went to such a Mass and made such a commitment in their youths. In Eastern Orthodox Christianity, copies of prayers that were specifically written for the creation of sworn brothers and sisters survive to this day.

So great was the political weight that such friendships could bear that they could effect changes in much the same way as a marriage. Another story Bray retraces demonstrates as much, from findings he made in Hereford Cathedral. Here, beneath the magnificent fourteenth century bishop's throne, there is another mysterious tombstone. Inscribed on it are two hands clasping, above which is written the words, 'In life united, in death not divided'.

This monument is the shared grave of Herbert Croft, bishop of Hereford, and George Benson, the dean of Hereford cathedral.

179

They died and were buried in the 1690s. Croft and Benson lived in tumultuous times, the English Civil War. Hereford Cathedral had witnessed the violence of those years: the library had been sacked and looted; monuments were defaced and destroyed; Croft and Benson had both come close to being murdered.

So, their shared grave is, on one level, an expression of the friendship forged in those years. But it is also much more than just a touching memorial to a private relationship. At the time, it was a powerful, political statement.

Today, we may have grown used to arguments in Christian churches. But during the thirteenth and fourteenth centuries the church was often, literally, at war with itself. In particular, the bishops of the church took up arms against the deans of its cathedrals. The arguments were usually over land and control. In 1328, for example, the Archbishop of York had to use force to enter Hereford Cathedral. He was, after all, a Lord claiming his estate.

The battle over Hereford was particularly long-lasting and intense. Two hundred and fifty years after York's forced entry, in 1559, bishops were still refused a way. One wrote to Queen Elizabeth's powerful secretary, William Cecil, accusing the dean of Hereford and his canons of 'blasphemy, whoredom, pryde and ignorance'. He could walk about Hereford city only with a guard.

But then in the second half of the seventeenth century the unthinkable happened. The bishop and the dean had found a settlement to the battle that had been going on for 500 years, and they became close friends in the process.

We do not know the exact details of the reconciliation, but we can now see how important their tombstone is. It is, in effect, a command to all subsequent bishops and deans: do not revisit the old quarrels of the past. That is why it was placed beneath the bishop's throne: Croft and Benson's successors would literally have had to step over it. Not only were Croft and Benson not divided in death, but the bishops and deans of Hereford should never again be divided in life. Their private friendship, therefore, carried enormous political significance: it effected a political reunion quite as strong as medieval marriage.

Sworn brotherhoods existed up to the seventeenth century. Another example, in the chapel of Christ's College, Cambridge, is the grave of John Finch and Thomas Baines from 1682. It is topped with a single flaming funerary urn that represents the mingling of their remains. The inscription reads:

> So that they who while living had mingled their interests, fortunes, counsels, nay rather souls, might in the same manner, in death, at last mingle their sacred ashes.

Another reflection of the popularity of the ideals of such sworn friendships is Jeremy Taylor's *Discourse of Friendship*. When it was published in 1657, it was reprinted several times in quick succession. He wrote:

> The more we love, the better we are and the greater our friendships are; let them be dear and let them be perfect ... it would be well if you could love and if you benefit all mankind; for I conceive that [heaven] is the sum of all friendships.

There is further evidence that friendships were sworn between women too and right into the nineteenth century, though less frequently and less publicly. The well documented friendship between Anne Lister and Ann Walker, recorded in enormous detail in the diary of Anne Lister, was one such. Bray believes that a sworn sisterhood is what Lister was referring to when she confided in her aunt that she and Walker had decided to settle as companions for life in a friendship that 'would be as good as marriage'. On Easter Sunday, 1834, they solemnised this commitment by receiving communion together in a church near York Minster. 'I had prayed that our union might be happy', she wrote. In other words, although their sworn friendship did not command the social significance that it might have done up to one hundred years before, the old religious forms of making a 'promise of mutual faith' were still available. They were still part of the public imaginary, still part of friendship.

The piety of friendship

So how are we to understand the philosophy, or rather theology, of friendship that underpins this commitment? This is where the element of religious piety comes in. During the medieval period, a number of Christian writers had reflected upon the importance of friendship in the monastic setting. Consider the writings of Anselm, the sometime Abbot of Bec and Archbishop of Canterbury who died in 1109. He is often remembered today for his 'proof' of the existence of God, which roughly runs that God must exist because existing is the greatest possession anyone can have, so God, of all beings, must have it. But when not proving God's existence, Anselm was a prolific letter writer to his monastic brethren. It is these letters that provide us with his thoughts on friendship.

What is notable about them is an extravagant use of, again, apparently affectionate terms: 'eye to eye, kiss for kiss, embrace for embrace', he signed off one. As between James I and Robert Carr, this kind of language is easily misunderstood and it is wrong to read it as sexual. Anselm's kisses are the same expression of connection, this time sealed by the monastic setting – a literal union of monks linked by their monastic vows and communal life. The extravagance of the language is an expression of the extravagant reward their commitment will bring them, the everlasting joys of Heaven.

In fact, and not unlike like James I and Robert Carr, it is possible that Anselm was not primarily thinking of human affection at all in these terms of spiritual endearment, strange as that may seem. When in 1093 he moved from Bec to Canterbury, many of his brothers suspected that he did so with little real regard for them as individuals. Anselm himself did not want the job, though not because he would miss his friends but mostly because of the dangers it would bring him. When he left, his brethren wondered whether his 'friendship' with them was based more in their being religious brothers than personal friends.

Anselm's theology of friendship is esoteric: his high doctrine was extended only to his monastic peers and even then there are grounds for thinking that he was drawn to a piety of spiritual connection that tended to diminish the friendships themselves. This arguably changes with Aelred of Rievaulx, for who the two elements fuse together. He was born in the year Anselm died and at the age of 37 was elected abbot of Rievaulx, a monastery of some 300 Cistercian monks, the remains of which stand to this day outside Thirsk in Yorkshire. His great work on friendship, *Spiritual Friendship*, was written soon after he arrived at Rievaulx. It is inspired by Cicero: if Cicero had written an account of friendship addressed to the late Roman republic, Aelred wanted to do the same for a Christian society. However, he is innovative too. Several things stand out.

First, he argues that friends should be willing to die for each other. His model in this respect is the life of Jesus: 'A man can have no greater love than to lay down his life for his friends', as the writer of John's Gospel has it. This saying has been co-opted today to express the sacrifice made by soldiers in war but in John's Gospel it means something rather different. It is actually a comment on the demands of discipleship. Earlier in John's Gospel Jesus says that he does not call his disciples servants but friends. Why? 'I call you friends because I have made known to you everything I have learnt from my Father.' In other words, the friends of Jesus both understand who he is and are prepared to pay the price of living by that conviction – even to the point of death. It is for this reason that 'friend' was almost a synonym for 'Christian' in the early, persecuted Church. Aelred implies the same should be true in his time.

Other things that Aelred thinks should be typical of friends follow from this. The love between friends should be undying in the sense that 'he that is a friend loves at all times'. Even if someone is unjustly accused, injured, cast into flames or crucified in ways that implicate their friends, as was the case for Jesus, the friendship should not cease or else it was 'never true friendship'.

Third, Aelred thinks that friends should share all things in common. This was a pattern of behaviour that was established in the very earliest days of the Church and is recorded in the Bible in the Acts of the Apostles. In Aelred's vision of friendship, sharing things in common comes to represent how friends are other selves to each other: 'And the multitude of believers had but one heart and one soul; neither did anyone say that aught was his own, but all things were common unto them.'

Conversely, Aelred is suspicious of lesser kinds of friendship, such as Aristotle's friendships of utility and pleasure. He believed that people either share true friendship or carnal friendship, the latter seeking worldly pleasures and material gains – sex and workplace advantages as I have described them here – and not love of another human being for who they are in themselves. Part of the reason for this rather harsh stance is that Aelred is very conscious of the Christian doctrine of original sin. After the fall of Adam and Eve, Aelred speculates, love 'cooled' and a range of evils including avarice, envy, contention, emulations and hates made inroads into love and 'corrupted the splendour of friendship'. It would be hard to beat such a summary of the ambiguities of friendship. At the same time, Aelred did not think that such ambiguities should be taken as to the detriment of friendship per se. In this way, he was in line with Thomas Aquinas rather than Augustine. Rather, they are themselves a reflection of his high ideals of friendship: he thought that friendship appeared first in the Garden of Eden, and so, although fallen friendship is certainly fallen, it is also a remembrance of the paradisical time that was. Moreover, he goes so far as to hold that God is friendship, like Thomas. So a friend is a guardian of heavenly love and friendship is a taste of paradise:

> Come now, beloved, open your heart, and pour into these friendly ears whatsoever you will, and let us accept gracefully the boon of this place, time, and leisure.

It used to be thought that Aelred's writings on friendship were a romantic vision of friendship within the cloister. But it now seems that his account of friendship was just one part of a more wide-spread piety, linked to the practice of sworn brotherhood. Thus, many people, not just monks, developed a devotion to their friends that they might interpret in a similar way to Aelred, and incorporate amity into their shared lives together.

That, in turn, is behind the phenomenon of shared graves. For Augustine, the death of a friend provoked a profound personal and theological crisis. But for Aelred, the death of a friend, something he also experienced, was the culmination of love, witnessed to by the love that lives on in the heart of the surviving friend. For all the agony of mourning, the death of a friend is an experience of eternity in the present. As Cicero put it, 'Even when he is dead, he is still alive.' Friendship's greatest gift is, thus, that it lifts the veil between this world and the next and provides a foretaste of the everlasting love of heaven here and now.

It is in this context that shared graves and the rites of sworn friendship in the Mass make the fullest sense. The shared grave is not just a private, romantic gesture of friendship at the end of two lives. It is the natural, final resting place of friends whose commitment in this world was both their ideal, amidst the

Figure 13: 'Even when he is dead, he is still alive.' Cicero, pictured here as a reading youth.

difficult demands of relating to others, and hope, as a foretaste of the love to be shared in eternity. Similarly, sharing the kiss of peace and receiving communion together was symbolic of the ethic that shaped their relationship with each other, their obligations to others, and ultimately their faith in God.

So seeing friendship within this Christian frame is not to paint it in pietistic gloss. Rather it adds a new dimension to the practice of friendship that builds on the advantages afforded it by the social conventions of pre-modern society. Friendship could not only become attached to various political demonstrations of connection, and so gain some public standing. It could achieve a semi-institutionalised status that far from being exceptional was part of a wider social order that many people understood and warmed to, whether or not they were sworn friends themselves. Again then: in the sense that the Middle Ages provided a social space within which friendships could be nurtured, we can see that it too was arguably more open to friendship in a way that was constitutive of society.

The issue of what has been lost, and its relevance to friendship today, needs to be pursued further: that is a matter for the next chapter. However, before we come to that, there is one more twist to add to the tale of sworn friendships.

I mentioned the friendship of Anne Lister and Ann Walker: there are two elements to draw out further in relation to it. The first I have already referred to, namely, that their friendship existed in the nineteenth century, 100 years after the tipping point when conventions changed: how can this be? The second is the one thing that anyone who has read about Lister and Walker knows: their friendship was sexual. So again, how could they take advantage of this form of friendship to secure their union when even suspicion of the sexual element could have branded them as sinners?

The two things are connected. For one thing, although social conventions changed, the reason sworn friendship was not erad-icated entirely is that religious pieties are not easily dislodged: friendship may have stopped carrying much social weight but that does not mean the sentiments that lay behind sworn friendship were abated. This meant, in turn, that although sworn friendships disappeared from view, that could be an advantage to those like Lister and Walker who both wished to celebrate their love in valid symbols, and did not want to draw too much attention to it, because it contained a sexual element.

In fact, Lister and Walker were not buried together. Anne died of a fever in Georgia after their 15-month journey together across Europe in 1840. As Bray suggests, it is significant that the other Ann did not leave her body there but went to the enormous lengths of having it returned to Halifax and buried in the church where they made their vows. Walker no doubt intended to be buried there alongside her – not just as a gesture of love and grief, but as the final and culminating act of their friendship.

Prophetic Friendship

'Every real friendship is a sort of secession, even a rebellion.'

C. S. Lewis

The final frame of Ridley Scott's movie *Thelma and Louise* is frozen: it holds a '66 Thunderbird car in midair above the Grand Canyon, lit brightly in orange pink sunshine. Thelma and Louise are in it. Behind and above them in patrol vehicles and helicopters are the massed ranks of the police who have chased them across the state. The two women are seconds from certain death. And yet just before they flew over the edge, they warmly embraced and smiled: 'You're a good friend', Thelma said, to which Louise replied, 'You too, sweetie, the best.' In other words, to see them only as about to die is to miss the moment. They are actually going to their freedom – the eternity of the final frozen frame. It captures the high point in their lives and their friendship has brought them to it.

The friendship of these two women, who were tired of being victimised by men, is evident from the opening scenes of the film. Thelma, played by Geena Davis, and Louise, played by Susan Sarandon, clearly know each other better than their respective husband and boyfriend know them. Their sense of one another is knit together to the extent that they can be critical of each other without ever questioning their bond. 'Friends share everything in common,' noted Plato. They have shared the road, a rape, a robbery and rude truck-drivers. It has brought them to that point high in the air. So what is it about their very modern friendship that finds its culmination in a glorious and defiant suicide?

The answer is a form of protest, based on friendship, that might be said to have begun to take shape in the very different time and place of Anne Lister and Ann Walker. (That Thelma and Louise's '66 Thunderbird becomes a 'shared grave' is particularly evocative).

Lister and Walker loved each other and borrowed the rites and sentiments of a form of friendship that used to be regarded as a pious celebration of two people's connection to make a commitment. That such sworn friendship had mostly disappeared in the nineteenth century in which they lived was convenient: it could be used to express the seriousness of their intent without having to seek the blessing of a society that would not give it. But their act was not just one of convenience. It was also a kind of complaint.

Relationships like theirs were becoming suspect and so theirs inevitably assumed a prophetic edge too. Lister and Walker probably thought of their sworn friendship as a kind of resistance; a way of quietly defying a society that sought to keep women and friendship in check. And a few years later such personal resistances had developed into a form of public protest which by the end of the twentieth century had evolved again to affect real change. It was as if the disappearance of the semi-institutional commitment of friends as part of the make-up of society, and the forgotten tradition of the Romans and Greeks who sought to celebrate friendship in their politics, made way for the reappearance of friendship as an important driving force in the demands of people who sometimes quietly, sometimes militantly, sought recognition and respect for their lives. In short, we can see a complete about turn: the constitutive role that friendship had played becomes subversive, the means of circumventing the new social norms that would outlaw its love, being based on a particular conception of the family and rigid roles for men and women. This movement, which we will now explore, has much to tell us about how friendship functions in modern society and also what friendship can be for us. To cut to the point: friendship holds out a promise for us of what a politically fairer, and emotionally richer, good life can be.

Suffragette city

The women's groups who fought for suffrage in the nineteenth and early part of the twentieth centuries provide a focus for the way in which personal resistance became public protest.

189

Friendship here becomes a relationship from which individuals find resources to refuse oppressive social conventions.

For a long time, suffragettes found little support within the corridors of power. Their public protests were often met with annoyed bemusement, even in circles that might be thought sympathetic. One newspaper of the time, *The Referee* (which carried the laudable strapline 'The paper that makes you think'), reports an incident in June 1914 that is typical. A liberal demonstration at Denmark Hill in South London was being addressed by David Lloyd George, who was to become British prime minister. These liberals, though, were far from tolerant of women's demands. 'At the outset Lloyd George had to submit to a Suffragist interruption', the paper reports, 'but the interrupters were quickly chased away from the scene.' There followed a series of 'extraordinary scenes' including one Revd Mr Wills being seized 'by people in the crowd and thrown into the pond at the back of the grounds of Bessemer House'.

> When he got out he came to blows with the man who pushed him in, and Mr Wills was very roughly handled. Another male sympathiser followed the reverend gentleman into the pond, and a Suffragette had a lot of her clothing torn off. The stewards were helpless in preventing the public from maltreating the interrupters.

Little wonder, then, that friendship was an important source of solidarity and succour amongst these women and their relatively few supporters.

The record of one friendship in particular has survived the passage of time and provides further details of how they functioned in this milieu. It was between two 'Ultras' (so-called because they were radical even for suffragettes), Elizabeth Cady Stanton and Susan B. Anthony.

> These celebrated women are of about equal ages, but of the most opposite characteristics, and illustrate the theory of counterparts in affection by entertaining for each other a friendship of

extraordinary strength. Mrs. Stanton is a fine writer, but a poor executant; Miss Anthony is a thorough manager, but a poor writer ... To describe them critically, I ought to say that opposite though they may be, each does not so much supplement the other's deficiencies as augment the other's eccentricities. Thus they often stimulate each other's aggressiveness and at the same time diminish each other's discretion.

Stanton and Anthony met in May 1851, the early days of the American women's movement before the Civil War. They were both already leading lights within it and their meeting was fortuitous: the Ultras were moving into the 'collective action stage', as Michael Farrell calls it in his book *Collaborative Circles*. Stanton and Anthony's friendship was central to this gearing up for battle and by the end of that first summer they had become close friends: Anthony stayed at Stanton's for much of July and August where she quickly became known as Aunt Susan to Stanton's several children. Thereafter their relationship could even be said to have been marriage-like in certain ways, though not sexual. For example, Stanton ensured that there was a room for Anthony permanently at the ready for when she came to stay.

Their friendship flourished on a number of levels. One was personal: Stanton describes how she and Anthony comforted each other when other members of the group wanted to tone down their fiery proclamations.

For Miss Anthony and myself, the English language had no words strong enough to express the indignation we felt in view of the prolonged injustice to women. We found, however, that after expressing ourselves in the most vehement manner, and thus in a measure giving our feelings an outlet, we were reconciled to issue the documents at last in milder terms.

Another level was practical. Stanton had family commitments to juggle with her political engagements and could not devote as much time to travelling and speaking as Anthony. In contrast,

Figure 14: 'We have indulged freely in criticism of each other when alone.' Elizabeth Candy Stanton on her friendship with Susan Anthony, pictured here.

Anthony felt inadequate in writing speeches. So their friendship enabled them to divide the labour. Anthony would do much of the research for the speeches, and Stanton would come up with the drafts: 'She supplied the facts and statistics, I the philosophy and rhetoric, and together we have made arguments that have stood unshaken by the storms of thirty long years ... the united products of our two brains.'

So the friendship was also vital when it came to their activism. Together they devised a programme of annual conventions at which participants gave speeches and read poems: the women realised that this mode of social action was effective both in terms of developing their philosophy and in terms of presenting women in different public roles. (Contemporary newspaper reports express surprise that women are actually as good at oratory as men.) The friendship was also a forum to discuss their experiments in how to dress and behave in public. Similarly, they talked about how women could set their own agenda in the pursuit of happiness, something that had hitherto been the prerogative of men. All in all, their friendship was a private powerhouse driving a prophetic way of life.

Having said that, the demands of the life they chose could cast a shadow over them too. For example, Anthony never married and whilst her collaboration with Stanton was for the most part premised on accommodating the responsibilities Stanton had for her family, Anthony did sometimes object: 'Woman must take to her soul a purpose and then make circumstances conform to this purpose, instead of forever singing the refrain, if and if and if!', she once argued in an implicit criticism of the compromises that marriage necessitates. But, it was actually the married Stanton whose mature politics did more to challenge their friendship towards the end.

Her final speech to the National American Woman Suffrage Association in 1892, entitled 'The Solitude of the Self' and often regarded as her masterpiece, was premised on an existential philosophy that implicitly marginalised friendship. In the speech, Stanton laid out an argument which said that women cannot depend on men because ultimately everyone is alone. This made a good case for suffrage because, if true, everyone must be allowed whatever means are available in society to guard themselves against such isolation. Stanton invoked the figure of Robinson Crusoe to demonstrate her case. He was an individual who lived in a world of his own, who was arbiter of his own destiny, and who used every faculty at his disposal to ensure his own safety and happiness. So, Stanton argued, should a woman be. She deployed the figure of Crusoe's companion, Friday, in her analogy; every woman would have her own woman, a Friday, she said. But what at first reads like an invocation of the early days of her friendship with Anthony turned out to distance them from each other, because she concluded that whilst a Friday brought benefits, ultimately no one could rely on anyone apart from themselves. The implication was that even Anthony had left her alone at certain moments:

In youth our most bitter disappointments, our brightest hopes and ambitions, are known only to ourselves. Even our

193

friendship and our love we never fully share with another ... Alone a woman goes to the gates of death to give life to every man that is born into the world; no one can share her fears, no one can mitigate her pangs; and if her sorrow is greater than she can bear, alone she passes beyond the gates into the vast unknown ... how few the burdens that one soul can bear for another!

Michael Farrell believes that this was Stanton's public 'divorce' of Anthony and that for what remained of her life she wanted to be independent of her. When, for example, Stanton's husband died, Anthony invited her to move in with her and form a new 'home for single women'. Stanton refused. Even close friends of forty years standing are never far from the unpredictable ambivalences of friendship.

As far as I know, Stanton and Anthony's friendship was never itself a source of public comment. Neither was it at the time interpreted, or meant, as an act of rebellion against the world of men – as if, for example, its marriage-like characteristics were a judgement on the bonds of real marriage within which women may have felt themselves to be trapped. In other words, the friendship fired a challenge to society but was not perceived as an affront in itself. But if we move forward a few years, to the feminist movement of the mid- to late twentieth century, then friendship itself becomes a form of protest. By this time, both contemporary and reconstructed historic friendships between women could be seen as acts of emancipation in their own right.

Political weight

A good example of this interpretation of friendship is found in Lillian Faderman's *Surpassing the Love of Men* – a study of women's friendships in the Victorian period whose title alone says much. (In the Bible it is the love of David and Jonathan whose love 'surpasses that of women'.) She examines what she calls romantic friendships between women such as Emily Dickinson and Sue

Gilbert, and finds them surprisingly common. However, Faderman's purpose in recovering these stories is not only historical. It is political and becomes explicit when in a deliberately provocative move, and no doubt with a wry smile on her face, she classifies them as lesbian. Not that she means they were necessarily sexual. In fact, she believes that is an uninteresting question. Rather, she uses the word lesbian to emphasise the social power of 'women on women' friendship that she wants to draw attention to within the context of the feminist politics of her time: 'a lesbian is a woman who makes women prime in her life, who gives her energies and her commitment to other women rather than to men', she explains.

This classification is not wholly anachronistic. Lesbianism has long been a trope for subversive women regardless of their sexual proclivities. In the Victorian writer Algernon Swinburne's posthumously published novel, *Lesbia Brandon*, he connects the high intellect and independent spirit of his lead female character to an 'inevitable' lesbianism, and indeed 'inevitable' eventual suicide. It is also the case that as the friendships Faderman documents blossomed, so they came to be regarded with anxiety, raising almost ridiculous concerns, such as the possibility that women everywhere might want to cease marrying and having relationships with men. But the subversive element is focused on something at once more subtle and pervasive. As Simone de Beauvoir observed in 1949, 'often women choose to become lesbians when they are absorbed in ambitious projects of their own, or when they simply want liberty and decline to abdicate in favour of another human being as the heterosexual relationship generally demands of females'. Faderman's goal is the same; to make an explicit link between the very fact of being friends and female emancipation. As she concludes:

> Many of the relationships that [men] condemned had little to do with sexual expression. It was rather that love between women, coupled with their emerging freedom, might conceivably bring about the overthrow of heterosexuality – which

has meant not only sex between men and women but patriarchal culture, male dominance and female subservience.

So how is it that friendship itself comes to be thought of as an act of rebellion, as opposed to just providing support for certain kinds of protest or, going further back to the times of Walker and Lister, merely being an act of personal resistance? It stems in large part from the critique of society that feminists have put forward: friendship is seen as an embodiment of that critique. This embraces a number of aspects. But take one.

As many feminists see it, many of the problems of the modern world arise from the dominance of individualism; the fact that being human is thought of in terms of being a 'social atom'. This is the same social atomism at the heart of post-Kantian ethics, though let us now frame it in a different way. Think of the model of human individuality that is often referred to as 'rational economic man' [sic]. According to this model, individuals make decisions according to the rule of maximising things for themselves, and themselves alone. Rational economic man views work as a place where he should gain as many advantages for himself as he can; he competes against his peers or competitors and balances out the pain of working hard (and reaping rewards) and the pleasure of an easy life (with few prospects). Alternatively, he views his political acts as a way to maximise the benefits he receives from society; he votes for whoever promises to improve his health care, to secure his job, and not to raise his taxes. More mundanely, when he travels he seeks to maximise the speed with which he can get somewhere; he pits his need to travel fast against other road-users' desire to do the same. All in all, decisions are taken primarily with himself in mind. Any consideration of others is judged by the disadvantage, inconvenience or pain such an action would cause to him. He operates as a social atom.

Now, of course, rational economic man does not exist in reality. Even the most selfish individual has family and friends whom they care about, at least some of the time: they will do favours for a colleague at work; will make allowances for a slow pedestrian crossing the road; will consider various policies when voting; a man may even shop for his wife. As Thomas Aquinas might have said, even egoism can reach out to others. However, the point about the model of a rational economic man is that the modern market economy favours behaviour that is like his. It is a competitive environment, driven by maximising utility, vying for scare resources, and encouraging predominantly instrumental, utility-based relationships. The net result is that behaving like rational economic individuals tends to be reinforced – in everything from government policy to the size of pay packets – and behaviour that is not like it tends to be marginalised.

Many thinkers, not just feminists, are unsettled by the implications of this. What they have in common is objecting to a conception of individuality based upon social atomism, and preferring instead an idea of people acting according to their attachments. Communitarianism is one alternative model. It is a way of thinking about socioeconomic behaviour based upon the belief that people make decisions about their actions in terms of their social, not individual, identity. As Alasdair MacIntyre puts it:

> I am someone's son or daughter, someone else's cousin or uncle; I am a citizen of this or that city, a member of this or that guild or profession; I belong to this clan, that tribe, this nation ... These are the given of my life, my moral starting point.

The problem with communitarianism for feminists is that although it takes people's attachments seriously, it can be blind to the possibility that these attachments may be oppressive. For example, if a woman is treated harshly by her husband, or a person of colour is ostracised in a predominantly white workplace, then communitarianism could inadvertently legitimise that abuse by celebrating the family connection, or professional association, regardless of its ramifications. Communitarians can, of course, share the values that abhor exploitation of this kind. But what critics of communitarianism argue is that it risks sidelining those values in the effort to shake off social atomism; valorising social networks like family, school, church or nation can validate the relationships out of which injustice can grow by taking them as 'the given' of life.

Right relationship

One feminist response to the inadequacy of alternatives like communitarianism has been to emphasise the necessity of choice in relationships. And this is where friendship as a model of social connection comes in because it is a relationship that is, in large part, characterised by voluntarism. Marilyn Friedman has written suggestively about this. Friendship, she argues, is a good way of thinking about what it is to be connected, particularly in the urban context in which many forms of connection are based on choice not obligation. Her point is not that friendship encourages people to have a friendly attitude towards each other which in turn reduces incidents of abuse: that would clearly be highly unlikely, to say nothing of the fact that cities can also be places of isolation, loneliness and alienation. Neither does she treat friendship idealistically, as if she were describing a society of friends in which division, dissent and disruption had ceased: we have seen that friendship can aspire to be noble but has little to do with utopias. Rather, she focuses on friendship to outline a way of engaging with society.

First, it promotes networks of support. In the urban context, this is manifested in the way that cities are home to all sorts of minorities. The city provides both the anonymity that allows someone to separate themselves from any oppressive origins and the networks around which to form common interest groups to resist that oppression. In bars and clubs, community centres and meeting rooms – 'amongst friends' – individuals can reinvent themselves without having to deal with the intolerance of crabby families or insular neighbours. Second, whilst such friendships may be politically passive, the city makes it highly likely that at least some people within such groups will become politically active – either fighting for their own interests or expressing solidarity with others. This is where the prophetic dynamic kicks in: friendship gains social weight and comes to be seen as an act of emancipation itself.

Another feminist thinker, Mary E. Hunt, develops this thought. For women, she argues, friendship is the context within which the political imperatives of mutuality, equality and reciprocity are best experienced. This is empowering at the personal level and becomes political because, as relational 'experts in the field', it gives women things to teach the world around them. In terms of the argument against individualism, what women's friendships teach is what she calls 'right relationship' – exemplified in a balance of four elements: love, feeling more united than separated; power, the power to fight for the right to choose what is best; embodiment, the struggle to love ourselves and each other particularly in relation to our bodies; and fourth what she calls spirituality, the sense of being concerned for quality of life. When friendships manifest such right relationships they become both liberative and witnesses to it.

Hunt realises that friendship has its weaknesses stemming from the ambiguities inherent in it. These may well stymie the attempt to find the right balance she seeks; such are its contingencies and vulnerabilities. However, she concludes that when friendship is regarded as the ethical norm, it reflects values that are different from those associated with social atomism. Rational economic man is exposed. This carries with it the potential for much social good. Something similar was said of friendships in the workplace: the dominant mode of relatedness there is individualistic and utilitarian; friendship overcomes that when individuals come to know and love each other for who they are, not simply what they give.

Hunt describes these friendships in abstract ideals – as empowered, embodied and so on. But what, we might ask, do they look like in practice? What are the ramifications of holding friendship as the predominant social norm? This is where the politics of friendship moves into another creative mode. Here it plays not only a critical role but also an inventive one, of asserting and perhaps devising alternative ways of relating. Hunt's notion of right relationship is certainly part of this. But let us now turn to another contemporary source of creative relational politics, namely, that of the friendships between self-identified gay men and women.

What are gay men for?

Consider friendship first from the gay men's point of view. There are many ways to tell this side of the story and scholars sometimes ferociously debate which is best. However, an interesting place to pick it up is to step back in time again to a particular moment in social history, the birth of the coffee house. During the latter half of the seventeenth century – that pivotal period for the emergence of modern society – several hundred coffee houses opened up in London alone. For a society that had come to consider commercial exchange, not social hierarchy, as its basis, they were places where people could relate as individuals on equal ground. They spread for very similar reasons in the US, if somewhat later, after the Civil War.

Having said that, they were not in general places for friends to meet. In fact, the rules of politeness that guided behaviour in them preferred people not to be close friends, or at least not to act as such; it was thought that conversation between intimates too easily descended into small talk. Rather, the coffee house was a place where for relatively modest amounts of cash – the price of coffee and possibly an entrance fee – all manner of mostly men could mingle for the serious business of discussing anything from Indian imports and Whigish scandals to German Idealism.

A small number of these coffee houses were called molly houses and they served a particular clientele: a male homosexual subculture with a rather different agenda. They formed, in a way, the original 'gay' scene and probably varied in character as much as gay bars do today. Some surviving descriptions of them emphasise the effeminacy of the men who frequented them. This sketch is by Edward Ward from his *Secret History of Clubs*:

> They adopt all the small vanities natural to the feminine sex to such an extent that they try to speak, walk, chatter, shriek and scold as women do, aping them as well in other respects. In a certain tavern in the City, the name of which I will not mention, not wishing to bring the house into disrepute, they hold parties and regular gatherings.

A more 'hard-core' picture comes from Samuel Stevens who was probably an agent for a collective organisation that went by the name of the Societies for the Reformation of Manners:

> I found between 40 and 50 men making love to one another as they called it. Sometimes they would sit in one another's laps, kissing in a lewd manner and using their hands indecently.

These sources were written by individuals who basically disapproved of molly houses. However, it would be a mistake to see them solely as scandalous places in which men met to flounce or frottage. More profoundly, they were the cultural product of a discontent that some men felt about the way their society thought they should be male, particularly in relation to the way they were supposed to relate to other men. As Michael Vasey has put it:

> [T]he male homosexual was now seen as an alternative to the masculine ideal of the culture; the role was becoming available as a social identity for those who were ill at ease with the prevailing masculine ideal within the culture ... It represented a borrowing of the cultural models for affectionate and sexual behaviour, as well as being a form of ironic criticism of the social order that was hostile to this form of same-sex affection.

In other words, when it came to the question of how men should relate in public, possibilities of affection found themselves ousted by the post-Lockean wariness of activities such as kissing and sleeping together, and molly houses provided 'a cultural counter-point' to the new social norms. They represented an alternative relational space. Men were affectionate in them, no doubt partly driven by the desire for sex but also by a need to explore intimacies and friendships that were limited elsewhere. It is perhaps only going slightly too far to say that the men who frequented them carried the remembrance of a way of relating between men that might otherwise have been increasingly excluded during this time of social change. If we ask tongue in cheek, what was the significance of these homosexuals to society at large, the answer in a word is friendship.

Lads, blokes and metrosexuals

Leaping to the present day, it is obvious that in many respects ideals of masculinity have shifted again. What is interesting about this, though, is that many aspects of male affection are still tied to notions of what we now call gayness. Take the phenomenon of David Beckham. He has shocked, transfixed and seduced the world because although unquestionably masculine he adopted many of the trappings associated with male homosexuality: his image says many things to men, but partly it says, you can push at gendered boundaries, look beautiful, and even risk public displays of affection. Alternatively, if you consider the return of the kiss as a common public greeting between men, I imagine that in the Anglo-Saxon world at least it has much to do with gay culture: one might also point to other factors such as the love of all things Italian (an association that was once itself a euphemism for homosexuality), but being at ease with physical expressions of affection, gay men have long kissed each other in greeting, and now this has arguably been passed back into society.

When it comes to contemporary attitudes towards male friendship, the evidence is mixed. Negatively, they can be coloured by homophobia, the negative response to the association with

gayness. This manifests itself as demonstrable rejectic
sexuality in the friendship, regardless of whether it is
Think of representations of men's friendship on teley
the cinema. They can show male relationships to be stinted and
stunted: the men might be concerned with little more than talking about bedding girls (in *Friends* think of Joey and Chandler);
nailing enemies (this genre of male friendship reaches back to
Miami Vice); or straightforwardly deriding homosexuality (think of
B-list war movies and the new recruits subjected to 'pansy-packed'
abuse from a sergeant). There is also the problem of loutish football fans: I wonder if the reason why some fans feel they must
trash town centres and attack their opponents is because, unconsciously, they feel they must indulge their machismo in order to
demonstrate that their friendships with other fans are not dodgy.
The point is to display a conspicuous heterosexuality that negates
any suggestion of what might be construed as affection. This is
the tragic side of modern friendship between men; it means that,
culturally speaking, friendship between men is often trivialised.

More positively, and apart from the increased visibility of gay
men themselves, contemporary culture is willing to explore the
more affectionate aspects of male friendship too. It is notable,
for example, that the films of the quintessential all-American
hero Tom Cruise routinely feature his friendships with men. In
Top Gun, the love that Cruise's character has for his flying partner exceeds the love that he has for his female flying instructor,
though inevitably the two of them do eventually 'bike off' into
the sunset. In Cruise's more recent film *Collateral*, the only relationship that his character has is with another man, though it is
driven by enmity. More widely, one can observe the emergence of
what Mark Simpson was the first to identify as the metrosexual
– a man who 'consumes in all the best gyms, clubs, shops and
hairdressers' because whether gay, straight or bisexual, his image
of his own masculinity allows him to do so. It is no surprise that
the narcissistic side of the metrosexual finds much in common
with the self-love inherent in much friendship; as Simpson notes,
his sense of self revolves around circles of friends. Alternatively,

the metrosexual conceives of marriage primarily in terms of friend-ship – as opposed to a relationship shaped by prescribed gender roles – and thinks that tying the knot should be an agreement between equals: 'the metrosexual is less interested in blood lines, traditions, family, class, gender than in choosing who they want to be and who they want to be with'. The male metrosexual also lurks within the female characters of soaps like *Sex and the City*, in molly house-like female guise. The message would seem to be this: if you want to enjoy deeper friendship, unleash your inner metrosexual.

That said, the extent to which even liberated modern man is good at friendship is debatable. Consider, Yasmina Reza's award winning play *Art*. The plot revolves around the friendship of three men: Serge who buys a painting of a featureless white canvass at vast expense; Marc who exclaims, 'You paid two hundred thou-sand francs for this shit'; and Yvan who is more tolerant and tries to placate them both. The play deals with the fragilities of their friendship which are exposed as a result of the purchase. Marc feels that Serge has betrayed him in what he sees as a pretentious purchase. Serge feels that an unattractive side of Marc is revealed by his attitude to the picture; it shows that he cannot see the dif-ference between cash value and true value. And they both come to see Yvan's friendship as insubstantial because all he can do as the crisis ensues is all he ever has done – try to make them laugh. In the final scene, Serge and Marc's 15-year friendship appears to come to an end because their masculinity refuses to allow them to admit to each other that they have been hurt. We might say that the friendship does not have the resources to carry them beyond the shock of being honest with one another; the art has exposed their usual habit of shallow friendliness and dissimulation.

Other portrayals of male friendship in novels such as those labelled 'lad-lit' are similarly ambiguous. For example, in Nick Hornby's novels *Fever Pitch* and *High Fidelity*, that tell of the blokeish love of soccer and music records respectively, the male characters flourish insofar as they are companionable with other men, but fail when they try to get close to them. This reflects what the sociologist Graham Allan has found: the dominant images of contemporary masculinity manage to show male sociability but are not so sure when it comes to male intimacy. It seems that male friendship still has its limits. Men are still subject to the dominance of the individualistic and competitive spirit released at the birth of privatising modernity, and an ideal of masculinity that finds affection tricky.

So there is a job for gay men to do yet! What, specifically, might that be for today? Andrew Sullivan is one contemporary writer to have thought about this. His answer focuses precisely on this question of male intimacy. The greatest difference between homosexual and heterosexual men, he thinks, is not to be found in their different sexual attractions or needs, but actually in their ability to sustain friendship. And sustaining friendship beyond the companionability found in football or music, and through the arguments that may break out over a piece of art, is key to the development of intimacy.

The reason for this 'ability' in gay men, Sullivan thinks, stems from the earliest experience of homosexuality. This is not merely one of illicit desire but is one of loneliness: it moves into openness if and only if the gay man finds a true friend, that is, someone who accepts that he is gay. 'Gay men value friendship because until they find their feet as human beings, and let's face it, it's not easy to be 16 and gay, friends are not just friends. They are allies against the world,' was how Tony Warren, creator of the soap *Coronation Street*, put it. So Sullivan's point is not to score points over heterosexuality: 'Gay men have sustained and nourished [friendship] in our culture only by default,' he continues. 'And they are good at friendship not because they are homosexual, but because, in the face of a deep and silent isolation, they are human.'

The job for gay men, then, is to open up closed possibilities of relationship to expansive notions of friendship. In this sense, gay liberation is a potential liberation for everyone:

It would be to open the heterosexual life – especially the male heterosexual life – to the possibilities of intimacy and support

205

that friendship offers, to vent the family with the fresh air of friendship, to expand the range of relationships and connections that every heterosexual person can achieve.

Having said that, gay men are still men. Their sexuality does not automatically free them from the competitive, evasive and proud features of much modern masculinity. Similarly, their friendship will be marked by the uncertainties, duplicities and confusions of amity. In fact there is an argument that they can develop an exceptional talent for friendly lying because of the need to conceal their sexuality from others. In other words, if there is any creative potential in gay friendship it would be more secure if it rested not just on the humanity of the individuals themselves but on the wider, prophetic impact of their very presence. This is the line of thought that was developed in the final years of his life by the French philosopher, Michel Foucault.

Queer lives

In 1982 Foucault gave an interview to the San Francisco-based magazine *Christopher Street*. In it, he argued that the battle for gay liberation is limited if it is thought of only in terms of gaining gay rights. The problem with merely fighting for rights is that it doesn't necessarily change anything fundamental: rights are extended as people become enfranchised, undoubtedly a good thing, but society itself and the way people think about themselves mostly remains the same. Think of something like the 'right' to go to a gay bar, perhaps construed as a right to freedom of expression. This would certainly be part of a liberal society. But the assertion of the right itself does not address the question of why gay bars are necessary to start with. For this reason, Foucault believed that the success of gay liberation is not just to be measured by the extent to which homosexuals are free to come out and live 'gay lives'. Nor by the extent to which it opens up the heterosexual life. Rather its true goal should be more radical. It should be one that begins a process by which people can find a way out of feeling the need to define themselves according to a particular sexuality at all.

What does he mean by that? Think again of the emergence of molly houses and, now, gay bars. The fundamental issue is the negative aspects of the social changes that led to the need for them to start with, which, if the history we've explored here is right, stems in turn from the collapse of the extended household and the dominance of a modern idea of society: it is this that has consequent ramifications for the way people relate to one another, particularly when it comes to affection. Gay liberation needs, therefore, to find ways of addressing these deeper issues too.

This is undoubtedly more difficult. However, in another interview entitled 'Friendship as a Way of Life', Foucault suggested a way forward when he noted the fact that modern society seems to be especially anxious about the way people behave in it. 'Society and the institutions which frame it have limited the possibility of relationships [to marriage] because a rich relational world would be very complex to manage.' According to this view, the challenge at the heart of gay liberation is the freedom to love, befriend and relate more widely; it is to create or imagine a society in which individuals have more options, one that permits many more possible types of relations to exist.

Now, it might be thought that this is to do with sex. But that is actually, I think, a distraction. What is far more disturbing at the social level is the possibility that same-sex men and women are loving each other. This is the point at which gay men and women are most prophetic and present their greatest challenge: as Foucault pointed out, when any serious attention is paid to the 'problem' of homosexuality, it rapidly becomes clear that the real problem is that of friendship; modern society has a problem with that.

It is for this reason that friendship, not sexual acts, lies at the heart of several current disputes about homosexuality. For example, it is no coincidence that the 'gay debate' is often at its most fierce in institutions that feel themselves least able to accommodate such love. Consider the question of gays in the military. The difficulty that the Forces have is that they straddle

Figure 15: 'The development towards which the problem of homosexuality tends is the one of friendship.' (Michel Foucault)

an uncomfortable contradiction when it comes to same-sex friendships. On the one hand, the military must promote them in the camaraderie that may even call on individuals to die for each other. But, on the other hand, it is an institution within which overtly homosexual love is routinely shamed, if not outlawed, for fear of the intense affections that might 'short-circuit' the rules and habits that soldiers are trained to obey. The matter is controversial because of the thought that military relationships are hard enough to police without the complication of actual love.

Alternatively, what of the current uproar in the Anglican Church over homosexuality? In the United States, this has focused on the consecration of the first openly gay man, Gene Robinson, as a bishop in New Hampshire. However the row started before that, with the appointment in the UK of Jeffrey John to the post of Bishop of Reading. He too was openly gay, but in a celibate relationship. In other words, he was neither engaging in 'sexual sin' nor was he going to teach anything that might be regarded as sexually immoral. The difficulty was that his way of life advocated an unconventional form of friendship. The challenge that posed provided quite enough unease for conservatives to leverage and get his appointment withdrawn. They say it's the sin they hate, but actually it's love between men that they find unsettling – evangelical conservatism merely serving to intensify a widespread unease about the changing roles of men and women in contemporary society.

Therein lies the creative iconoclasm of friendship – its contemporary subversiveness. It presents a challenge that is more than just the introduction of another category of partners; the coupledom of the nuclear family could readily embrace more couples. Rather it opens up the far larger matter of how men and women relate to one another. Foucault continued:

> [H]ow is it possible for men to be together? To live together, to share their time, their meals, their room, their leisure, their grief, their knowledge, their confidences? What is it, to be 'naked' among men, outside of institutional relations, family, profession and obligatory camaraderie?

The significance of gay friendship is, then, that it is a way of life that seeks to be simultaneously innovative and subversive. It embodies a freedom that stems not only from the early experiences of homosexuality but also from the fact that it emerges in spite of attempts to control and manage relationships. The 'advantage' that gay men and women have is in a sense negative: until very recently at least, they do not have access to the institutions that others adopt to shape and understand their relationships, notably marriage. They must literally make it up, partly no doubt by imitating marriage, but also by having to transcend contemporary relational constraints within a context of friendship. It might be thought of as a kind of social experiment, a struggle of invention because of the paucity of the received relational imagination, though, perhaps not unlike Lister and Walker, it can find resources in the older ways of friendship that we have examined.

The paradox is that whilst gay men and women are routinely discriminated against in society, the 'experiments' they undertake in their relationships may actually be a rich resource for others to draw on, not least in terms of friendship. Angela Mason, former director of the UK lobby group Stonewall, described it thus:

> My argument is that lesbians and gay men who have been the most sexually stigmatised group within society, who are derided as promiscuous and immoral, may have a contribution to make to a new ethic of personal relationships that is not exclusively based on sexual gratification or demeaning sexual stereotypes.

Foucault captured the experience of the freedom that gay men and women might find in friendship by considering the kind of relationship that can exist between two same-sex individuals of very different age – the age difference emphasising the inaccessibility of conventional institutions for them to model their relationship on, should they want to. 'What code would allow them to communicate?', he pondered:

> They face each other without terms or convenient words, with nothing to assure them about the meaning of the movement that carries them towards each other. They have to invent, from A to Z, a relationship that is still formless, which is friendship: that is to say, the sum of everything through which they can give each other pleasure.

Again, it is important not to romanticise such relationships in the temptation to idealise gayness and friendship. In fact, Foucault's example deliberately discourages that since the freedom that these two individuals might enjoy could as easily become something that is feared; the anxiety of a relationship that is formless, that floats free of any norms to guide it or conventions with which to express it. This is undoubtedly a fear that many gay men and women will have experienced, particularly as they struggle to form long-lasting partnerships. However, it is a fear that is also seen in the reaction that other people can have to relationships like it. The tendency here is to assume that it must be mostly sexual, in the case of the older person, and mostly for some kind of financial benefit, in the case of the younger. What is hard to admit is that it may be a friendship, one that overturns conventional ideas about physical beauty or material gain. Or, to put it another way, one that manages to negotiate certain ambiguities of friendship. Being open to the possibility that it may be genuinely affectionate, mutual, faithful and companionable is for many too much to stomach.

Of course the possibilities represented by friendship depend to a degree upon the success that the individuals may or may not be able to make of it. However, the alternative way of life that they can embody is both a personal and a social opportunity. As Foucault summarises:

> Homosexuality is an historic occasion to re-open affective and relational [possibilities], not so much through the intrinsic qualities of the homosexual, but due to the biases against the position he occupies; in a certain sense diagonal lines that he can trace in the social fabric permit him to make these [possibilities] visible.

It matters to anyone for whom friendship matters at all.

Sociological evidence

So much for the theory. What about the practice? The sociologist Jeffrey Weeks headed up a team that researched gay relationships, or as they called them 'same-sex intimacies'. They interviewed people in a variety of such non-traditional relationships, and found that the 1990s saw a growing acceptance of same-sex partnerships, and to a lesser extent parenting, which was in turn reflected in changes in the meaning of family. Within these wider social shifts, they also identified the emergence of a complex but durable friendship ethic. In fact, friendship was the most common way that the interviewees identified their relationships. 'Friendships particularly flourish when overarching identities are fragmented in periods of rapid social change, or at turning points in people's lives, or when lives are lived at odds with social norms,' Weeks writes. The friendship ethic he uncovered exhibits a number of characteristics that I think demonstrate the creative political potential of friendship.

On one level, it has much to do with simply being gay in a relatively hostile world. For example, Weeks identifies a role for the friendship ethic in supporting the individual through what he calls 'fateful moments' in homosexual experience. The significance of friendship in this case is its necessity for survival and self-actualisation in a hostile world: family and other institutions of belonging won't do and may in fact be associated with the hostility. This might manifest itself in a number of ways. Many of the interviewees said that being able to talk frankly about sexual experiences with certain individuals was what distinguished them as close friends. A related factor is the permanence of close friends, or at least an assumption that they will be permanent: 'In contrast to the vagaries of one-to-one relationships, friends ... are a focus of long-lasting engagement, trust and commitment.'

Alternatively, he draws attention to aspects of the relationships he examined that are key simply because friendship itself is highly valued. For example, they are regarded as freely chosen, though many social factors limit the choice in practice; they take time to form; they come in many shapes and sizes running from mere acquaintances to those thought of as family; and they must be 'constantly negotiated and renegotiated if friendships are to work and survive'. This last issue points to another facet of the weight of its freedom: friendships are not socially legitimised like relationships of kin, and so gay men and women who depend upon them must finds ways of strengthening them and making them stand up.

However, it is in relation to Aids – another 'fateful' factor – that the friendships perhaps most clearly show the potential for innovative forms of relationship. Aids is a catalyst for extended notions of family because traditional family members are often absent or not able to cope with the crisis. Alternatively, Aids deepens the friendship ethic because of the way it impacts attitudes towards care, responsibility and respect:

> Care involves an active concern for the lives, hopes, needs and potentialities of others. It is a highly gendered activity in western culture, seen typically as the prerogative of women. But from our evidence, it is as likely to occur in male as it is female non-heterosexual relationships ... Responsibility as a voluntary act, revealing our response to the needs, latent or explicit, of others, and receiving in return the responsible behaviour of others, is a clearly expressed ideal of our interviewees. Respect, for one's individual autonomy, and for the dignity of others, is a motivating force of many of the friendship circles of our interviewees. These are all features of the friendship ethic at its best.

Weeks also highlights a common concept amongst those he talked to which he calls the 'good friend' – friendship based upon values such as sharing, support, openness, interests, trust and commitment. His interviewees realise that the good friend may be hard to realise in practice. But what is notable is that they are also alert to trying to strike the right balance that makes for it, the balance between being useful and feeling used, sexual possessiveness and individual autonomy, distance and involvement, choice and obligation – that is, they are aware of negotiating the perils of friendship and realising its promise.

Of course, homosexuality does not necessary make for successful let alone innovative forms of friendship. As Weeks notes, circles of homosexual friends can be as insular and conventional as any other. Moreover, some may fear the freedom associated with being gay and use friendship as a refuge from the personal ramifications of being homosexual, reinforcing social stereotypes rather than encouraging experimentation. In terms of Foucault's analysis, this is a ghettoised form of friendship that preserves, not

dissolves, the homosexual identity. But in general, Weeks is optimistic about the significance of the gay friendship ethic for the
relational landscape of the early twenty-first century.

Friendship in other relationships

Gay men and women have no intrinsic monopoly on these
political possibilities: they are not the only individuals against
which society is biased. Friendship between people of different
race, creed or class may well represent relationships with which a
majority are uneasy and which therefore have social significance.
Moreover, non-institutional but committed ways of relating have
become widespread in western societies and these in turn present
certain challenges to relationships that are set within a traditional
frame.

Anthony Giddens, for example, has coined the term 'pure relationship' to identify not just a type of relationship but a common
characteristic of perhaps most modern relationships: 'It refers to a
situation where a social relation is entered into for its own sake,
for what can be derived by each person from a sustained association with another.' He believes that the pure relationship has
arisen because the social function of marriage has changed: it is
no longer required to secure the future population but has
become an option in the enactment of romantic love. The pure
relationship is also a product of a social change in which people
value an integrity in their relationships based upon trust, an attitude which makes the older economic necessities that underpinned traditional marriage seem outdated if not repugnant. As
Foucault might have put it, the pure relationship has arisen
in part because society has impoverished relational institutions:
couples may not want to marry for many complex reasons but a
perception that the institution is moribund is one of them.

Giddens only mentions friendship in passing in his work,
perhaps aware that it is a notoriously difficult relationship for sociologists to define. Indeed, it seems to me that the pure relationship
is not necessarily synonymous with friendship. For example, the

pure relationship's association with romantic notions of love may actually scupper the evolution of deeper kinds of friendship. If the romantic enactment of marriage is focused on a possessive notion of union – two becoming one – then friendship may be compromised; friendship requires a recognition of the distance as well as the proximity of another self. At the same time, the freedom associated with the pure relationship and the fact that it is entered into for its own sake may provide fertile grounds for friendship; the focus here is not on union but on loving someone for who they are, which according to Aristotle is the essence of friendships of the highest kind.

Two other sociologists, Liz Spencer and Ray Pahl, have addressed the question of friendship in modern relationships head on in their book *Rethinking Friendship: Hidden Solidarities Today*. In part, what they see is an interpenetration of notions of family and friends in people's 'personal communities', making the point that many do not think of family and friends as polar opposites (as if family consisted solely of given relationships, and friends solely of those who are chosen). Spencer and Pahl interpret this using the idea of 'suffusion'; personal communities that incorporate family relationships and wider circles of friends. The personal communities of some individuals conform to strict definitions of family. But, for others, they may be family-based in the sense that friends come to seem like family, or friend-based in the sense that family relationships are thought of as friends. All in all, they conclude that most people's personal communities fall onto one of these types:

1. A friend-like community, where a person depends more on friends than family.
2. A friend-enveloped community, with close relatives at the centre, and a larger group of friends around the family.
3. A family-like community in which family members outnumber friends.
4. Family-dependent – family outnumber friends.
5. Partner-focused, in which a couple keep friends and relatives at a distance.

215

6. Neighbourhood-focused.
7. Professional-dependent.

The return of trust

It is against this background that we can return to the question of regaining a sense of trust in friendship. We explored the notion that the secular reinterpretation of Christianity's unease with friendship was to regard it as a selfish and particular relationship that operates outside, and perhaps even undermines, the best ethical concerns. Spencer and Pahl's evidence that suffusions of family and friends are to be found within personal communities implies that this distrust of friendship is misplaced, because – at the risk of stating the obvious – people do rely on friends and see friendship as part and parcel of a good life. To a degree, then, networks of family and friends are part of the informal and perhaps hidden fabric of an admittedly changing society already: the implication is that friendship needs to be brought in from the cold.

Against this, though, is the subversive nature of friendship which whilst not negative in intent – the aim is to vent the family not undermine it, to extend the ways people love not limit them – is premised on a philosophy that is discontent with the status quo. This may well fuel the sense of distrust in friendship since for all that friendship is critical at a personal level, it may be viewed as destabilising society as a whole. The alarm that feminist and queer ideas can generate is obvious. Alternatively, a conservative point of view will see the spread of Gidden's pure relationship, for example, as wilful and indulgent, not liberated, a notion that is, say, detrimental to the raising of children who require commitment beyond the couple's own interests, not relationships entered into for their own sake. There's no doubt much in that concern.

But if friendship is so important to people, as it clearly is, then how might it be supported in society, and how might its contribution to a richer understanding of human relationships be nurtured? Might it be, say, productive to reinvent institutions of committed friendship, much like the medieval sworn brothers and sisters?

You could argue that contemporary attitudes towards marriage and cohabitation are already re-embracing friendship. Individuals may think of their marriages as founded primarily on friendship, and if they do not get married that may well be because they want their relationship to be one of friendship, which they see the old institution as undermining. Indeed, it is in way remarkable that, for all the liturgical changes embraced by Christian churches, the marriage service still contains no explicit reference to friendship. There must be a reason for that. One can speculate that friendship, with its ambiguities on the one hand and subversive associations on the other, is thought too fragile or fraught to form the fundamental unity of society. Or, to put it in terms we've used, it is still distrusted.

The same thing can be said of the new legislation recognising gay marriages and civil partnerships. They are conceived of in terms of extending the legal benefits of marriage to couples whose personal relationships otherwise miss out. It is true that they are a recognition of the relationships of same-sex citizens – in the words of Jacqui Smith, the former British Minister for Equality, 'The Civil Partnership Act sends a clear message that we value and support the contribution committed same-sex couples make to each other and to our society.' However, none of the acts being discussed by various governments is framed in the context of friendship or uses the language of friendship, as far as I know. Rather, civil partnerships are conceived of as extensions of civil rights and thus are strictly legal entities, really no more than contracts. There is not, or at least not yet, any new institution of friendship. Moreover, in the few years that gay marriage has been a possibility in some countries, it seems that the predominant model upon which people are drawing is one of old-style marriage, rather than any new possibility for friendship. And when you make the case that civil partnerships may represent an opportunity for friendship to be publicly celebrated in western society once more, as I should say I've tried to do, the argument appears to fall on deaf ears. It's an uncompromising demand for mono-chrome equality that most gay activists want, not the diversity of relational opportunities that our medieval forebears apparently enjoyed.

There is another kind of contemporary social friendship worth considering too, namely civic friendship – something closer to Aristotle's model of a city and community that is based upon a mutual concern for one's fellows. It's a more difficult thing to assess. At one level, it is clear that there is such a thing as civic friendliness. One only needs to think of the wide variety of charities and NGOs that are concerned with the quality of other people's lives. They work, in part, by promoting networks of concerned individuals, from business, government and other organisations like the church. The relationships that evolve out of this concern are often based on certain types of friendship and certainly promote friendliness. But valuable though this may be, can we say any more than that vis-à-vis friendship?

First, a brief reminder of what civic friendship has meant. The basis of it was a positive regard for friendship as constitutive of society. For Aristotle, civic friendship was therefore a concern shared between citizens for each others' wellbeing, a result of the city-state nurturing life in two senses. One was the provision of the means for feeding oneself, defending oneself, and so on. The other addressed the deeper aspect of humanity's aspirations as a spiritual animal, namely, that of not only wanting to live, but to live well. This is what he meant by civic friendship: the shared desire in a city-state for the good life.

In the Middle Ages, a related kind of civic friendship obtained. It perhaps gained its clearest expression in the institution of sworn friendship. This existed in various forms over a long period of time, and made a link between the personal commitment of two individuals and their social lives. At one level, it provided a com-plementary set of personal links alongside the web of relations focused on the extended household, and, at another, it con-tributed to the formation of medieval society by making for affinities in addition to those of family or fiefdom.

What these two periods of history show is that for civic friendship to flourish, society must have a place for it. In ancient Greece, that receptiveness was manifest in a long tradition of concern about what friendship was and how it might be nurtured, demonstrated by everything from the statues they placed in their public squares to the books written by philosophers. In the Middle Ages, civic friendship found a place because social institutions were inclusive enough to embrace it; marriage and feudal ties were inter-, over- and under-woven with bonds of friendship. So, it seems that there are good grounds for suggesting that contemporary, western society is limited on two critical fronts.

First, modern democracy has rich mechanisms for looking after citizens' wellbeing in an economic sense – that is, life in terms of staying well, staying alive, staying safe. But it flounders when it comes to the kind of wellbeing of which Aristotle's friendship was a sign. Possibilities for civic friendship in the full sense are in fact rather squeezed. On the one hand, the success of modern economic life arguably leaves less time for friends and for the higher concerns of wellbeing, perhaps even promoting ways of life that can be positively inimical to friendship. As Ray Pahl puts it in an essay entitled 'Friendly Society', for all that some people are looking for friendly families and families of friends, why is it that so many still put the consumption of things over the cultivation of friendship in their pursuit of happiness? As we've seen, in practice we appear to be more in love with work, romance, mobility and ourselves than we are with the love called friendship, for all that many would confess otherwise. The structure of modern life, and the choices that people make in it, demonstrate as much.

On the other hand, although our contemporary cultural life can undoubtedly be rich, it seems that it falls short of the aspirations of the past. Simon Goldhill's *Love, Sex and Tragedy* amply demonstrates the perhaps inevitable 'poverty of cultural ambition' today when set alongside the Great Dionysia of ancient Athens. This 'enabled and fostered participation and self-reflection on the personal, familial, intellectual and political issues of general concern.

Where in the public life of western society could we look for any such equivalent critical and emotional civic engagement?' – though it is hardly surprising that a political culture dominated by management and the market is so lacking.

Second, modern democracy is characterised by a radical separation of the private and the public. For a variety of reasons, as we've seen, friendship has come to be seen as a private concern. We don't really trust it as a form of politics. Hence the reason that when it does infringe on public life, it is regarded as subversive. Remember the political friendship between George W. Bush and Tony Blair. It is widely treated with Disraeli-like scepticism. Even publications like *The Economist*, a keen supporter of Anglo-American relations, carried pictures of the two leaders on its front cover under the headline, 'Wielders of Mass Deception'. Not much of a celebration of amity there. It means that though the notion of the family is changing, and new forms of belonging focused on friendship may be gaining ground, friendship has become socially significant again only in the limited sense that individuals are seeking legal adjustments that better accommodate their personal lives. Thus, civil partnerships are not a sign that friendship is being conceived of as either a quasi-Aristotelian contribution to the good life of citizens or as a medieval-like institution of affection-based bonding. In other words, the contemporary politics of friendship does not unsettle the strict division of public and private.

It is possible that our limited aspirations for friendship are not only all that a large, plural democracy can hope for, but that they are all it *should* hope for. The reason: friendship might actually be destabilising of the representative democracy we enjoy now. The issue here is the dark side of democracy that Aristotle recognised in calling it a deviant constitution. If it can liberate the spirit and encourage participation amongst the masses, it can also turn in on itself when the majority disregards the life of the minority. Mob rule is always a threat, and so perhaps it is better to think of mass democracy as an arrangement made amongst strangers than friends. After all, friendships in practice – particularly political friendships – can readily rest on the hostility shown to common enemies, the notion that my enemy's enemy is my friend, as the philosopher Carl Schmitt's politics of friendship shows. As such, more profound notions of civic friendship today could by hijacked by a reactionary social conservatism and the politics of fear. The ambiguities of friendship raise their head again; it is not without some reason that contemporary politics is wary of it.

The Spirituality of Friendship

> 'Of the things which wisdom provides for the blessedness of one's whole life, by far the greatest is the possession of friendship.'
>
> Epicurus

Spirituality is something of a buzz word. As Jeremy Carrette and Richard King argue in *Selling Spirituality: the Silent Takeover of Religion*, it is a concept that, first, has become highly individualised – it's about 'me' and 'my' quality of life – and, second, has been adopted by organisations from car manufacturers to art galleries, with churches laying claim somewhere in between, whose primary aim is commercial – increasing audiences and shifting products.

The spirituality of friendship is similarly something to be rather sceptical about, at least at first. If asked what it might mean probably the most common answer would have to be soul friendship. But the idea of soul friendship is one almost irredeemably 'taken-over' by maudlin, marketable associations too. Type 'soul friends' (or even worse 'soulmate') into an internet search engine and some of the most syrupy aphorisms on friendship will be returned for your edification: 'A soulmate is someone who has locks that fit our keys', 'You are my fire, my titanic ocean', etc. The search will also throw up hundreds of dating agencies, websites promoting relationships with 'celebrity soulmates', and others that proffer advice on things like 'soulmate health'. Such is the commercial value of the notion that one electronics manufacturer has named its MP3 music player SoulMate.

The trouble with this sentimental haze and commodification is that it cheapens an idea of enormous human value: the spirituality of friendship is not something that can simply be ceded to the market. It must be recovered because it captures the attitude best able to negotiate the ambiguities of friendship we have discussed, and make friendship nothing less than a way of life.

The first thing to do is to expose the spiritual veneer of the friendship of the marketplace. Consider again, the Aristotelian conception of the friend as another self. The very ambivalence of the phrase is indicative of a characteristic that is key to any significant spirituality of friendship. 'Another self' captures both the intimacy of close friendship in conveying the idea that this friend is another person like yourself; to discover such a person is to discover someone who at least some of the time mirrors your own thoughts, beliefs and feelings – someone with whom the apparently intractable distance between human beings collapses until it is vanishingly small. And the phrase also includes the vital qualifier that, for all the closeness, soul friends still recognise that they are separate individuals. Each is 'an other self' to the other. Unlike Narcissus who looked in the mirror and saw only himself, the source of the delight of soul friends is that they recognise not only themselves but another human being. 'The essence of friendship lies, I suggest, in the exercise of a capacity to perceive, a willingness to respect, and a desire to understand the differences between persons,' said the philosopher Richard Wollheim. Friends may share an intensity of feeling for each other, including joys and sorrows – 'I am happy because she is happy', 'I am sad when he is sad' – alongside successes and failures: they bask in each other's reflected glory, or languish in each other's mistakes. But they never seek to consume each other or fall into a perpetual embrace.

This is one aspect of spiritual friendship that the marketplace conveniently overlooks: its sentimentalisation of soulmateship arises by conflating that with the union to which romantic love aspires, a trope which commercially plays much better than advocating difference. The human value of the former, and the cash value of the latter, is illustrated in the way soul friends behave and lovers are portrayed. Soul friends' qualified need of each other, in the sense of respecting each others' individuality, means that they do not mind being physically apart for periods

223

of time. Screen lovers, however, spend the whole time that they are apart yearning for the moment when they will be reunited – and when they are together, they are haunted by fears that they may not be together forever. Alternatively, soul friends understand one another to the extent that they trust one another implicitly: when they befriend others, if to a lesser degree, the seeds of jealousy are not sown between them. Screen lovers, though, cannot in general even countenance a wandering eye, quickly detecting betrayal and the promiscuity of desire.

Deep respect. Implicit trust. No distorting neediness. Even a first look at soul friendship shows that it is nothing if not an exceptional state. Aristotle implied that it could only form between certain individuals. He argued that if someone is not at peace with themselves, virtuous in their habits, attitudes and passions, and honestly conscious of their own self-worth to such an extent that they can get over themselves, they will not be able to befriend themselves, let alone another. He is surely right. The rarity of soul friendship does not imply that connection and belonging may not be found in other more common relationships, just that they are not necessarily of the same quality. For example, many find a tremendous sense of belonging in a partner, others in their families, both representing profound bonds: husbands and wives, boyfriends and girlfriends share a jealous love, and family ties can arguably never be wholly eradicated. The point is that they are not necessarily bonds of friendship – indeed, they may be exploitative or oppressive. To put it another way, friendship is not the fundamental human relationship, though any acquaintance, partnership, association, marriage or relationship of blood or love may be friendly, to greater or less degrees. Rather, friendship is something that may grow from them, on occasion perhaps to share features of the closest friendships.

Timing and exceptionality

Michel de Montaigne, who we briefly met before, is particularly illuminating on this scarcer type of amity. His argument is that because the individuals capable of soul friendship are so rare, then soul friendship itself will be even rarer; a frequency of about once every three centuries was his estimate. Unsurprisingly, he regarded his friendship with La Boëtie as the winning million to one shot, certainly grounds for questioning the low odds he gives everyone else. However, if his estimation does seem exaggerated it also serves a purpose. It highlights the exceptional value of the friendship to him and carries the more general implication not so much that soul friendship is literally rare but that when it does come about it feels to the friends as if it cannot possibly be matched. There is something about such intimacy that seems unique; its worth seems inimitable and hardly communicable to others.

So what then is it? It is not primarily characterised as other kinds of relationships might be, nor as other friendships – say in relation to a project done in common or a passion that is shared. Soul friendship is fundamentally the unrepeatable experience of knowing, and being known, by that one, particular person. Conveying what this is like is as impossible as describing

Figure 16: 'In everything we were halves.' (Michel de Montaigne)

the experience of thinking; it can only be experienced by doing it, by living it. Other people may be able to view and sense some of the effects of soul friendship, which is partly why it can be confused with falling in love or conflated with sentimental romance. But the only way truly to know of such friendship is from the inside. Montaigne again:

> If you press me to say why I loved him I feel that it cannot be expressed except by replying: 'Because it was him: because it was me.' Mediating this union there was, beyond all my reasoning, beyond all that I can say specifically about it, some inexplicable force of destiny.

However, for all that it felt like a 'force of destiny', the circumstances that provided such fertile grounds for the friendship between Montaigne and La Boëtie are not so elusive. Happenstance was key to its formation; timing was everything. The fact is that the historical period in which they lived made them natural allies, so one can say something of how it comes about.

Montaigne admits as much when he explains how the two knew of each other before they met. The most obvious aspect of the common ground between them was that they were both committed humanists in an age when to be religiously unorthodox was dangerous. Montaigne was a close associate of the Protestant King of Navarre, who became the Catholic monarch Henri IV when he married Margot de Valois just before the infamous St Bartholomew's Day massacre. This meant that he had many enemies, and prudence in his public pronouncements was nothing short of a matter of life and death. Alternatively, his dedication to the classical author Plutarch, whose *Lives* he called his breviary, could easily have been reason enough for him to be targeted by fanatics. La Boëtie ran similar risks. He was the author of a treatise called *On Willing Slavery*, a controversial analysis of the religious hegemony of the times that led to him being accused of republicanism. So charged was this aspersion that in his essay on their friendship, Montaigne found it necessary to defend his friend by watering down his republican convictions with assertions of his respect for the Christian laws of the land. Montaigne had read La Boëtie's treatise before they met, and that is how he came to his attention.

When they did meet, it was therefore almost to be expected that they would fall into a friendship based upon the relief of being able to share their passionate nonconformity. Montaigne indicates the joy of having such a confidant when he says, 'not only did I know his mind as well as I knew my own but I would have entrusted myself to him with greater assurance than to myself'. He is not just talking about the emotional trust that existed between them but the trust he placed in someone whose betrayal could have forfeited his life. That possibility, Montaigne says, was as unthinkable between them as killing their own children. He would have been in sympathy with Dante who put Brutus in the lowest circle of Hell for betraying his friend rather than his country.

So circumstance and timing were necessary conditions for the birth of their friendship. But that is true of any friendship: it is not a sufficient condition for the depth of the soul friendship that subsequently emerged. So another element to add to the alchemy that made their friendship exceptional is not just that they lived in exceptional times but also that they were exceptional individuals: as human beings they met the conditions for close friendship that Aristotle identified. A combination of historic circumstances, good timing and human character is, then, what makes for soul friendship.

There is one final characteristic of soul friendship that Montaigne draws attention to. As it turned out, his friendship with La Boëtie was short lived. La Boëtie died four years after they met. Montaigne experienced his death as a severe loss, and he saw it as a pivotal episode in the transformation of his life. The relatively brief length of their friendship therefore serves as a final way of interpreting soul friendship's exceptionality: it does not just mean that it may be only for a chosen few, but more importantly that, if it is known, it is an exceptional experience in the context of any life taken as a whole. It might be said that only some friendships have the qualities necessary to exhibit the characteristics of soul friendship, and then only from time to time – rather like the occasions when feigning in friendship gives way to moments of truth.

So the story of Montaigne and La Boëtie's friendship draws attention to the various contingencies that must come together for two people to form a soul friendship: character and circumstance in particular make for its exceptionality and inimitability. But even if we think that these conditions allow for such friendship more often than once every 300 years – perhaps interpreting Montaigne's exaggeration as conveying the sense that any individual lifetime allows only one or two exceptional relationships – the implication is still that the friendship enjoyed by most individuals, for much of the time, will not attain friendship's greatest potential, or know its deepest loves. In other words, the really difficult question with regards to soul friendship is not what it is and how it comes about: the conditions for its emergence are relatively straightforward, though that does not make it any more likely; it is also pretty clear how it differs from other sorts of friendship, though the experience of soul friendship can only be fully comprehended by soul friends themselves. The harder and perhaps more pressing question for most, much of the time, is quite simply how to live without it.

This was not Montaigne's concern. He thought he'd had it. It was, though, the interest of another essayist of friendship, the American philosopher Ralph Waldo Emerson. He concurred with the basic insight: 'Friendship may be said to require natures so rare and costly, each so well tempered and so happily adapted, and withal so circumstanced, that its satisfaction can very seldom be assured.' He also recognised the sense in which a friend is another self, namely at once as familiar as you are to yourself and as strange too: 'Let him not cease an instant to be himself. The only joy I have in his being mine, is that the *not mine* is *mine*.' That you are simultaneously entirely comfortable with a close friend, and yet still conscious of wanting to know them better, is what makes for the expansiveness of friendship, the way it encourages you to forget yourself and discover, first, another human being and, then, the world aside from your own world. Only a friend like you, and unlike you, provides such an invitation, makes for such excitement.

The difference between Emerson and Montaigne is that Emerson did not claim to have experienced friendship in all its fullness. Rather he believed that he could imagine what it would be like in some of the closer friendships he did have: 'I have never known so high a fellowship as others. I please my imagination more with a circle of god-like men and women variously related to each other and between whom subsists a lofty intelligence.' He does not therefore celebrate the exceptionality of soul friendship as Montaigne does, but seeks instead a more practical, day-by-day account of a life lived in friendship, and yet still hoping for the best. This is what makes him our man here, the last of our wise guides on our journey through the perils and promise of friendship.

Telling it slant

Emerson belonged to the school of American philosophy called New England Transcendentalism. What these individuals had in common was the conviction that the divine could be discerned in everything, that nature was symbolic of deeper realities, and that a strong character was key to throwing off the deceptions of conformity, tradition and mere appearances. Their method was very much one of engagement. They met, published articles and gave speeches in order to progress along what they saw as a kind of spiritual journey, informed by poets and philosophers. Times of solitude were part of this exchange too. Emerson himself lived for many years in a peaceful, rural town outside Boston suitably called Concord.

His essays can be thought of as philosophical sermons: in his early adult life he had been a Unitarian preacher. They are provocative reflections, rather than analytical discourses, designed to unsettle, inspire and exhort. Mary Oliver describes their effect well:

> The best use of [them] bends not toward the narrow and the absolute but to the extravagant and the possible. Answers are no part of it; rather it is the opinions, the rhapsodic persuasions, the ingrafted logics, the clues that are to the mind of the reader the possible keys to his own self-quarrels, his own predicament. This is the crux of Emerson, who does not advance straight ahead but wanders to all sides of an issue; who delivers suggestions with a kindly gesture; who opens doors and tells us to look at things for ourselves.

This commentary on his writing is worth quoting because it also conveys his idea of friendship, and we might suppose the attitude he had towards soul friendship: in Emily Dickinson's phrase, it is found 'in circuit'. So he rejoices more in opinions, persuasion and clues than in narrow and absolute convictions; he wanders, thinks kindly, and opens doors through which he and his readers can look together. He devoted one essay solely to friendship, and it too is not merely an abstract account of the characteristics of amity but in its style and approach evokes the dynamics of the friendships he formed within the transcendentalist circle. This is important for the spirituality of friendship that he wants to convey; it is not like a mathematical formula that can be simply read off the page but must be inhabited by the reader. Again, it's an art, not a science.

We can get a sense of that here by coming to the essay via arguably the most famous of Emerson's friendships, the one he shared with Margaret Fuller. They met when Fuller visited the Emerson household for three weeks in the summer of 1836. He was 33 and did not take to her at first, commenting in his journal on her extreme plainness, distracting eye movements and nasal voice. However, her mind won him over:

> She has the quickest apprehension and immediately learned all we knew and had us at her mercy when she pleased to make

us laugh. She has noble traits and powers and cannot fail of a permanent success.

Strangely though, their friendship developed an uneasy under-current – some have said a fault – that resulted from an imbal-ance in their affections. He deeply respected her intellect but she was put off by his apparent emotional coolness towards her.

It is easy to read this as some kind of psychological defect in Emerson: he had already remarried once after the death of his first wife, and perhaps feared losing the affections of another woman. Even so, he did not reject her. Far from it. He invited her to attend meetings of the transcendentalist circle to which she contributed so much that he then asked her to edit their journal *The Dial*. Then, 12 years after their first meeting, Fuller went to Italy. When, two years later, the ship on which she was returning was disas-trously hit by a hurricane and wrecked within sight of Fire Island, killing her, Emerson was grief-struck and showed it; he begged that the wreckage be searched for personal effects, anything by which to remember her, though none were found.

His essay on friendship was written before this disaster but expresses his feelings towards her, I think, when he talks of friends 'going to Europe'. He admits he will have languid moods and will regret 'the lost literature of your mind, and wish you were by my side again'. He will feel robbed for a while of some joy. However, he is consoled by the thought that he will be repaid later with more, and that the spiritual tie he seeks in friendship is far stronger than that offered by romantic love and physical proxim-ity. And anyway, Europe is hardly a destination likely to keep anyone for ever, he thinks, being only an 'old faded garment of dead persons'.

The tragedy is that it was not Europe that stole Fuller from him but the storms of the American Atlantic coast. His essay carries lines that almost seem to have foreseen this disaster: 'Ah! Seest thou not, O brother, that thus we part only to meet again on a higher platform, and only be more each other's because we are more our own?' Therefore, it is wrong, I think, to put Emerson's lack of a soul friend down to an inability to connect emotionally. Something more subtle is going on, something about the spirituality of friendship and the very possibility of soul friendship that his essay provokes us to ponder and reflect on ourselves.

Mere friendship

It begins by celebrating the little wells of friendliness that are to be found in many parts of life: 'We have a great deal more kindness than is ever spoken.' This is particularly clear when it comes to the affection individuals routinely show to complete strangers. If, for example, we welcome a stranger into our house, it is possible to show them a wealth of hospitality, conviviality and generosity that we might never have agreed to give in advance. Moreover, we receive back from them the blessing of their acquaintance as a result. However, there are certain conditions attached to such mere friendliness, for it is quickly scuppered if the stranger oversteps the mark: if he 'intrude[s] his partialities, his definitions, his defects into the conversation, it is all over'. The risk is that affront and then familiarity breed contempt. In other words, though friendliness bathes the human family with 'an element of love like a fine ether', it is also as thin; disturb it with even a slight current of indignity and it disperses like smoke.

Much of the essay describes such thin friendship, shared in pleasant enough but ephemeral relationships. Emerson sounds quite Nietzschean: even relatively good friendships can be buffeted by 'baffled blows', 'sudden, unseasonable apathies', 'epilepsies of wit and of animal spirits', he says. Such subtle antagonisms begin to play on the friendship and turn its 'poetry into stale prose'; 'in the golden hour of friendship we are surprised with shades of suspicion and unbelief'. This can be distressing and, in response, many are tempted to overestimate even obviously weak friendships. They prefer to be in denial of friendship's pains and disappointments than admit that these and perhaps most friendships are woven of 'cobwebs not cloth', of 'wine and dreams', not the 'tough fibres of the heart'.

Others aim at the petty benefits of friendship; they are cherry-pickers in the business of friendship, going for the quick wins and low-hanging fruit, rather than waiting for the deeper friendship that 'many summers and many winters must ripen'. In a similarly horticultural vein, Emerson notes that it is only natural to want to pick the beautiful flowers thrown up by the majority of friendships, and to hope that the wiry roots buried in the damp, dark soil of another's character, soul or mind do not come with them. Nature provides another way of analysing this predicament: 'Is it not that the soul puts forth friends as the tree puts forth leaves, and presently, by the germination of new buds, extrudes the old leaf?' Rotation is a law of human relationships as much as a law of nature.

What is the problem with friendship? Why is it in general so readily altered and so rarely simply true? The fundamental reason is again familiar from Nietzsche:

> Every man alone is sincere. At the entrance of a second person, hypocrisy begins. We parry and fend the approach of our fellowman by compliments, by gossip, by amusements, by affairs. We cover up our thought from him under a hundred folds.

Later Emerson adds: 'To most of us society shows not its face and eye, but its side and its back.'

So for friendship to grow into something closer, people must first be able to be themselves: 'We must be our own before we can be another's ... There can never be deep peace between two spirits, never mutual respect, until in their dialogue each stands for the whole world.' That this is hard to achieve, as Aristotle and Montaigne pointed out, means that friendship is too often a kind of descent or a compromise: 'What a perpetual disappointment is actual society, even of the virtuous and gifted!' If most friends were to write truly honest letters to each other, Emerson speculates, they would have to confess how often they had failed one another.

233

If Emerson is majoring on the ambiguity of dissimulation, I suspect that his tone would have been similar if he had considered the ambiguity associated with sexuality (hence I suspect the perception that he was aloof towards Fuller – he sought a friendship not an affair) and the ambiguity that derives from a work-like, utility-driven culture (the transcendentalists stood against this, valuing 'useless' things like beauty in nature over and against the commercial milieu of nineteenth-century America). But for all that it might be tempting to derive an overwhelming sense of disappointment towards friendship from this side of his essay, it is not, I think, the final reaction he intended. Emerson did not lose faith in friendship but rather sought to identify what was often compromised in it. His hope is that, in so doing, the superior value of a deeper kind of friendship might become clearer. Such friendship is not of the merely friendly kind, for all that that sociability makes the world pleasant and bearable. Rather, it overcomes the 'thick walls of individual character, relation, age, sex, circumstance'. It is a friendship that deepens lives: 'High thanks I owe you, excellent lovers, who carry out the world for me to new and noble depths, and enlarge the meaning of all my thoughts.'

All in all, Emerson's aim is to derive a positive attitude from the uncertainties of friendship. It is only by entering into the ambiguities of friendship that its higher possibilities may be discerned; it is only then that the weaknesses of character and the contingencies of time that would inhibit it are overcome. His essay is an exercise in sifting the wheat from the chaff, and treating the matter of friendship with what he calls the 'roughest courage'.

'To do without it'

This is good advice: it takes courage to acknowledge that shallower friendships, though pleasant, are only cursory, and that deeper friendships because they are real need not be handled with kid gloves but can cope with the rougher, tougher exchanges of transformative, significant relationships: 'they are not glass threads or frost-work, but the solidest thing we know'. It is also key to a practical spirituality of friendship – 'friendship, like the immortality of the soul, too good to be believed' – to which he is now in a position to turn.

He does not actually use the phrase soul friendship. His transcendentalist language prefers the phrase 'divine friendship', perhaps echoing some of the earlier Christian writers who came to feel that God is friendship. Emerson himself has a pantheistic idea of God. The divine is not above but is found within the people and things around him: 'My friends have come to me unsought. The great God gave them to me', he says. So soul friendship is therefore divine in two senses. First, it shows a god-like honesty of mind. Second, it enjoys a god-like honesty of affection. This is what he imagines soul friendship is like. Consider these aspects in turn.

A god-like honesty of mind exhibits itself as a truthfulness between individuals that is uncompromised and unmediated: 'Who hears me, who understands me, becomes mine – a possession for all time'; 'A friend is a person with whom I may be sincere. Before him I may think aloud.' It can indeed be characterised as like those rare encounters in which dissimulation, second-guessing what someone wants to hear, and even courtesy for courtesy's sake, are dropped. Then people deal with each other in simplicity and wholeness: 'A friend is a sane man who exercises not my ingenuity, but me.'

In his essay, Emerson does not just stick to lofty phrases but illustrates what he imagines such friendship to be like in practice. This is doubly informative because the occasion he turns to is not with an intimate such as Fuller, but refers unexpectedly back to the time when he was still working as a preacher. He was a minister in the Second Church (Unitarian) in Boston for three years, having graduated from Harvard Divinity School in 1829. He left the church at the age of 29 because he experienced a vocational change of heart: he came to believe that holy communion was not sacramental. Such a theological change profoundly undermines the role of a minister whose vocation revolves around the administration of the sacraments, and unsurprisingly it was not something his congregation readily understood or liked. However, they did respect his forthrightness – his honesty – and it is for this reason that he came to remember the departure as one of friendship: it had been a moment of god-like truthfulness with the congregation. Further, that he shared this with his congregation again underlines his point: as any minister of religion will tell you, concern with things divine is a rarity compared to the daily grind of indulging a congregation's 'whims of religion and philanthropy', as Emerson himself put it.

In fact, his congregation did at first think him mad, apparently linking his apparent loss of faith to the loss of his wife. But as they listened they came to understand him better, a testament to his desire for truthfulness: 'To stand in true relations with men in a false age is worth a fit of insanity, is it not?' It was therefore an intimation of soul friendship.

The second aspect, honesty of affection, must similarly cut through much 'mush of concession'. The ambiguity that causes the difficulty here is that people are tied to each other in all sorts of ways – by blood, pride, fear, hope, money, lust, hate, admiration – but rarely by love alone. To be able to offer another tenderness as a result of pure love and not some more compromised affection is to achieve a blessed state indeed: 'When a man becomes dear to me I have touched the very goal of fortune.'

Emerson is interesting in the way he chooses to expand on this quality of soul friendship too because he again suggests that it is best glimpsed in utterly practical and perhaps unexpected ways. He says there is something more emotionally honest in friendship with 'ploughboys' and 'tin-peddlers', in the shared frivolity and rides – today we could add friendship in chat rooms or pubs – than there is in a pretence of high friendship with more 'learned acquaintances'. His point is that friendship must plant its feet on the ground 'before it vaults over the moon', and friends must learn to be good citizens to one another before they are 'cherubs'. If they do not, then their so-called divine love will risk revealing itself as a token wrapped up in sentimental affection. Such friends exchange gifts, offer loans, pretend at good neighbourliness, and so on, for the benefit it brings them, not in the hope of genuine relationship itself.

By way of illustration, and no doubt recalling its worst excesses, he contemplates that great institution of middle-class friendliness, the dinner party.

> Why insist on rash personal relations with your friend? Why go to his house, or know his mother and brother and sisters? Why be visited by him at your own? Are these things material to our covenant? Leave this touch and clawing. Let him be to me a spirit. A message, a thought, a sincerity, a glance from him, I want, but not news, or pottage. I can get politics and chat and neighbourly conveniences from cheaper companions. Should not the society of my friend be to me poetic, pure, universal and great as nature itself?

Nietzsche could not have composed a wittier aphorism when Emerson wrote: 'Are you a friend of your friend's buttons, or of his thought?'

It is almost as if Emerson envisages three broad categories of friendship. One is common, mundane and passing, though warm-hearted, honest within its own limits, and friendly as a result. Another is rare, 'divine', and demands a searching integrity and immediacy of encounter. This is the sort that may even on occasion be called soul friendship, though more often is experienced in the best moments of good friendship. In between the two lies a third and arguably the worst: friendship that hopes or pretends it is more but ultimately rests on a wish or facade. There will almost certainly be movement between the different types. But it is particularly in admitting to the existence of the third group of friends that the right attitude towards soul friendship is found. The temptation is to think or hope that these ones are more than they are. But fooling yourself of that is actually to plump for less.

This is, therefore, the key to the spirituality of friendship: 'The condition which high friendship demands is the ability to do without it.' Paradoxically, soul friendship is not best sought by striving for it. The best thing to do is, in a sense, to forget it and practise truthfulness instead – honesty in oneself, towards others, and in any friendship that arises. As truthfulness is something that must be practised and is rarely perfected, this is another way of expressing the rarity of soul friendship.

To put it another way, the best stance to adopt to be open to the potential in friendship is in hope – to live expectantly though with the expectation that it will never be wholly realised or experienced unalloyed. Perhaps, in fact, all love is like this: when you tell someone you love them – in an erotic relationship as in a friendship – you love, in part, that which you don't yet know, and that which you hope might be disclosed to you. Alexander Nehamas has reflected that beauty – the thing which we see in someone we want to know, whether in their face or in their soul – 'points to the future, and we pursue it without knowing what it will yield.' He continues: 'Beauty inspires desires without letting me know what they are for.' Or we might say that to love someone is the promise, but only the promise, of happiness. Even Montaigne only had a soul friend for a short while; even he had to reconcile himself to the reality of normal life when La Boëtie died.

This is not so odd or fatalistic as it may first seem. For example, it is very similar to what is often said about happiness: the thing that kills it is wanting it; but living as if happiness were not the goal of life actually makes for it. (Not that such a neat summary makes the actual living any easier.) For many, like Aristotle, happiness is friendship, at least in part, so, in the same way that most people keep faith with happiness when they do not have it, Emerson advocates never losing faith in the highest aspirations of friendship. 'I awoke this morning with devout thanksgiving for my friends, the old and the new,' he writes. And again: 'I chide society, I embrace solitude, and yet I am not so ungrateful as not to see the wise, the lovely and the noble-minded, as from time to time they pass my gate.' This paradox is not meant to decry close friendship. It is designed to provoke a recognition of the everyday limitations of friendship, and ultimately of being human – limitations that are never more keenly felt than in encounters with others. It provokes the development of an ethos, a spirituality of friendship, that makes for the possibility that these limitations may on occasion be overcome.

The brilliance of Emerson's wandering essay is that its oscillations between high ideals and lower reality precisely reflects the possibility of something more in friendship; it mirrors what friendship is like in life. For most of the time friendship exists within the limits of its inherent ambiguities, but sometimes, if only fleetingly, it shows itself to be capable of much more.

A number of Emerson's aphorisms resonate with these moments of transcendence:

> Let him be to thee for ever a sort of beautiful enemy, untamable, devoutly revered, and not a trivial conveniency to be soon outgrown and cast aside.

> [Friendship] treats its object as a god, that it may deify both.

At other times he adopts an eschatological tone to capture the promise:

> Let the soul be assured that somewhere in the universe it should rejoin its friend, and it would be content and cheerful alone for a thousand years.

> The higher the style we demand of friendship, of course the less easy to establish it with flesh and blood ... But a sublime hope cheers ever the faithful heart, that elsewhere, in other regions of the universal power, souls are now acting, enduring and daring, which can love us and which we can love.

> Leave to the diamond its ages to grow, nor expect to accelerate the births of the eternal.

The 'rougher courage' required for this attitude towards friendship is similarly expressed. For example, Emerson can say that he does not fear the times when he is not with a close friend, or the times when such friendship is absent in the relationships he has, because the spiritual nature of the connection once made is no less vivid for not being currently present: 'my relation with them is so pure that we hold by simple affinity'. Alternatively, the long days or moments of relative loneliness, when life is felt to be humdrum and full of longing, should be thought of as preparation for the moment of true friendship: 'Happy is the house that shelters a friend! It might well be built, like a festal bower or arch, to entertain him a single day.' And, Emerson adds, even if the longing for soul friendship is ultimately unrequited, it will still enlarge the soul: 'It never troubles the sun that some of his rays fall wide and vain into ungrateful space, and only a small part on the reflecting planet.'

The spirituality of friendship is therefore dynamic; it moves from below up. It does not posit a high ideal of friendship as if it were

Figure 17: 'I hate the prostitutions of the name of friendship to signify modish and worldly alliances.' (Ralph Waldo Emerson)

240

merely a goal to achieve, and which if achieved would suggest that the quest was somehow over. After all, friendship itself would come to an end if the desire to get to know another some more ceased. Nor does it analyse the 'low' vicissitudes of friendship solely to reveal the shape and extent of the ambiguities that is the stuff of most relationships, and leave it at that. But, on the assumption that all friendships start from below, it suggests a dynamic process of sifting, discernment, patience, personal struggle and gratitude – sometimes moving up, sometimes sliding down – that opens up the possibility for some friendships to aspire to and realise the best.

And when life is lived less than fully – 'I have often had fine fancies about persons which have given me delicious hours; but the joy ends in the day; it yields no fruit. Thought is not born of it; my action is not modified' – the ability to do without it is not without its consolations either. Two stand out.

First, a high, dynamic doctrine of friendship will tend to value all kinds of friendship and refuse to allow any one to remain as 'mere' friendship. Rather, because such an attitude demands much of friendship, the result is that many good friendships are likely to be enjoyed. This is what is meant when we say someone has a gift for friendship: not that they necessarily have a soul friend but that they value friends.

Second, should it come about, soul friendship is not something that only benefits the individuals when actually possessed. Rather, when momentarily or over time two people form a connection unsullied by the usual ambiguous affections of life, free of the complexities of feigning, it is something that potentially stays with them for ever. We say that a connection has been made – 'we connected' – and the remembrance of that is in some ways as important as the moment itself. It is enough. As Menander once commented: 'A man is happy if he has merely encountered the shadow of a friend.'

241

Friendship Beyond Self-help

'The bird a nest, the spider a web, man friendship.'
William Blake

We have searched through the philosophical tradition and other cultural resources to illuminate the perils and promise of friendship. I have had Tom Stoppard's comments in mind, when, reflecting on the romp that is his play *Jumpers* in a radio interview, he said:

> The area of moral philosophy [is] an open house for the layman, the non-philosopher, the curious human being because most of the questions which preoccupy professional philosophers are only an elevated more technical version of the kind of question which any sentient human being asks himself or herself while burning the toast.

What's striking, then, is that today, when people ask themselves about friendship – when their curiosity is peaked – they don't generally turn to philosophy. They turn, instead, to self-help. Philosophers must bear much of the blame for that, for philosophy needn't be arid and dry when it comes to the richest and most animating questions we have. But it's not just that by missing out on philosophy we miss out on its insights. Rather, there are good grounds for fearing that when it comes to friendship, the broad characteristics of the self-help tradition may be doing us a profound disservice. It's that concern which will be a good one to end on.

Self-help's fatal flaw

The central problem with self-help books on friendship is this: by placing you yourself at the centre of the universe, as self-help almost invariably does, it treats everyone else in the universe as bit players in the story of your life. Hence friends cease to be other people, who you might know and love as persons in their own right, and are regarded as sources for the various elements that you need in your life – one friend to shop with, another friend to cry with; another again to laugh with, and someone else to rebel with. Friends, in short, as service providers. And as everyone knows, the minute your friends start to feel used, for all that they may otherwise be happy to be useful, is the minute your friendship starts to fall apart.

Hence, self-help books on friendship run a grave risk, namely of destroying friendships. It's a point that seems supported by the evidence. It's 150 years since the self-help genre was born, when Samuel Smiles published his book *Self-Help* in 1859. It was a bestseller. Readers wanted more. It was only a question of time before *How To Win Friends And Influence People* appeared. Only why, one might ask, the retrospective sense of inevitability about the burgeoning self-help industry, today worth billions of dollars. Surely, there's only one explanation. Self-help doesn't really work. People need to keep buying more. If Smiles had been right, there would only have been one self-help book written, his.

There's a related problem. Perhaps the key to a fulfilled life is not to be self-centred but other-centred, to lose yourself in order to find it. That's a common religious sentiment, and it's one attested to by the experience of friendship too. Aristotle has a particularly powerful account of it, when he talks of the friend being another self, the person not just in whom you see yourself reflected but in who you discover yourself. There is no being human on a desert island, anymore than there are such things as solitary ants. The good life is the attempt to live for others in life. As Iris Murdoch has it, love is 'the painful realisation that something other than myself exists'.

This perhaps partly explains why there is no end to self-help books. They are condemned to struggle with this conundrum: the solution they offer – attend to yourself – is actually part of the problem, being self-centred. To be fair, some self-help books realise this. One of the best sellers of all time, *The Purpose Driven Life*, by Rick Warren, opens with the line: 'It's not about you.' Only the rest of the book is entirely about you.

How have we reached this point? What's gone wrong? One key issue is that it's very easy, in the modern world, to become your own project: it's as if there is no other point to life apart from your own interests. To put it another way, we are social animals, and yet much of the time the contemporary environment encourages us to live solipsistic lives. There are many examples of this crux. In fact, once you become aware of it, you start to see it everywhere.

I live in London, and the skyline along the River Thames is dominated by two buildings: the dome of St Paul's Cathedral and the gerkin shape of the Swiss Re skyscraper. They stand out because of their striking curves. And yet those shapes represent two very different views of life. St Paul's is a building designed to hold people and, when congregations assemble under that dome, they look up and are presented with a vision of another world: the celestial heights. The goal of your life is not located in your own life, the dome says: it is to be found outside of yourself. Contrast that with the Swiss Re skyscraper, another building designed to hold people: go in and look up. What you see are mostly just ceiling panels concealing wires and ducts. There is no other world in the gerkin. People are there to work on the project that is their career.

Here's another example that strikes me as I write. It's the month of Ramadan, the period during which Muslims fast. Fasting is, of course, very common in modern society, only usually it is called dieting. And therein lies the difference: fasting is supposed to open you up to a wider view of things; dieting is solely to attend to yourself.

Another very current case concerns environmentalism. The vast majority of scientists agree that climate change is a threat, and that we must alter our behaviour now. However, climate change is not much of a threat to us now, at least those of us who live in the developed world: it's worst will not become apparent for at least a generation or two. In other words, if people are to be persuaded to act for the sake of the environment, they must be persuaded to do it for others, not themselves. That, it seems, is a very hard case to make.

Another example comes from the life of the philosopher John Stuart Mill. He wrote a lot on happiness, not least because in his late teens he had a massive breakdown, even contemplating suicide for a while. He felt there was no way out, until he discovered the poetry of the Romantics, and their rich appreciation of the countryside. Mill realised that his mistake had been to think that he would discover happiness by working on his own life. Now he knew he would not. Rather, as his awakening to the beauty of the natural world around him showed, he had to centre his projects in life on things and people beyond himself. 'Those only are happy who have there minds fixed on some other project than their own happiness,' he wrote.

It is surely no coincidence that once he realised this, and began to pull out of his depression, he formed a powerful friendship with Harriet Taylor. It prompted a virtual paen to the blessings of other-love, of amity, as in his *Autobiography*, he writes:

It was at the period of my mental progress which I have now reached that I formed the friendship which has been the honour and chief blessing of my existence, as well as the source of a great part of all that I have attempted to do, or hope to effect hereafter, for human improvement ... To her outer circle she was a beauty and a wit, with an air of natural distinction, felt by all who approached her: to the inner, a woman of deep and strong feeling, of penetrating and intuitive intelligence, and of an eminently meditative and poetic nature ... Into this circle I had the good fortune to be admitted, and I soon perceived that she possessed in combination, the qualities which in all other persons whom I had known I had been only too happy to find singly ... To be admitted into any degree of mental intercourse with a being of these qualities, could not but have a most beneficial influence on my development;

though the effect was only gradual, and many years elapsed before her mental progress and mine went forward in the complete companionship they at last attained. The benefit I received was far greater than any which I could hope to give ... What I owe, even intellectually, to her, is, in its detail, almost infinite; of its general character, a few words will give some, though a very imperfect, idea.

There's a related problem embedded in Mill's experience, which exposes another facet of the self-help nexus, how it sees the business of love. It too is too focused on the self-interested aspects of loving, missing out how love is actually love of another.

The psychologist, Erich Fromm, provides an excellent analysis of the matter in his book, *The Art of Loving*. When two people meet, he noted, they are, by definition, strangers. If they then suddenly feel close to one another, and the walls between them come down – which is to say they start to fall in love – that leads to what can be possibly the most exhilarating and exciting experience in life. It seems wonderful and miraculous, not least for someone who has for some time being looking for the 'right person', their lost half. Surely this is it, they are bound to ask, or hope. Sexual attraction is the powerful, physical expression of that newfound intimacy. Loneliness appears banished to memory.

However, in Fromm's analysis, falling in love cannot be lasting. It is premised on the meeting of strangers. Once you stop being a stranger to this new person, and they stop feeling delightfully strange to you, the feeling of falling for them, and its exhilaration, will ease off too. What was miraculous starts to feel humdrum. The risk is that disappointment rushes in, quite possibly followed by the resurfacing of irritations and anxieties. They conspire to negate the previous experience. It's easy to assume that if you were falling in love, you've now fallen out of love; the temptation is to call the whole thing off. Your life looks boring again, which is presumably why marketers do not try to sell it to us.

This sets up a paradox though. The passion associated with falling in love is not actually a measure of true love, but rather is a measure of the speed with which you collapsed into the arms of a stranger. At best, falling in love is just one element of love. At worst, it has little to do with love at all – as the notion of 'falling' might suggest. The danger is that individuals become addicted to the thrill of falling in love, much as they might to the heights induced by drugs. Such an individual has a series of relationships, in succession or concurrently, and finds it hard to hold a relationship down. They are living a life of self-centred love affairs, where the determining factor is the pleasure or security or companionship their lover delivers to them.

Standing in love is different. Unlike falling in love, which is premised on the fact that the lovers are still more or less strangers, to stand in love is to love a person because they are as well known to you as you are to yourself. Falling in love becomes standing in love, if it does, when the thrill of the unknown becomes the delight of knowing another and being known by them. It is the love of friendship and whilst it will no doubt not be perfect, it is focused on the other person.

Just how unlike standing in love is compared with falling in love can be gleaned by thinking about the difference between being with individuals who are falling in love and with individuals who are standing in love. The first couple – the new lovers – are typically discomforting to be with. They are so in love with each other that they have little concern for anyone else. It's the lovey-dovey syndrome. It is annoying to have to share an evening with them or sit opposite them on the train. They are so absorbed in each other that they do not notice the rest of the world. You are left out. You feel alone when with them.

Being with people who are standing in love is entirely different. It is a joy. The nicest people to know are those who are in love with each other and who make you feel part of their love. Standing in love bids you welcome too. Such lovers have learnt the art of love with each other and it results in generating a care and concern for others.

Fromm's analysis of the difference between falling in love and standing in love continues in this way. When you fall in love, you want your partner to be faithful to you because if they are not, it threatens you with loneliness again. The lover might leave you, and leave you desolate. This is one source of the possessiveness that love can exhibit. When you stand in love, though, you still want your partner to be faithful to you but not because of any possessiveness. Rather, it is because the relationship has come to represent the trust that ideally exists between all human beings when they relate well to each other. It is an expression of an inclusive love for others, potentially perhaps for all humankind. That, again, might be called friendship. It's a facet of human life that self-help either undermines or at least finds difficult to accommodate.

A mutual scratching of backs

There's a third self-oriented facet of contemporary culture that shapes self-help, and represents a threat to friendship. It's the way in which the worth of everything is assessed by way of a cost-benefit analysis: we are encouraged to do things – like say thank you or smile at strangers – not because it is good to be grateful and friendly but because exhibiting gratitude and friendliness comes with the promise of personal happiness in return. It makes you feel good. It's the morality not of do as you would be done unto, but do because it delivers.

There's a particularly insidious form of this cost-benefit analysis that colours many contemporary discussions of friendship, and focuses on the concept of reciprocal altruism. Reciprocal altruism can be crudely translated as 'if you scratch my back, I'll scratch yours', though it is more sophisticated than that. A discipline within economics, game theory, has provided a fuller account. What the theory shows is that when playing hypothetical games, a successful strategy is one in which individuals act as if in the interests of others. Take the game of tit-for-tat. It turns out that a good way to win is to treat the other players as you have yourself been treated. If another player has cooperated, then cooperation is reciprocated. If not, then cooperation is withheld. Now the tit-for-tat tactic appears to favour the other players, and so appears to be an act in their interest, which is why it has been labelled altruism. But the altruism is only adopted because of the reciprocal element: if it's good for them, it's first good for you. That's why you do it. Game theory propagates the reductive idea that my self-interest is served by pretending to be interested in others. In truth, that's the self-help doctrine in scientific guise.

Incidentally, the individualistic approach to moral behaviour implicit in game theory was not one that Charles Darwin shared, for all that evolutionary theory today goes by the name of Darwinism. He believed that social animals, like human beings, are social to their very core, not that they are essentially selfish and must somehow strap altruism onto their nature. So, in *The Descent of Man*, he rejects the reductive assumption that the foundation of moral behaviour lies in selfishness, and asserts that 'the moral sense is fundamentally identical with the social instincts'. Hence, there is no need for the moral gymnastics implicit in reciprocal altruism and enlightened self-interest. Darwin continues: 'The reproach of laying the foundation of the most noble part of our nature in the base principle of selfishness is removed.' Not that the great man's observations have stopped subsequent evolutionists from impugning human beings with selfish essences, as game theory tends to do, and as self-help tends to build into its fundamental philosophy too.

From that theory a self-help thought follows: if natural selection favours the optimal organisation of personal relationships then maybe we should favour it too. And herein lies the insidious effect that the analysis of reciprocal altruism has upon friendship. It applauds calculation. In the how-to-win-friends world, we should do unto others because it's good for us. Do the cost–benefit analysis.

Defenders of reciprocal altruism attempt to defend its virtue on two fronts. First, they argue that it explains why we make the strangers who surround us 'honorary friends'. That's good, since it makes for a functioning society. Second, they argue that the science supports friendship as a natural tendency, and as such it should be valued. The world may be driven by self-interest, but actually that is no terminal state of affairs: like Adam Smith's invisible hand, much good is the result.

However, I'm not sure this adds up. For one thing, the science itself is highly speculative. Just because game theory and its derivatives comes up with the concept of reciprocal altruism does not mean that many tens of thousands of years ago, when human beings were evolving, tit-for-tat operated on the Savannah. We've already seen how the economists' model of rational economic man is flawed. Perhaps reciprocal altruism is too.

Then there is the cost-benefit ideology itself. Sympathy, even friendship, is a phenomenon that undoubtedly exists in nature, and is not limited to human beings. One of the most important studies of altruism amongst chimpanzees and bonobos has been carried out by Frans de Waal. He has seen these apes perform remarkable acts for one another, and even for different species. It's led him to conclude that whilst they are quite capable of calculation, and understand that generosity pays dividends, the concept of reciprocal altruism is not adequate as an explanation for everything he has observed. Why would an ape help a bird, an act he once saw? Why risk its own death to save a member not of its own kin but of another species?

Behind the selfish imperatives that are deployed as biological explanations, de Waal detects something else at work. We are being hauled into 'a Hobbesian arena in which it's every man for himself, where people show generosity only to trick others. Love is unheard of, sympathy is absent, and goodness a mere illusion,' he writes. De Waal certainly believes that our altruistic instincts are natural. Only they are genuine too. He continues: 'We should be happy that this dark, forbidding place is pure fantasy, that it differs radically from the actual world in which we laugh, cry, make love, and fawn over babies.' The actual world is one in which others can matter for their own sake. The implication is that game theory's cost–benefit analysis is not something read out of nature but into nature.

A related point is that without a prior concept of friendship, it is hard to see how forms of human interaction that are purely instrumental could be thought of as friendship at all. Why would tit-for-tat suggest anything above a contractual arrangement characterised by commitment but indifference? The suspicion is that friendship is being read back into the situations the economists and biologists observe. It is suggested that friendship arises as a kind of excess of feeling: in small groups, as presumably existed in times past, an individual's welfare was so caught up with others that it left a legacy so that even when my welfare now will be compromised by helping you, I will do so. Charity was born and the rest is history. But friendship isn't like that. For one thing, putting anything down to an excess is obfuscation not explanation. For another, it doesn't account for the non-fungibility of friendship: my sense of connection to my friend doesn't become so deep because our mutual welfare becomes so entwined, though it may do; it becomes so deep because it's you, the person who is my friend. No one else will do. Reciprocal altruism misses out on that fundamentally important characteristic of the most humanly significant relationships we have. Or again, there is the fact that human beings do things that are bizarre and inexplicable in the cost–benefit world: greater love hath no man than to lay down his life for a friend. That surely is going too far – only in real life, people value such acts not as irrational and excessive but as inspiring and heroic.

The situation interestingly mirrors Aristotle's categorisation of friendship. The first two types he observed – utility friendships such as those typically found at work, and pleasure friendships such as those shared by people who enjoy doing something together – depend upon the shared activity that is external to the relationship itself. Take away the work, or the enjoyment, and the friendship will stumble too. His third sort of friendship – knowing and loving someone for who they are in themselves regardless of benefit or exchange – is, therefore, the quintessential type, the kind because of which we think of the other types of human interaction as friendship too; they share some of the characteristics of the best. In logical terms, Aristotle's quintessential friendship is prior to the other, lesser types. Those other types can only be thought of as friendship because we have an idea, or a hope, of friendship in its best sense, where there is no exchange or utility but only the delight of knowing another person, and being known by them. The lesson seems to be that we

251

too should value friendship for its own sake if we want to live lives of friendship.

Failing to do that is perhaps why so much self-help on friendship misses out on what Aristotle makes clear as basic: close friendship requires an individual to possess a greater range of qualities than just a fulsome capacity for reciprocal goodwill. It requires a proper sort of self-regard – the kind that allows the individual to get over themselves; and a wider love of life itself – so that the individual is capable of pursuing interests that are not their own.

All in all, the problem with importing a cost–benefit analysis into our accounts of friendship – as the evolutionary explanations do, and as self-help picks up on in response – is that it leads us to treat others as ends to our interests, not as ends in themselves. Friendship requires the opposite, for us to realise that others are persons who should be nurtured for their own sake. We don't need calculation, we need compassion. Aristotle's pithy aphorism comes to mind once more: friends do not put the scales centre-stage.

So what to do, if you want to deepen your capacity for friendship no less? What tips ought one to follow? A better strategy, I'd suggest, is not to seek out some formula for friendship, but is instead to examine it yourself. This is precisely the approach adopted by Aristotle and Plato before him. They were committed to the concept of working on yourself in a pursuit of the good life. 'Know thyself!' was their motto. However, their approach was to seek wisdom, not to-do lists. They envisaged life as an exploration, not a programme. It's the insight I've tried to follow here.

What has been the result? First, we looked at how friendship engages with the utility-obsessed side of our culture, since, for all the good things it brings, the danger is that the law of productivity and consumption holds sway and friendship cannot rise above being instrumental; it risks being always determined by workplace-like demands. If, though, individuals come to like one another for who they are, and not just for what they do, a deeper friendship becomes possible.

When it comes to friends and lovers, friendship's calling is to engage with the complex maelstrom of erotic feelings that can exist between two people and from that to discern a mutually shared passion that moves above the desire for romantic union to the desire to know (not to have) the other person, and be known by them. This higher passion is focused on things beyond the couple. It is, therefore, the same as that shared between friends who are lovers of life. It is sustainable, will grow, and should flourish.

Third, pretty much all friendship knows of the issue of dissimulation – the feigning that is kind, because even virtuous individuals find blunt honesty too harsh all of the time; that is wise, because even discerning individuals can make mistakes when judging others; and that is realistic, for most relationships depend upon a friendliness of measured not mounting affection. Once again, there is a promise that hides behind this peril: dissimulation can give way to honesty given the right circumstances, time and care. Candid friendships can transform a life with truthfulness.

An apparently new environment for friendship is the internet, a place in which genuine amity is shared, and depressing animosity has become a way of life too. Only, the internet is arguably only the latest manifestation of a desire for mobility and connection that has gathered apace since the birth of the modern world. So the older philosophy of friendship still holds in the new world. Remember that screens screen, that friending is not the same as befriending, and that it is quite possible to seek a crowd and feel lonely, not loved.

Then, there is the secular appropriation of Christianity's tendency to distrust friendship as a form of love. This can leave us suspicious of friendship in a way that marginalises and even outlaws it. What makes this particularly complicated is that it is the democratic systems that have given us universal rules and rights, which we rightly value, that are often the ones most antithetical to friendship. There are a number of issues to tease out if the value of friendship is to be revived: the subtle interplay of altruistic and egoistic motives are a major part of that. However, what is also vital is the factor identified by Thomas Aquinas, namely, the need to restore faith in the best sorts of friendship, the insight found in the belief that God is friendship, or in secular guise as the conviction that friendship is fundamentally a form of other love.

The politics of friendship is another kind of struggle. In one mode friendship resists the limiting constraints of inherited social conventions, notably in terms of the dictates of tight notions of family; in another mode it is a protest against individualistic, competitive conceptions of what it is to be human; and in another it is an effort to create new forms of relationship founded upon the freedom of friendships that go against the norm. Friendships may flourish for us in all these contexts.

Finally, I have tried to outline a spirituality of friendship based upon the essays of Montaigne and Emerson. Success is found in circuit, to quote one poet. Or to use Keats's phrase, soul friendship would seem to be a prime candidate for his 'negative capability', that ability to live life without certainty, but with an expectant open-heartedness.

Given that philosophy illuminates the nature, potential and limits of the love called friendship, there is one further, final observation to make. It centres on the figure of Socrates. He has regularly popped up throughout the course of the book. At one level, this is unsurprising; he is nothing if not an emblem of wisdom. But to see his presence here solely as a result of the fact that he is a big-hitter is to miss a more subtle point. For Socrates, I think, philosophy and friendship are ultimately one and the same thing.

According to Plato, Socrates understood the wily ambiguities of erotic love and argued that they should be seized upon as an opportunity to propel lovers along a course to a relationship based upon friendship. He also understood that true friendship is scarce. One may be friends with many, as indeed he was, the outcome of a way of life which took him around the streets of Athens seeking individuals to talk with. The complicating factor for him was that his vocation as a philosopher meant that he did not seek friends to be chummy but to encourage people to understand the errors in their beliefs and the failures of their character – in fact nothing less than the limits of their humanity. Rare is the individual who can embrace a relationship like that, and he was often left isolated, wondering whether he would ever find a true friend. At the same time, he never gave up hope.

Putting it another way, Socrates thought that friends should not primarily hope for happiness in one another, though that might come, but should seek together to live fuller, truer lives. This happens, he believed, when individuals become wise to their ignorance; the wisdom gained when one understands the limits of one's capabilities is of supreme value. It is best gained in discoursing with others, particularly when the exchange is marked by the kind of honesty that can exist between the closest of friends. Then the individuals have the opportunity not only to learn about the limitations of the beliefs that they hold true but also about the flaws in their character and the vulnerabilities of their temperaments. These are, after all, far deeper sources of delusion than mere rational confusion. Thus it is possible, I think, to construe the Socratic way of life as one that puts friendship centre stage. Epicurus, who in many ways followed in the same footsteps, agreed: 'The noble man is most involved with wisdom and friendship.'

Plato's dialogues deploy a number of metaphors and encounters that describe and portray Socrates' approach. Probably the most famous is that of the midwife: he takes his role to be that of one who knows he knows nothing but is committed to asking questions; sometimes his interlocutors 'give birth' to certain insights as a result – 'It is I, with God's help, who deliver them of this offspring [wisdom]', he says in the *Theaetetus*. Alternatively, in the *Meno*, Socrates describes his method by drawing a contrast with the eristic ways of his contemporary philosophical rivals, the sophists: 'If they are friends, as you and I are, and want to discuss with each other, they must answer in a manner more gentle and more proper to discussion.' The implication is that his way of doing philosophy is in part the attempt to form a friendship.

Socratic friendship is also a tough kind of love; it requires the roughest courage. Consider what he says to another character, Callicles, on the purpose of philosophy:

> I think that someone who is to test adequately the soul which lives aright and the soul which does not, needs to have three qualities: knowledge, goodwill and willingness to speak freely

... You [Callicles] would never have agreed with me simply because you did not know better or were too ashamed to admit you did not know, nor to deceive me; for you are my friend, as you say yourself.

As it happens Socrates is speaking ironically, for by the end of the dialogue in which this exchange is recorded, the *Gorgias*, Callicles has betrayed every one of the intimacies that they might have shared. His vanity could not take Socrates' probing enquiry. However, what Socrates says to Callicles reads like a summary of friendship. It includes goodwill and a willingness to speak freely. It does not require individuals to be knowledgeable; rather they must have a passion for wisdom in Socrates' sense. Finally, the most promising candidates for friendship will show themselves to be honest, particularly when it comes to their self-awareness.

So it is not just Montaigne and Nietzsche, Emerson and Aelred who developed a dynamic ethos or spirituality of friendship characterised as the struggle to rise above life's everyday ambiguities. At the origins of western philosophy is the same notion in which, at its best, doing philosophy and becoming friends are one and the same thing. Socratic friendship suggests that at least one conception of philosophy is itself caught up in this same dynamic. Friendship is the desire to know another and be known by them – in Emerson's phrase, they delight as they exclaim to one another, 'Do you see the same truth?' Philosophy is not, therefore, just illuminating of friendship. The very possibility of friendship lies at the heart of philosophy. They come together partly because as Aristotle commented, 'we are better able to observe our friends than ourselves and their actions than our own'. But more so because to truly befriend others is to stare life's uncertainties, limits and ambiguities in the face. To seek friendship is to seek wisdom.

Further Reading and References

Introduction

Ray Pahl's research mentioned here was carried out for the launch of the Blackberry Pearl.

Aristotle's examination of friendship is found in his *Nicomachean Ethics* chapters VIII and IX. A new translation, introduction and commentary by Sarah Broadie and Christopher Rowe published by Oxford University Press (2002) is clear and helpful. All my quotes from Aristotle come from this *Ethics* unless stated. He does discuss friendship elsewhere, notably in the *Eudemian Ethics* which is usually taken to be the main source for the *Nicomachean Ethics*. And also in the *Art of Rhetoric* 6.2.4.

The thought experiment of Nietzsche is from *Human, All Too Human* Volume I, 376.

In writing the new edition of this book, I've been indebted to Alexander Nehamas' Gifford Lectures of 2008, entitled '"Because it was he, because it was I": Friendship and its place in life', available online.

1   Friends at work

The Gallop research was published in Tom Rath's *Vital Friends: The People You Can't Afford To Live Without* (2006).

The Aristotle references are from his *Nicomachean Ethics* chapters VIII and IX.

The Theory of Moral Sentiments, by Adam Smith, is available from a number of publishers and can also be downloaded;

Prometheus Books produce a cheap edition. An academic but readable article, 'Adam Smith on Friendship and Love', by Douglas J. Den Uyl and Charles L. Griswold Jr., can be found in the *Review of Metaphysic* 49 (March 1996): 609–37.

Smith is compared with Ferguson and Hume in Lisa Hill and Peter McCarthy's article 'Hume, Smith and Ferguson: Friendship in Commercial Society', in the excellent book *The Challenge to Friendship in Modernity*, edited by Preston King and Heather Devere and published by Frank Cass (2000).

Friendship at work as an area of research has established quite a niche for itself in many business schools. Geraldine Perreault of the University of Northern Iowa, for example, has written on leadership as friendship.

2   Friends and lovers

Montaigne's essay 'On Friendship' where he discusses his relationship with La Boëtie can be found in any collection of his *Complete Essays*, though Penguin's Great Ideas series includes an attractive publication of it alone, if without introduction.

John Evelyn and Margaret Godolphin's friendship is examined in wonderful detail by Frances Harris in *Transformations of Love*, published by Oxford University Press (2002).

Simon Callow's *Love Is Where It Falls: an Account of a Passionate Friendship* is a highly readable, witty and moving book published by Penguin (1999).

C. S. Lewis's essay on friendship in *The Four Loves* (reissued in HarperCollins Signature Classics edition, 2002) is idiosyncratic and insightful in equal measure.

The quotes from Nietzsche are from *The Gay Science* Book 1, 14.

The classic on Greek homosexuality is Kenneth Dover's eponymous book *Greek Homosexuality* (Duckworth, 1997), though James Davidson's *The Greeks and Greek Love* (Weidenfeld and Nicolson, 2006) has revised the older view in several crucial respects.

There are many discussions of Plato's ideas about love; any introduction to Plato will include one. The translations of the *Symposium* and the *Phaedrus*, by Alexander Nehamas and Paul Woodruff, are engaging with accessible introductions. Martha Nussbaum is an oft-quoted source too: *The Fragility of Goodness* (Cambridge University Press, 1986) contains many illuminating discussions though I think many of her conclusions about Plato have been superceded by studies such as Mary P. Nichols's *Socrates on Friendship and Community* (Cambridge University Press, 2009).

When it comes to Plato on friendship in particular (and his dialogue the *Lysis*) the first chapter of Lorraine Smith Pangle's *Aristotle and the Philosophy of Friendship* (Cambridge University Press, 2003) is an academic examination of the *Lysis*, as is Anthony Price's rich and challenging first chapter in *Love and Friendship in Plato and Aristotle* (Clarendon Press, 1990). For another alternative translation and commentary on the dialogue David Bolotin captures the drama as well as the philosophy – *Plato's Dialogue on Friendship* (Cornell University Press, 1979).

For general philosophical comparisons of love and friendship I enjoyed Allan Bloom's *Love and Friendship* (Simon & Schuster, 1993) and the chapter on love in Andre Comte-Sponville's *A Short Treatise on the Great Virtues* (Vintage, 2003), though I am not sure he gets friendship quite right. Alain de Botton's *Essays in Love* (Picador, 1994) is an excellent novelised portrayal of love that touches on friendship too.

3 Faking it

The quotes from Nietzsche in this chapter come from three books, unless otherwise stated. A more or less complete list of his aphorisms on friendship in this middle period is:

Human, All Too Human Volume I, 354, 368, 376, 378, 390, 406, 499; Volume II, 241, 242, 251, 259, 260.

The Gay Science Book 1, 14, 16; Book 2, 61; Book 4, 279, 328; Book 5, 364, 366; and from the Prelude, Rhymes 14 and 25.

Daybreak Book 4, 287, 313; Book 5, 489.

Ruth Abbey puts them into academic context in her article 'Circles, Ladders and Stars: Nietzsche on Friendship', in *The Challenge to Friendship in Modernity*, edited by Preston King and Heather Devere, published by Frank Cass (2000).

To read more of Kant's view see 'Of Friendship' from *Lectures on Ethics* translated by Peter Heath and J. B. Schneewind, published by Cambridge University Press (1997).

The article by Giorgio Agamben, entitled 'Friendship', is published in the online journal *Contretemps*, 5 (December 2004).

Proust's attitude to friendship is examined in Duncan Large's 'Proust on Nietzsche: the Question of Friendship', *Modern Language Review*, 88/3 (July 1993): 612–24.

For more on Stanley Cavell's thoughts his *Conditions Handsome and Unhandsome: the Constitution of Emersonian Perfectionism* (University of Chicago Press, 1991) is a good place to start.

4   Friending online

An earlier and shorter version of this chapter was published as part of the Institute of Ideas 'Battle of Ideas' weekend in 2007.

David Holmes is an academic at Manchester Metropolitan University interested in psychology and social change, to whom I spoke to gain these statistics.

Sherry Turkle's ideas first appeared in *The Second Self: Computers and the Human Spirit*, published by Simon & Schuster (1984).

Susan Greenfield pursues her fears in *ID: The Quest for Meaning in the 21st Century*, published by Spectre (2009).

David Smallwood made his comments to the journalist Sophie Goodchild, health editor of *The Evening Standard* in an article for the paper published on 22nd October 2008.

Jerald Block's research is published in *The American Journal of Pyschiatry* 165: 306–7, March 2008. The figures for South Korea and China come from the same article.

The research from the University of California was led by Mizuko Ito and announced at the 2008 American Anthropological Association meeting.

The research about losing friends in London comes from YouGov. The reference for the research about similar trends in the US is M. McPherson, L. Smith-Lovin and M. E. Brashears (1996), 'Social isolation in America: changes in core discussion networks over two decades', *American Sociological Review* 71(3): 353–75.

The more positive research, conducted by Hua Wang and Barry Wellman, is in an article entitled 'Social Connectivity in America: Changes in Adult Friendship Network Size from 2002 to 2007', dated 6 June 2009 and forthcoming in the *American Behavioral Scientist.*

5 Unconditional love

Maria Boulding's translation of Augustine's *Confessions* (Hodder and Stoughton, 1997) captures the remarkably modern feel of the autobiography. Peter Brown's classic biography of the saint is called *Augustine of Hippo: a Biography* (Faber and Faber, 1967).

The relevant sections from Kierkegaard's *Works of Love* are usefully collated in *Other Selves: Philosophers on Friendship*, edited by Michael Pakaluk and published by Hackett (1991).

As indeed are the key paragraphs from Thomas's *Summa Theologiae*. For an examination of his philosophy and theology, Brian Davies's *The Thought of Thomas Aquinas* (Clarendon, 1993) is hard to beat.

The Kant lecture is in Pakaluk's book too with an introduction.

John Henry Newman's sermon is in *Parochial Sermons, Volume II*, Sermon V, 'The Feast of St John the Evangelist, Love of Relations and Friends', published by Rivington and Parker (1843).

Alasdair MacIntyre's reflections come from *After Virtue* (University of Notre Dame Press, 1984).

To follow up on Iris Murdoch's idea of the good, see *The Sovereignty of Good* (Routledge, 1970).

Few contemporary Christian writers have sought to reconcile friendship and theology at book length which is itself notable given the ink spilt on divine love. P. Waddell's *Friendship and the Moral Life* (University of Notre Dame Press, 1989) and G. Meilaender's *Friendship: a Study in Theological Ethics* (University of Notre Dame Press, 1981) are two that are often cited. For a latter-day Kierkegaard, see Anders Nygren's *Agape and Eros. Friendship and the Ways to Truth*, by David Burrell (University of Notre Dame Press, 2000), weaves philosophy and faith together. Elizabeth Stuart's *Just Good Friends* (Mowbray, 1995) approaches the issue from a lesbian and gay perspective. Stanley Hauerwas has an article 'Companions on the Way: the Necessity of Friendship', in *The Ashbury Theological Journal* Vol. 45 (1990): 1. My Postscript to Jeremy Carrette's book *Religion and Culture by Michel Foucault* (Routledge, 1999), 'I Am Not What Am', offers a view of friendship through theological eyes.

6 Politics of friendship

David Konstan's *Friendship in the Classical World* (Cambridge University Press, 1997) discusses everything you could want to know about the matter and more.

G. Herman in *Ritualised Friendship and the Greek City* (Cambridge University Press, 1987) is anthropological. Paul Cartledge's *The Greeks: a Portrait of Self and Others* (Oxford University Press, 1993) paints the broader picture.

The Aristotle references are from his *Nicomachean Ethics* chapter VIII and his civic friendship is discussed by Richard Mulgan in his article 'The Role of Friendship in Aristotle's Political Theory', in *The Challenge to Friendship in Modernity*, edited by Preston King and Heather Devere. David Cohen in *Law, Sexuality and Society: the Enforcement of Morals in Classical Athens* (Cambridge University Press, 1991) is fascinating on the place of the household in political friendships.

The longest discussion of friendship in Plato's *Republic* occurs in Book 1 [334b ff], though not directly in relation to the ideal city-state. In the *Laws*, friendship is raised in a variety of contexts, for example, at [693c], [729d], [738d–e], [743c] and [757a].

The surviving texts of Epicurus are available in a number of readers. Suzanne Stern-Gillet brings Epicurean friendship to life, given the limited sources, in an article 'Epicurus and Friendship', in the journal *Dialogue*, 28 (1989): 275–88.

Cicero's dialogue on friendship, *Laelius*, can be found in the Penguin Classics volume *On the Good Life* (translated by Michael Grant, 1971).

Alan Bray's *The Friend* is published by University of Chicago Press (2003). Diarmaid MacCulloch's *Reformation: Europe's House Divided* (Penguin, 2004) discusses changing attitudes to love, family and marriage. John Bossy's *Christianity in the West 1400–1700* (Oxford University Press, 1985) captures the essence and function of the medieval notion of charity. John Boswell's *Same-Sex Unions in Premodern Europe* (Vintage, 1995) offers an alternative, and to my mind slightly less convincing, account of sworn friendship.

Frances Bacon's essay 'Of Friendship' addresses the particular issue of friendship with kings. (It can be found in any collection of his essays. Everyman publish a cheap edition.) His point is that those who are otherwise above reproach because of the power they wield need friends in order to keep their feet on the ground. Friendship, as Bacon puts it, 'opens the understanding', 'waxeth wiser', and 'there is no such remedy against flattery of a man's self as the liberty of a friend'. However, this friend cum special advisor on personal integrity can only speak the truth to power because he has minimal political interests of his own. If political concerns influence the friend, his advice loses its personal edge and his intimacy becomes sycophancy; friendship matters to Bacon because it is above affairs of state.

John Locke's *Essay concerning the True Original, Extent, and End of Civil Government* is available online for free.

There is an interesting discussion of Anselm on friendship in an article entitled 'Friendship', by David Moss, in *Radical Orthodoxy*, edited by John Milbank, Catherine Pickstock and Graham Ward (Routledge, 1998).

Aelred's *Spiritual Friendship* is available from Cistercian Publications. Excerpts can be found in *Other Selves: Philosophers on Friendship*, edited by Michael Pakaluk.

I Know My Own Heart: the Diaries of Anne Lister, 1791–1840 is published by Virago (1988). Bray discusses the relationship at length.

7   Prophetic friendship

Michael Farrell's *Collaborative Circles: Friendship Dynamics and Creative Work* is published by University of Chicago Press (2003). My quotes come from his book. *Not For Ourselves Alone*, a film of Stanton and Anthony's life from PBS, is available on DVD from Warner Home Video.

Lillian Faderman's *Surpassing the Love of Men: Romantic Friendship and Love between Women from the Renaissance to the Present* is published by HarperCollins (1998). The quote of Simone de Beauvoir comes from *The Second Sex* (Vintage Classics, 1997).

Marilyn Friedman's essay 'Feminism and Modern Friendship: Dislocating the Community' can be found in a mixed collection of essays, *Friendship: a Philosophical Reader*, edited by Neera Kapur Badhwar (Cornell University Press, 1993).

Mary E. Hunt discusses her politics of friendship in *Fierce Tenderness: a Feminist Theology of Friendship* (Crossroad, 1991).

My discussion of molly houses draws historical material from David Greenberg's *The Construction of Homosexuality* (University of Chicago Press, 1988). Michael Vasey's interpretation of their significance is in *Strangers and Friends* (Hodder and Stoughton, 1995).

For more on Mark Simpson see www.marksimpson.com.

Love Undetectable: Reflections on Friendship, Sex and Survival, by Andrew Sullivan, is where his discussion of gay friendship can be found (Vintage, 1999).

Foucault's work on friendship can be hard to find, especially since it has become fashionable to attribute extreme constructionist accounts of sexuality to him. However, the thoughtful interview 'Friendship as a Way of Life' is in *Foucault Live*, edited by S. Lotringer (Semiotext(e), 1989). Jeremy Carrette's *Religion and Culture by Michel Foucault* (Routledge, 1999) also contains useful material.

Jeffrey Weeks's research is published in *Same-Sex Intimacies: Families of Choice and Other Life Experiments* (Routledge, 2001). Anthony Giddens's ideas are found in *The Transformation of Intimacy* (Stanford University Press, 1993).

Liz Spencer and Ray Pahl's latest research is in *Hidden Solidarities: Friendship and Personal Communities Today* from Princeton University Press (2005). Pahl's *On Friendship* (Polity Press, 2000) is an accessible essay on friendship with a sociological slant.

For a less empirical take, try *Bowling Along*, by Robert Putnam (Simon and Schuster, 2000).

8   The spirituality of friendship

The quote of Richard Wollheim comes from chapter IX of *The Thread of Life* (Yale University Press, 1999).

Montaigne's essay 'On Friendship' can be found in any collection of his *Complete Essays*, and Penguin's Great Ideas series includes an edition of it alone.

Emerson's essay 'Friendship' comes from his First Series and is in *The Essential Writings of Ralph Waldo Emerson* (Modern Library, 2000), edited by Brooks Atkinson and with an introduction by Mary Oliver, whom I quote too. *The Woman and the Myth: Margaret Fuller's Life and Writings*, edited by Bell Gale Chevigny (Northeastern University Press, 1994), provides much more about Fuller.

9   Friendship beyond self-help

John Stuart Mill's *Autobiography* is a Penguin Classic.

Paul Seabright's book is *The Company of Strangers: A Natural History of Economic Life*, published by Princeton University Press (2004).

For more on the Socratic way of life though not so much on friendship, Pierre Hadot's *What Is Ancient Philosophy?* (Belknap Press, 2004) is a great read.

Index

Figures in **bold** refer to illustrations.

Index